Java™ NIO

Related titles from O'Reilly

Also available

Java™ NIO

Ron Hitchens

O'REILLY®

Beijing · Cambridge · Farnham · Köln · Paris · Sebastopol · Taipei · Tokyo

Java™ NIO
by Ron Hitchens

Published by O'Reilly & Associates, Inc., 1005 Gravenstein Highway North, Sebastopol, CA 95472.

O'Reilly & Associates books may be purchased for educational, business, or sales promotional use. Online editions are also available for most titles (*safari.oreilly.com*). For more information contact our corporate/institutional sales department: (800) 998-9938 or *corporate@oreilly.com*.

Editor:	Mike Loukides
Production Editor:	Matt Hutchinson
Cover Designer:	Hanna Dyer
Interior Designer:	Melanie Wang

Printing History:

August 2002:	First Edition.

Library of Congress Cataloging-in-Publication Data

Hitchens, Ron.
    Java NIO/Ron Hitchens
        p. cm.
    ISBN 0-596-00288-2
    1. Java (Computer program language) 2. Computer input-output equipment. 3. Object-
        oriented programming (Computer science) I. Title.

QA76.73.J38 H58 2002
005.13'3--dc21   2002074959

ISBN: 0-596-00288-2
[C]   [11/02]

To my wife, Karen.
What would I do without you?

Table of Contents

Preface

Computers are useless. They can only give you answers.
—Pablo Picasso

This book is about advanced input/output on the Java platform, specifically I/O using the Java 2 Standard Edition (J2SE) Software Development Kit (SDK), Version 1.4 and later. The 1.4 release of J2SE, code-named Merlin, contains significant new I/O capabilities that we'll explore in detail. These new I/O features are primarily collected in the java.nio package (and its subpackages) and have been dubbed *New I/O* (NIO). In this book, you'll see how to put these exciting new features to work to greatly improve the I/O efficiency of your Java applications.

Java has found its true home among Enterprise Applications (a slippery term if ever there was one), but until the 1.4 release of the J2SE SDK, Java has been at a disadvantage relative to natively compiled languages in the area of I/O. This weakness stems from Java's greatest strength: Write Once, Run Anywhere. The need for the illusion of a virtual machine, the JVM, means that compromises must be made to make all JVM deployment platforms look the same when running Java bytecode. This need for commonality across operating-system platforms has resulted, to some extent, in a least-common-denominator approach.

Nowhere have these compromises been more sorely felt than in the arena of I/O. While Java possesses a rich set of I/O classes, they have until now concentrated on providing common capabilities, often at a high level of abstraction, across all operating systems. These I/O classes have primarily been stream-oriented, often invoking methods on several layers of objects to handle individual bytes or characters.

This object-oriented approach, composing behaviors by plugging I/O objects together, offers tremendous flexibility but can be a performance killer when large amounts of data must be handled. Efficiency is the goal of I/O, and efficient I/O often doesn't map well to objects. Efficient I/O usually means that you must take the shortest path from Point A to Point B. Complexity destroys performance when doing high-volume I/O.

The traditional I/O abstractions of the Java platform have served well and are appropriate for a wide range of uses. But these classes do not scale well when moving large amounts of data, nor do they provide some common I/O functionality widely available on most operating systems today. These features—such as file locking, non-blocking I/O, readiness selection, and memory mapping—are essential for scalability and may be required to interact properly with non-Java applications, especially at the enterprise level. The classic Java I/O mechanism doesn't model these common I/O services.

Real companies deploy real applications on real systems, not abstractions. In the real world, performance matters—it matters a lot. The computer systems that companies buy to deploy their large applications have high-performance I/O capabilities (often developed at huge expense by the system vendors), which Java has until now been unable to fully exploit. When the business need is to move a lot of data as fast as possible, the ugly-but-fast solution usually wins out over pretty-but-slow. Time is money, after all.

JDK 1.4 is the first major Java release driven primarily by the Java Community Process. The JCP (*http://jcp.org/*) provides a means by which users and vendors of Java products can propose and specify new features for the Java platform. The subject of this book, Java New I/O (NIO), is a direct result of one such proposal. Java Specification Request #51 (*http://jcp.org/jsr/detail/51.jsp*) details the need for high-speed, scalable I/O, which better leverages the I/O capabilities of the underlying operating system. The new classes comprising `java.nio` and its subpackages, as well as `java.util.regex` and changes to a few preexisting packages, are the resulting implementation of JSR 51. Refer to the JCP web site for details on how the JSR process works and the evolution of NIO from initial request to released reference implementation.

With the Merlin release, Java now has the tools to make use of these powerful operating-system I/O capabilities where available. Java no longer needs to take a backseat to any language when it comes to I/O performance.

Organization

This book is divided into six chapters, each dealing with a major aspect of Java NIO. Chapter 1 discusses general I/O concepts to set the stage for the specific discussions that follow. Chapters 2–4 cover the core of NIO: buffers, channels, and selectors. Following that is a discussion of the new regular expression API. Regular expression processing dovetails with I/O and was included under the umbrella of the JSR 51 feature set. To wrap up, we take a look at the new pluggable character set mapping capabilities, which are also a part of NIO and JSR 51.

For the impatient, anxious to jump ahead, here is the executive summary:

Buffers

The new Buffer classes are the linkage between regular Java classes and channels. Buffers implement fixed-size arrays of primitive data elements, wrapped inside an object with state information. They provide a rendezvous point: a Channel consumes data you place in a Buffer (write) or deposits data (read) you can then fetch from the buffer. There is also a special type of buffer that provides for memory-mapping files.

We'll discuss buffer objects in detail in Chapter 2.

Channels

The most important new abstraction provided by NIO is the concept of a *channel*. A Channel object models a communication connection. The pipe may be unidirectional (in *or* out) or bidirectional (in *and* out). A channel can be thought of as the pathway between a buffer and an I/O service.

In some cases, the older classes of the java.io package can make use of channels. Where appropriate, new methods have been added to gain access to the Channel associated with a file or socket object.

Most channels can operate in nonblocking mode, which has major scalability implications, especially when used in combination with selectors.

We'll examine channels in Chapter 3.

File locking and memory-mapped files

The new FileChannel object in the java.nio.channels package provides many new file-oriented capabilities. Two of the most interesting are file locking and the ability to memory map files.

File locking is an essential tool for coordinating access to shared data among cooperating processes.

The ability to memory map files allows you to treat file data on disk as if it was in memory. This exploits the virtual memory capabilities of the operating system to dynamically cache file content without committing memory resources to hold a copy of the file.

File locking and memory-mapped files are also discussed in Chapter 3.

Sockets

The socket channel classes provide a new method of interacting with network sockets. Socket channels can operate in nonblocking mode and can be used with selectors. As a result, many sockets can be multiplexed and managed more efficiently than with the traditional socket classes of java.net.

The three new socket channels, ServerSocketChannel, SocketChannel, and DatagramChannel, are covered in Chapter 3.

Selectors

> Selectors provide the ability to do *readiness selection*. The Selector class provides a mechanism by which you can determine the status of one or more channels you're interested in. Using selectors, a large number of active I/O channels can be monitored and serviced by a single thread easily and efficiently.
>
> We'll discuss selectors in detail in Chapter 4.

Regular expressions

> The new java.util.regex package brings Perl-like regular expression processing to Java. This is a long-awaited feature, useful for a wide range of applications.
>
> The new regular expression APIs are considered part of NIO because they were specified by JSR 51 along with the other NIO features. In many respects, it's orthogonal to the rest of NIO but is extremely useful for file processing and many other purposes.
>
> Chapter 5 discusses the JDK 1.4 regular expression APIs.

Character sets

> The java.nio.charsets package provides new classes for mapping characters to and from byte streams. These new classes allow you to select the mapping by which characters will be translated or create your own mappings.
>
> Issues relating to character transcoding are covered in Chapter 6.

Who Should Read This Book

This book is intended for intermediate to advanced Java programmers: those who have a good handle on the language and want (or need!) to take full advantage of the new capabilities of Java NIO for large-scale and/or sophisticated data handling. In the text, I assume that you are familiar with the standard class packages of the JDK, object-oriented techniques, inheritance, and so on. I also assume that you know the basics of how I/O works at the operating-system level, what files are, what sockets are, what virtual memory is, and so on. Chapter 1 provides a high-level review of these concepts but does not explain them in detail.

If you are still learning your way around the I/O packages of the Java platform, you may first want to take a look at *Java I/O* by Elliote Rusty Harold (O'Reilly) (*http://www.oreilly.com/catalog/javaio/*). It provides an excellent introduction to the java.io packages. While this book could be considered a follow-up to that book, it is not a continuation of it. This book concentrates on making use of the new java.nio packages to maximize I/O performance and introduces some new I/O concepts that are outside the scope of the java.io package.

We also explore character set encoding and regular expressions, which are a part of the new feature set bundled with NIO. Those programmers implementing character sets for internationalization or for specialized applications will be interested in the java.nio.charsets package discussed in Chapter 6.

And those of you who've switched to Java, but keep returning to Perl for the ease of regular expression handling, no longer need to stray from Java. The new `java.util.regex` package provides all but the most obscure regular expression capabilities from Perl 5 in the standard JDK (and adds a few new things as well).

Software and Versions

This book describes the I/O capabilities of Java, particularly the `java.nio` and `java.util.regex` packages, which first appear in J2SE, Version 1.4. Therefore, you must have a working version of the Java 1.4 (or later) SDK to use the material presented in this book. You can obtain the Java SDK from Sun by visiting their web site at *http://java.sun.com/j2se/1.4/*. I also refer to the J2SE SDK as the Java Development Kit (JDK) in the text. In the context of this book, they mean the same thing.

This book is based on the final JDK version, 1.4.0, released in February 2002. Early access (beta) versions of 1.4 where widely available for several months prior. Important changes were made to the NIO APIs shortly before final release. For that reason, you may see discussions of NIO published before the final release that conflict with some details in this book. This text has been updated to include all known last-minute changes and should be in agreement with the final 1.4.0 release. Later releases of J2SE may introduce further changes that conflict with this text. Refer to the documentation provided with your software distribution if there is any doubt.

This book contains many examples demonstrating how to use the APIs. All code examples and related information can be downloaded from *http://www.javanio.info/*. Additional examples and test code are available there. Additional code examples provided by the NIO implementation team are available at *http://java.sun.com/j2se/1.4/docs/guide/nio/example/*.

Conventions Used in This Book

Like all programmers, I have my religious beliefs regarding code-formatting style. The samples in this book are formatted according to my preferences, which are fairly conventional. I'm a believer in eight-column tab indents and lots of separating whitespace. Some of the code examples have had their indents reduced to four columns because of space constraints. The source code available on the web site has tab indents.

When I provide API examples and lists of methods from a class in the JDK, I generally provide only the specific methods referenced in the immediate text. I leave out the methods that are not of interest at that point. I often provide the full class API at the beginning of a chapter or section, then list subsets of the API near the specific discussions that follow.

These API samples are usually not syntactically correct; they are extracts of the method signatures without the method bodies and are intended to illustrate which methods are available and the parameters they accept. For example:

```
public class Foo
{
        public static final int MODE_ABC
        public static final int MODE_XYZ

        public abstract void baz (Blather blather);
        public int blah (Bar bar, Bop bop)
}
```

In this case, the method baz( ) is syntactically complete because abstract declarations consist of nothing but signature. But blah( ) lacks a semi-colon, which implies that the method body follows in the class definition. And when I list public fields defining constants, such as MODE_ABC and MODE_XYZ, I intentionally don't list the values they are initialized to. That information is not important. The public name is defined so that you can use it without knowing the value of the constant.

Where possible, I extract this API information directly from the code distributed with the 1.4 JDK. When I started writing this book, the JDK was at Version 1.4 beta 2. Every effort has been made to keep the code snippets current. My apologies for any inaccuracies that may have crept in. The source code included with the JDK is the final authority.

Font Conventions

I use standard O'Reilly font conventions in this book. This is not entirely by choice. I composed the manuscript directly as XML using a pure Java GUI editor (XXE from *http://www.xmlmind.com/*), which enforced the DTD I used, O'Reilly's subset of DocBook (*http://www.oasis-open.org/*). As such, I never specified fonts or type styles. I'd select XML elements such as <filename> or <programlisting>, and O'Reilly's typesetting software applied the appropriate type style.

This, of course, means nothing to you. So here's the rundown on font conventions used in this text:

Italic is used for:

- Pathnames, filenames, and program names
- Internet addresses, such as domain names and URLs
- New terms where they are defined

Constant Width is used for:

- Names and keywords in Java code, including method names, variable names, and class names

- Program listings and code snippets
- Constant values

Constant Width Bold is used for:

- Emphasis within code examples

 This icon designates a note, which is an important aside to the nearby text.

 This icon designates a warning relating to the nearby text.

How to Contact Us

Although this is not the first book I've written, it's the first I've written for general publication. It's far more difficult to write a book than to read one. And it's really quite frightening to expound on Java-related topics because the subject matter is so extensive and changes rapidly. There are also vast numbers of very smart people who can and will point out the slightest inaccuracy you commit to print.

I would like to hear any comments you may have, positive or negative. I believe I did my homework on this project, but errors inevitably creep in. I'm especially interested in constructive feedback on the structure and content of the book. I've tried to structure it so that topics are presented in a sensible order and in easily absorbed chunks. I've also tried to cross-reference heavily so it will be useful when accessed randomly.

Offers of lucrative consulting contracts, speaking engagments, and free stuff are appreciated. Spurious flames and spam are cheerfully ignored.

You can contact me at *ron@javanio.info* or visit *http://www.javanio.info/*.

O'Reilly and I have verified the information in this book to the best of our ability, but you may find that features have changed (or even that we have made mistakes!). Please let us know about any errors you find, as well as your suggestions for future editions, by writing to:

O'Reilly & Associates, Inc.
1005 Gravenstein Highway North
Sebastopol, CA 95472
(800) 998-9938 (U.S. and Canada)
(707) 829-0515 (international/local)
(707) 829-0104 (fax)

You can also contact O'Reilly by email. To be put on the mailing list or request a catalog, send a message to:

info@oreilly.com

We have a web page for this book, where we list errata, examples, and any additional information. You can access this page at:

http://www.oreilly.com/catalog/javanio/

To ask technical questions or comment on the book, send email to:

bookquestions@oreilly.com

For more information about O'Reilly books, conferences, Resource Centers, and the O'Reilly Network, see O'Reilly's web site at:

http://www.oreilly.com/

Acknowledgments

It's a lot of work putting a book together, even one as relatively modest in scope as this. I'd like to express my gratitude to several people for their help with this endeavor.

First and foremost, I'd like to thank Mike Loukides, my editor at O'Reilly, for affording me the chance join the ranks of O'Reilly authors. I still wonder how I managed to wind up with a book deal at O'Reilly. It's a great honor and no small responsibility. Thanks Mike, and sorry about the comma splices.

I'd also like to thank Bob Eckstein and Kyle Hart, also of O'Reilly, for their efforts on my behalf: Bob for his help with early drafts of this book and Kyle for giving me free stuff at JavaOne (oh, that marketing campaign may be helpful too). Jessamyn Read turned my clumsy pictures into professional illustrations. I'd also like to thank the prolific David Flanagan for mentioning my minuscule contribution to *Java in a Nutshell, Fourth Edition* (O'Reilly), and for letting me use the regular expression syntax table from that book.

Authors of technical books rely heavily on technical reviewers to detect errors and omissions. Technical review is especially important when the material is new and evolving, as was the case with NIO. The 1.4 APIs were literally a moving target when I began work on this project. I'm extremely lucky that Mark Reinhold of Sun Microsystems, Specification Lead for JSR 51 and author of much of the NIO code in JDK 1.4, agreed to be a reviewer. Mark reviewed a very early and very rough draft. He kindly set me straight on many points and provided valuable insight that helped me tremendously. Mark also took time out while trying to get the 1.4.1 release in shape to provide detailed feedback on the final draft. Thanks Mark.

Several other very smart people looked over my work and provided constructive feedback. Jason Hunter (*http://www.servlets.com/*) eagerly devoured the first review draft within hours and provided valuable organizational input. The meticulous John G. Miller, Jr., of Digital Gamers, Inc. (*johnmiller@digigamers.com*, *http://www.digigamers.com/*), carefully reviewed the draft and example code. John's real-world experience with NIO on a large scale in an online, interactive game environment made this book a better one. Will Crawford (*http://www.williamcrawford.info/*) found time he couldn't afford to read the entire manuscript and provided laser-like, highly targeted feedback.

I'd also like to thank Keith J. Koski and Michael Daudel (*mgd@ronsoft.com*), fellow members of a merry band of Unix and Java codeslingers I've worked with over the last several years, known collectively as the Fatboys. The Fatboys are thinning out, getting married, moving to the suburbs, and having kids (myself included), but as long as Bill can suck gravy through a straw, the Fatboy dream lives on. Keith and Mike read several early drafts, tested code, gave suggestions, and provided encouragement. Thanks guys, you're "phaser enriched."

And last but not least, I want to thank my wife, Karen. She doesn't grok this tech stuff but is wise and caring and loves me and feeds me fruit. She lights my soul and gives me reason. Together we pen the chapters in our book of life.

CHAPTER 1

Introduction

Get the facts first. You can distort them later.
—Mark Twain

Let's talk about I/O. No, no, come back. It's not really all that dull. Input/output (I/O) is not a glamorous topic, but it's a very important one. Most programmers think of I/O in the same way they do about plumbing: undoubtedly essential, can't live without it, but it can be unpleasant to deal with directly and may cause a big, stinky mess when not working properly. This is not a book about plumbing, but in the pages that follow, you may learn how to make your data flow a little more smoothly.

Object-oriented program design is all about encapsulation. Encapsulation is a good thing: it partitions responsibility, hides implementation details, and promotes object reuse. This partitioning and encapsulation tends to apply to programmers as well as programs. You may be a highly skilled Java programmer, creating extremely sophisticated objects and doing extraordinary things, and yet be almost entirely ignorant of some basic concepts underpinning I/O on the Java platform. In this chapter, we'll momentarily violate your encapsulation and take a look at some low-level I/O implementation details in the hope that you can better orchestrate the multiple moving parts involved in any I/O operation.

I/O Versus CPU Time

Most programmers fancy themselves software artists, crafting clever routines to squeeze a few bytes here, unrolling a loop there, or refactoring somewhere else to consolidate objects. While those things are undoubtedly important, and often a lot of fun, the gains made by optimizing code can be easily dwarfed by I/O inefficiencies. Performing I/O usually takes orders of magnitude longer than performing in-memory processing tasks on the data. Many coders concentrate on what their objects are doing to the data and pay little attention to the environmental issues involved in acquiring and storing that data.

Table 1-1 lists some hypothetical times for performing a task on units of data read from and written to disk. The first column lists the average time it takes to process one unit of data, the second column is the amount of time it takes to move that unit of data from and to disk, and the third column is the number of these units of data that can be processed per second. The fourth column is the throughput increase that will result from varying the values in the first two columns.

Table 1-1. Throughput rate, processing versus I/O time

Process time (ms)	I/O time (ms)	Throughput (units/sec)	Gain (%)
5	100	9.52	(benchmark)
2.5	100	9.76	2.44
1	100	9.9	3.96
5	90	10.53	10.53
5	75	12.5	31.25
5	50	18.18	90.91
5	20	40	320
5	10	66.67	600

The first three rows show how increasing the efficiency of the processing step affects throughput. Cutting the per-unit processing time in half results only in a 2.2% increase in throughput. On the other hand, reducing I/O latency by just 10% results in a 9.7% throughput gain. Cutting I/O time in half nearly doubles throughput, which is not surprising when you see that time spent per unit doing I/O is 20 times greater than processing time.

These numbers are artificial and arbitrary (the real world is never so simple) but are intended to illustrate the relative time magnitudes. As you can see, I/O is often the limiting factor in application performance, not processing speed. Programmers love to tune their code, but I/O performance tuning is often an afterthought, or is ignored entirely. It's a shame, because even small investments in improving I/O performance can yield substantial dividends.

No Longer CPU Bound

To some extent, Java programmers can be forgiven for their preoccupation with optimizing processing efficiency and not paying much attention to I/O considerations. In the early days of Java, the JVMs interpreted bytecodes with little or no runtime optimization. This meant that Java programs tended to poke along, running significantly slower than natively compiled code and not putting much demand on the I/O subsystems of the operating system.

But tremendous strides have been made in runtime optimization. Current JVMs run bytecode at speeds approaching that of natively compiled code, sometimes doing even better because of dynamic runtime optimizations. This means that most Java applications are no longer CPU bound (spending most of their time executing code) and are more frequently I/O bound (waiting for data transfers).

But in most cases, Java applications have not truly been I/O bound in the sense that the operating system couldn't shuttle data fast enough to keep them busy. Instead, the JVMs have not been doing I/O efficiently. There's an impedance mismatch between the operating system and the Java stream-based I/O model. The operating system wants to move data in large chunks (buffers), often with the assistance of hardware Direct Memory Access (DMA). The I/O classes of the JVM like to operate on small pieces—single bytes, or lines of text. This means that the operating system delivers buffers full of data that the stream classes of java.io spend a lot of time breaking down into little pieces, often copying each piece between several layers of objects. The operating system wants to deliver data by the truckload. The java.io classes want to process data by the shovelful. NIO makes it easier to back the truck right up to where you can make direct use of the data (a ByteBuffer object).

This is not to say that it was impossible to move large amounts of data with the traditional I/O model—it certainly was (and still is). The RandomAccessFile class in particular can be quite efficient if you stick to the array-based read( ) and write( ) methods. Even those methods entail at least one buffer copy, but are pretty close to the underlying operating-system calls.

As illustrated by Table 1-1, if your code finds itself spending most of its time waiting for I/O, it's time to consider improving I/O performance. Otherwise, your beautifully crafted code may be idle most of the time.

Getting to the Good Stuff

Most of the development effort that goes into operating systems is targeted at improving I/O performance. Lots of very smart people toil very long hours perfecting techniques for schlepping data back and forth. Operating-system vendors expend vast amounts of time and money seeking a competitive advantage by beating the other guys in this or that published benchmark.

Today's operating systems are modern marvels of software engineering (OK, some are more marvelous than others), but how can the Java programmer take advantage of all this wizardry and still remain platform-independent? Ah, yet another example of the TANSTAAFL principle.*

The JVM is a double-edged sword. It provides a uniform operating environment that shelters the Java programmer from most of the annoying differences between operating-system environments. This makes it faster and easier to write code

---

* There Ain't No Such Thing As A Free Lunch.

because platform-specific idiosyncrasies are mostly hidden. But cloaking the specifics of the operating system means that the jazzy, wiz-bang stuff is invisible too.

What to do? If you're a developer, you could write some native code using the Java Native Interface (JNI) to access the operating-system features directly. Doing so ties you to a specific operating system (and maybe a specific version of that operating system) and exposes the JVM to corruption or crashes if your native code is not 100% bug free. If you're an operating-system vendor, you could write native code and ship it with your JVM implementation to provide these features as a Java API. But doing so might violate the license you signed to provide a conforming JVM. Sun took Microsoft to court about this over the JDirect package which, of course, worked only on Microsoft systems. Or, as a last resort, you could turn to another language to implement performance-critical applications.

The java.nio package provides new abstractions to address this problem. The Channel and Selector classes in particular provide generic APIs to I/O services that were not reachable prior to JDK 1.4. The TANSTAAFL principle still applies: you won't be able to access every feature of every operating system, but these new classes provide a powerful new framework that encompasses the high-performance I/O features commonly available on commercial operating systems today. Additionally, a new Service Provider Interface (SPI) is provided in java.nio.channels.spi that allows you to plug in new types of channels and selectors without violating compliance with the specifications.

With the addition of NIO, Java is ready for serious business, entertainment, scientific and academic applications in which high-performance I/O is essential.

The JDK 1.4 release contains many other significant improvements in addition to NIO. As of 1.4, the Java platform has reached a high level of maturity, and there are few application areas remaining that Java cannot tackle. A great guide to the full spectrum of JDK features in 1.4 is *Java In A Nutshell, Fourth Edition* by David Flanagan (O'Reilly).

I/O Concepts

The Java platform provides a rich set of I/O metaphors. Some of these metaphors are more abstract than others. With all abstractions, the further you get from hard, cold reality, the tougher it becomes to connect cause and effect. The NIO packages of JDK 1.4 introduce a new set of abstractions for doing I/O. Unlike previous packages, these are focused on shortening the distance between abstraction and reality. The NIO abstractions have very real and direct interactions with real-world entities. Understanding these new abstractions and, just as importantly, the I/O services they interact with, is key to making the most of I/O-intensive Java applications.

This book assumes that you are familiar with basic I/O concepts. This section provides a whirlwind review of some basic ideas just to lay the groundwork for the discussion of how the new NIO classes operate. These classes model I/O functions, so it's necessary to grasp how things work at the operating-system level to understand the new I/O paradigms.

In the main body of this book, it's important to understand the following topics:

- Buffer handling
- Kernel versus user space
- Virtual memory
- Paging
- File-oriented versus stream I/O
- Multiplexed I/O (readiness selection)

Buffer Handling

Buffers, and how buffers are handled, are the basis of all I/O. The very term "input/output" means nothing more than moving data in and out of buffers.

Processes perform I/O by requesting of the operating system that data be drained from a buffer (write) or that a buffer be filled with data (read). That's really all it boils down to. All data moves in or out of a process by this mechanism. The machinery inside the operating system that performs these transfers can be incredibly complex, but conceptually, it's very straightforward.

Figure 1-1 shows a simplified logical diagram of how block data moves from an external source, such as a disk, to a memory area inside a running process. The process requests that its buffer be filled by making the read( ) system call. This results in the kernel issuing a command to the disk controller hardware to fetch the data from disk. The disk controller writes the data directly into a kernel memory buffer by DMA without further assistance from the main CPU. Once the disk controller finishes filling the buffer, the kernel copies the data from the temporary buffer in kernel space to the buffer specified by the process when it requested the read( ) operation.

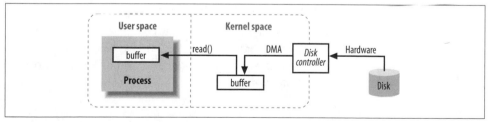

Figure 1-1. Simplified I/O buffer handling

This obviously glosses over a lot of details, but it shows the basic steps involved.

Note the concepts of *user space* and *kernel space* in Figure 1-1. User space is where regular processes live. The JVM is a regular process and dwells in user space. User space is a nonprivileged area: code executing there cannot directly access hardware devices, for example. Kernel space is where the operating system lives. Kernel code has special privileges: it can communicate with device controllers, manipulate the state of processes in user space, etc. Most importantly, all I/O flows through kernel space, either directly (as decsribed here) or indirectly (see the section "Virtual Memory").

When a process requests an I/O operation, it performs a *system call*, sometimes known as a *trap*, which transfers control into the kernel. The low-level open( ), read( ), write( ), and close( ) functions so familiar to C/C++ coders do nothing more than set up and perform the appropriate system calls. When the kernel is called in this way, it takes whatever steps are necessary to find the data the process is requesting and transfer it into the specified buffer in user space. The kernel tries to cache and/or prefetch data, so the data being requested by the process may already be available in kernel space. If so, the data requested by the process is copied out. If the data isn't available, the process is suspended while the kernel goes about bringing the data into memory.

Looking at Figure 1-1, it's probably occurred to you that copying from kernel space to the final user buffer seems like extra work. Why not tell the disk controller to send it directly to the buffer in user space? There are a couple of problems with this. First, hardware is usually not able to access user space directly.* Second, block-oriented hardware devices such as disk controllers operate on fixed-size data blocks. The user process may be requesting an oddly sized or misaligned chunk of data. The kernel plays the role of intermediary, breaking down and reassembling data as it moves between user space and storage devices.

Scatter/gather

Many operating systems can make the assembly/disassembly process even more efficient. The notion of *scatter/gather* allows a process to pass a list of buffer addresses to the operating system in one system call. The kernel can then fill or drain the multiple buffers in sequence, scattering the data to multiple user space buffers on a read, or gathering from several buffers on a write (Figure 1-2).

This saves the user process from making several system calls (which can be expensive) and allows the kernel to optimize handling of the data because it has information about the total transfer. If multiple CPUs are available, it may even be possible to fill or drain several buffers simultaneously.

---

* There are many reasons for this, all of which are beyond the scope of this book. Hardware devices usually cannot directly use virtual memory addresses.

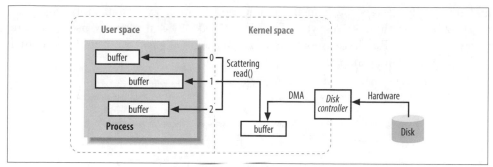

Figure 1-2. A scattering read to three buffers

Virtual Memory

All modern operating systems make use of *virtual memory*. Virtual memory means that artificial, or *virtual*, addresses are used in place of physical (hardware RAM) memory addresses. This provides many advantages, which fall into two basic categories:

1. More than one virtual address can refer to the same physical memory location.

2. A virtual memory space can be larger than the actual hardware memory available.

The previous section said that device controllers cannot do DMA directly into user space, but the same effect is achievable by exploiting item 1 above. By mapping a kernel space address to the same physical address as a virtual address in user space, the DMA hardware (which can access only physical memory addresses) can fill a buffer that is simultaneously visible to both the kernel and a user space process. (See Figure 1-3.)

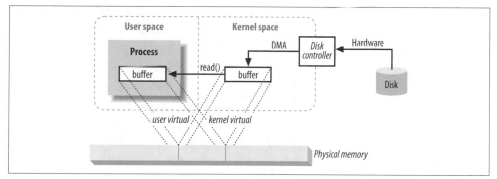

Figure 1-3. Multiply mapped memory space

This is great because it eliminates copies between kernel and user space, but requires the kernel and user buffers to share the same *page alignment*. Buffers must also be a multiple of the block size used by the disk controller (usually 512 byte disk sectors). Operating systems divide their memory address spaces into *pages*, which are fixed-size groups of bytes. These memory pages are always multiples of the disk block size and are usually powers of 2 (which simplifies addressing). Typical memory page sizes are 1,024, 2,048, and 4,096 bytes. The virtual and physical memory page sizes are always the same. Figure 1-4 shows how virtual memory pages from multiple virtual address spaces can be mapped to physical memory.

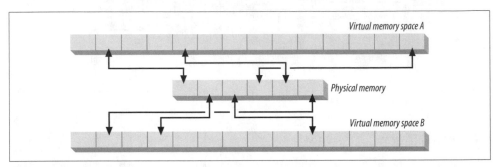

Figure 1-4. Memory pages

Memory Paging

To support the second attribute of virtual memory (having an addressable space larger than physical memory), it's necessary to do *virtual memory paging* (often referred to as *swapping*, though true swapping is done at the process level, not the page level). This is a scheme whereby the pages of a virtual memory space can be persisted to external disk storage to make room in physical memory for other virtual pages. Essentially, physical memory acts as a cache for a *paging area*, which is the space on disk where the content of memory pages is stored when forced out of physical memory.

Figure 1-5 shows virtual pages belonging to four processes, each with its own virtual memory space. Two of the five pages for Process A are loaded into memory; the others are stored on disk.

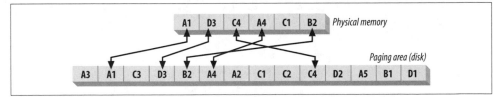

Figure 1-5. Physical memory as a paging-area cache

Aligning memory page sizes as multiples of the disk block size allows the kernel to issue direct commands to the disk controller hardware to write memory pages to disk or reload them when needed. It turns out that *all* disk I/O is done at the page level. This is the only way data ever moves between disk and physical memory in modern, paged operating systems.

Modern CPUs contain a subsystem known as the Memory Management Unit (MMU). This device logically sits between the CPU and physical memory. It contains the mapping information needed to translate virtual addresses to physical memory addresses. When the CPU references a memory location, the MMU determines which page the location resides in (usually by shifting or masking the bits of the address value) and translates that virtual page number to a physical page number (this is done in hardware and is extremely fast). If there is no mapping currently in effect between that virtual page and a physical memory page, the MMU raises a *page fault* to the CPU.

A page fault results in a trap, similar to a system call, which vectors control into the kernel along with information about which virtual address caused the fault. The kernel then takes steps to *validate* the page. The kernel will schedule a *pagein* operation to read the content of the missing page back into physical memory. This often results in another page being *stolen* to make room for the incoming page. In such a case, if the stolen page is *dirty* (changed since its creation or last pagein) a *pageout* must first be done to copy the stolen page content to the paging area on disk.

If the requested address is not a valid virtual memory address (it doesn't belong to any of the *memory segments* of the executing process), the page cannot be validated, and a *segmentation fault* is generated. This vectors control to another part of the kernel and usually results in the process being killed.

Once the faulted page has been made valid, the MMU is updated to establish the new virtual-to-physical mapping (and if necessary, break the mapping of the stolen page), and the user process is allowed to resume. The process causing the page fault will not be aware of any of this; it all happens transparently.

This dynamic shuffling of memory pages based on usage is known as *demand paging*. Some sophisticated algorithms exist in the kernel to optimize this process and to prevent *thrashing*, a pathological condition in which paging demands become so great that nothing else can get done.

File I/O

File I/O occurs within the context of a filesystem. A filesystem is a very different thing from a disk. Disks store data in *sectors*, which are usually 512 bytes each. They are hardware devices that know nothing about the semantics of files. They simply provide a number of slots where data can be stored. In this respect, the sectors of a disk are similar to memory pages; all are of uniform size and are addressable as a large array.

A filesystem is a higher level of abstraction. Filesystems are a particular method of arranging and interpreting data stored on a disk (or some other random-access, block-oriented device). The code you write almost always interacts with a filesystem, not with the disks directly. It is the filesystem that defines the abstractions of filenames, paths, files, file attributes, etc.

The previous section mentioned that all I/O is done via demand paging. You'll recall that paging is very low level and always happens as direct transfers of disk sectors into and out of memory pages. So how does this low-level paging translate to file I/O, which can be performed in arbitrary sizes and alignments?

A filesystem organizes a sequence of uniformly sized data blocks. Some blocks store meta information such as maps of free blocks, directories, indexes, etc. Other blocks contain file data. The meta information about individual files describes which blocks contain the file data, where the data ends, when it was last updated, etc.

When a request is made by a user process to read file data, the filesystem implementation determines exactly where on disk that data lives. It then takes action to bring those disk sectors into memory. In older operating systems, this usually meant issuing a command directly to the disk driver to read the needed disk sectors. But in modern, paged operating systems, the filesystem takes advantage of demand paging to bring data into memory.

Filesystems also have a notion of pages, which may be the same size as a basic memory page or a multiple of it. Typical filesystem page sizes range from 2,048 to 8,192 bytes and will always be a multiple of the basic memory page size.

How a paged filesystem performs I/O boils down to the following:

- Determine which filesystem page(s) (group of disk sectors) the request spans. The file content and/or metadata on disk may be spread across multiple filesystem pages, and those pages may be noncontiguous.
- Allocate enough memory pages in kernel space to hold the identified filesystem pages.
- Establish mappings between those memory pages and the filesystem pages on disk.
- Generate page faults for each of those memory pages.
- The virtual memory system traps the page faults and schedules pageins to validate those pages by reading their contents from disk.
- Once the pageins have completed, the filesystem breaks down the raw data to extract the requested file content or attribute information.

Note that this filesystem data will be cached like other memory pages. On subsequent I/O requests, some or all of the file data may still be present in physical memory and can be reused without rereading from disk.

Most filesystems also prefetch extra filesystem pages on the assumption that the process will be reading the rest of the file. If there is not a lot of contention for memory, these filesystem pages could remain valid for quite some time. In which case, it may not be necessary to go to disk at all when the file is opened again later by the same, or a different, process. You may have noticed this effect when repeating a similar operation, such as a grep of several files. It seems to run much faster the second time around.

Similar steps are taken for writing file data, whereby changes to files (via write( )) result in dirty filesystem pages that are subsequently paged out to synchronize the file content on disk. Files are created by establishing mappings to empty filesystem pages that are flushed to disk following the write operation.

Memory-mapped files

For conventional file I/O, in which user processes issue read( ) and write( ) system calls to transfer data, there is almost always one or more copy operations to move the data between these filesystem pages in kernel space and a memory area in user space. This is because there is not usually a one-to-one alignment between filesystem pages and user buffers. There is, however, a special type of I/O operation supported by most operating systems that allows user processes to take maximum advantage of the page-oriented nature of system I/O and completely avoid buffer copies. This is *memory-mapped I/O*, which is illustrated in Figure 1-6.

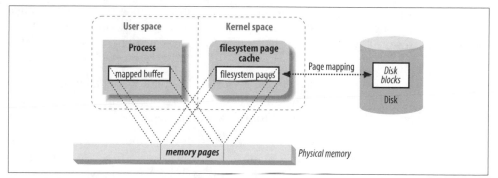

Figure 1-6. User memory mapped to filesystem pages

Memory-mapped I/O uses the filesystem to establish a virtual memory mapping from user space directly to the applicable filesystem pages. This has several advantages:

* The user process sees the file data as memory, so there is no need to issue read( ) or write( ) system calls.

* As the user process touches the mapped memory space, page faults will be generated automatically to bring in the file data from disk. If the user modifies the mapped memory space, the affected page is automatically marked as dirty and will be subsequently flushed to disk to update the file.

* The virtual memory subsystem of the operating system will perform intelligent caching of the pages, automatically managing memory according to system load.

- The data is always page-aligned, and no buffer copying is ever needed.
- Very large files can be mapped without consuming large amounts of memory to copy the data.

Virtual memory and disk I/O are intimately linked and, in many respects, are simply two aspects of the same thing. Keep this in mind when handling large amounts of data. Most operating systems are far more effecient when handling data buffers that are page-aligned and are multiples of the native page size.

File locking

File locking is a scheme by which one process can prevent others from accessing a file or restrict how other processes access that file. Locking is usually employed to control how updates are made to shared information or as part of transaction isolation. File locking is essential to controlling concurrent access to common resources by multiple entities. Sophisticated applications, such as databases, rely heavily on file locking.

While the name "file locking" implies locking an entire file (and that is often done), locking is usually available at a finer-grained level. File *regions* are usually locked, with granularity down to the byte level. Locks are associated with a particular file, beginning at a specific byte location within that file and running for a specific range of bytes. This is important because it allows many processes to coordinate access to specific areas of a file without impeding other processes working elsewhere in the file.

File locks come in two flavors: *shared* and *exclusive*. Multiple shared locks may be in effect for the same file region at the same time. Exclusive locks, on the other hand, demand that no other locks be in effect for the requested region.

The classic use of shared and exclusive locks is to control updates to a shared file that is primarily used for read access. A process wishing to read the file would first acquire a shared lock on that file or on a subregion of it. A second wishing to read the same file region would also request a shared lock. Both could read the file concurrently without interfering with each other. However, if a third process wishes to make updates to the file, it would request an exclusive lock. That process would block until all locks (shared or exclusive) are released. Once the exclusive lock is granted, any reader processes asking for shared locks would block until the exclusive lock is released. This allows the updating process to make changes to the file without any reader processes seeing the file in an inconsistent state. This is illustrated by Figures 1-7 and 1-8.

File locks are either *advisory* or *mandatory*. Advisory locks provide information about current locks to those processes that ask, but such locks are not enforced by the operating system. It is up to the processes involved to cooperate and pay attention to the *advice* the locks represent. Most Unix and Unix-like operating systems

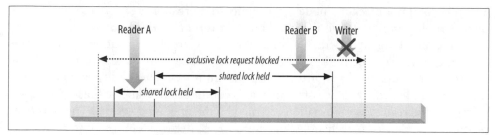

Figure 1-7. Exclusive-lock request blocked by shared locks

Figure 1-8. Shared-lock requests blocked by exclusive lock

provide advisory locking. Some can also do mandatory locking or a combination of both.

Mandatory locks are enforced by the operating system and/or the filesystem and will prevent processes, whether they are aware of the locks or not, from gaining access to locked areas of a file. Usually, Microsoft operating systems do mandatory locking. It's wise to assume that all locks are advisory and to use file locking consistently across all applications accessing a common resource. Assuming that all locks are advisory is the only workable cross-platform strategy. Any application depending on mandatory file-locking semantics is inherently nonportable.

Stream I/O

Not all I/O is block-oriented, as described in previous sections. There is also stream I/O, which is modeled on a pipeline. The bytes of an I/O stream must be accessed sequentially. TTY (console) devices, printer ports, and network connections are common examples of streams.

Streams are generally, but not necessarily, slower than block devices and are often the source of intermittent input. Most operating systems allow streams to be placed into *nonblocking mode*, which permits a process to check if input is available on the stream without getting stuck if none is available at the moment. Such a capability allows a process to handle input as it arrives but perform other functions while the input stream is idle.

A step beyond nonblocking mode is the ability to do *readiness selection*. This is similar to nonblocking mode (and is often built on top of nonblocking mode), but offloads the checking of whether a stream is ready to the operating system. The operating system can be told to watch a collection of streams and return an indication to the process of which of those streams are ready. This ability permits a process to *multiplex* many active streams using common code and a single thread by leveraging the readiness information returned by the operating system. This is widely used in network servers to handle large numbers of network connections. Readiness selection is essential for high-volume scaling.

Summary

This overview of system-level I/O is necessarily terse and incomplete. If you require more detailed information on the subject, consult a good reference—there are many available. A great place to start is the definitive operating-system textbook, *Operating System Concepts, Sixth Edition*, by my old boss Avi Silberschatz (John Wiley & Sons).

With the preceding overview, you should now have a pretty good idea of the subjects that will be covered in the following chapters. Armed with this knowledge, let's move on to the heart of the matter: Java New I/O (NIO). Keep these concrete ideas in mind as you acquire the new abstractions of NIO. Understanding these basic ideas should make it easy to recognize the I/O capabilities modeled by the new classes.

We're about to begin our Grand Tour of NIO. The bus is warmed up and ready to roll. Climb on board, settle in, get comfortable, and let's get this show on the road.

CHAPTER 2

Buffers

It's all relative.
—Big Al Einstein

We begin our sightseeing tour of the java.nio packages with the Buffer classes. These classes are the foundation upon which java.nio is built. In this chapter, we'll take a close look at buffers, discover the various types, and learn how to use them. We'll then see how the java.nio buffers relate to the channel classes of java.nio. channels.

A Buffer object is a container for a fixed amount of data. It acts as a holding tank, or staging area, where data can be stored and later retrieved. Buffers are filled and drained, as we discussed in Chapter 1. There is one buffer class for each of the non-boolean primitive data types. Although buffers act upon the primitive data types they store, buffers have a strong bias toward bytes. Nonbyte buffers can perform transla-tion to and from bytes behind the scenes, depending on how the buffer was created.* We'll examine the implications of data storage within buffers later in this chapter.

Buffers work hand in glove with *channels*. Channels are portals through which I/O transfers take place, and buffers are the sources or targets of those data transfers. For outgoing transfers, data you want to send is placed in a buffer, which is passed to a channel. For inbound transfers, a channel deposits data in a buffer you provide. This hand-off of buffers between cooperating objects (usually objects you write and one or more Channel objects) is key to efficient data handling. Channels will be covered in detail in Chapter 3.

Figure 2-1 is a class diagram of the Buffer class-specialization hierarchy. At the top is the generic Buffer class. Buffer defines operations common to all buffer types, regardless of the data type they contain or special behaviors they may possess. This common ground will be our jumping-off point.

---

* This implies byte-ordering issues, which we'll discuss in the section "Byte Ordering."

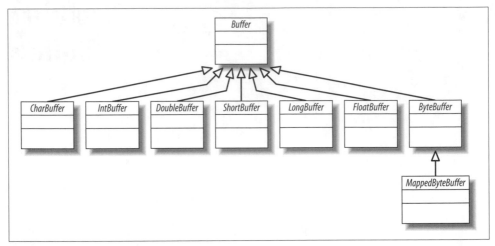

Figure 2-1. The Buffer family tree

Buffer Basics

Conceptually, a buffer is an array of primitive data elements wrapped inside an object. The advantage of a Buffer class over a simple array is that it encapsulates data content and information about the data into a single object. The Buffer class and its specialized subclasses define a API for processing data buffers.

Attributes

There are four *attributes* all buffers possess that provide information about the contained data elements. These are:

Capacity
> The maximum number of data elements the buffer can hold. The capacity is set when the buffer is created and can never be changed.

Limit
> The first element of the buffer that should not be read or written. In other words, the count of live elements in the buffer.

Position
> The index of the next element to be read or written. The position is updated automatically by relative get( ) and put( ) methods.

Mark
> A remembered position. Calling mark( ) sets mark = position. Calling reset( ) sets position = mark. The mark is undefined until set.

The following relationship between these four attributes always holds:

```
0 <= mark <= position <= limit <= capacity
```

Let's look at some examples of these attributes in action. Figure 2-2 shows a logical view of a newly created ByteBuffer with a capacity of 10.

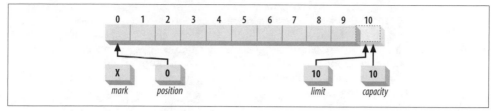

Figure 2-2. A newly created ByteBuffer

The position is set to 0, and the capacity and limit are set to 10, just past the last byte the buffer can hold. The mark is initially undefined. The capacity is fixed, but the other three attributes can change as the buffer is used.

Buffer API

Let's take a look now at how we can use a buffer. These are the method signatures for the Buffer class:

```
package java.nio;

public abstract class Buffer {
        public final int capacity( )
        public final int position( )
        public final Buffer position (int newPosition)
        public final int limit( )
        public final Buffer limit (int newLimit)
        public final Buffer mark( )
        public final Buffer reset( )
        public final Buffer clear( )
        public final Buffer flip( )
        public final Buffer rewind( )
        public final int remaining( )
        public final boolean hasRemaining( )
        public abstract boolean isReadOnly( );
}
```

One thing to notice about this API is that methods you would normally expect to return void, such as clear( ), instead return a Buffer reference. These methods return a reference to the object they were invoked upon (this). This is a class design technique that allows for *invocation chaining*. Chaining invocations allows code like this:

```
buffer.mark( );
buffer.position(5);
buffer.reset( );
```

to be written like this:

```
buffer.mark().position(5).reset( );
```

The classes in java.nio were designed with invocation chaining in mind. You may have seen invocation chaining used with the StringBuffer class.

 When used wisely, invocation chaining can produce concise, elegant, and easy-to-read code. When abused, it yields a cryptic tangle of muddled gibberish. Use invocation chaining when it improves readability and makes your intentions clearer. If clarity of purpose suffers when using invocation chaining, don't use it. Always make your code easy for others to read.

Another thing to note about this API is the isReadOnly( ) method. All buffers are readable, but not all are writable. Each concrete buffer class implements isReadOnly( ) to indicate whether it will allow the buffer content to be modified. Some types of buffers may not have their data elements stored in an array. The content of MappedByteBuffer, for example, may actually be a read-only file. You can also explicitly create read-only view buffers to protect the content from accidental modification. Attempting to modify a read-only buffer will cause a ReadOnlyBufferException to be thrown. But we're getting ahead of ourselves.

Accessing

Let's start at the beginning. Buffers manage a fixed number of data elements. But at any given time, we may care about only some of the elements within the buffer. That is, we may have only partially filled the buffer before we want to drain it. We need ways to track the number of data elements that have been added to the buffer, where to place the next element, etc. The *position* attribute does this. It indicates where the next data element should be inserted when calling put( ) or from where the next element should be retrieved when get( ) is invoked. Astute readers will note that the Buffer API listed above does not contain get( ) or put( ) methods. Every buffer class has these methods, but the types of the arguments they take, and the types they return, are unique to each subclass, so they can't be declared as abstract in the top-level Buffer class. Their definitions must be deferred to type-specific subclasses. For this discussion, we'll assume we're using the ByteBuffer class with the methods shown here (there are additional forms of get( ) and put( ), which we'll discuss in the section "Bulk Moves"):

```
public abstract class ByteBuffer
        extends Buffer implements Comparable
{
        // This is a partial API listing

        public abstract byte get( );
        public abstract byte get (int index);
        public abstract ByteBuffer put (byte b);
        public abstract ByteBuffer put (int index, byte b);
}
```

Gets and puts can be *relative* or *absolute*. In the previous listing, the relative versions are those that don't take an index argument. When the relative methods are called, the position is advanced by one upon return. Relative operations can throw exceptions if the position advances too far. For put( ), if the operation would cause the position to exceed the limit, a `BufferOverflowException` will be thrown. For get( ), `BufferUnderflowException` is thrown if the position is not smaller than the limit. Absolute accesses do not affect the buffer's position, but can throw `java.lang.IndexOutOfBoundsException` if the index you provide is out of range (negative or not less than the limit).

Filling

Let's try an example. We'll load the byte values representing the ASCII character sequence `Hello` into a `ByteBuffer` object named `buffer`. After the following code is executed on the newly created buffer from Figure 2-2, the resulting state of the buffer would be as shown in Figure 2-3:

```
buffer.put((byte)'H').put((byte)'e').put((byte)'l').put((byte)'l').put((byte)'o');
```

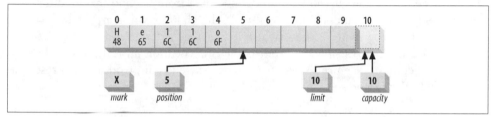

Figure 2-3. Buffer after five put( )s

Notice that each character must be cast to byte in this example. We can't do this:

```
buffer.put('H');
```

without casting because we're putting bytes, not characters. Remember that in Java, characters are represented internally in Unicode, and each Unicode character occupies 16 bits. The examples in this section use bytes containing the numeric values of the ASCII character set. By casting a char to a byte, we're discarding the high-order eight bits to create an eight-bit byte value. This generally works for Latin characters but not for all possible Unicode characters. To keep things simple, we're intentionally ignoring character set mapping issues for the moment. Character encoding is covered in detail in Chapter 6.

Now that we have some data sitting in the buffer, what if we want to make some changes without losing our place? The absolute version of put( ) lets us do so. Suppose we want to change the content of our buffer from the ASCII equivalent of `Hello` to `Mellow`. We can do this with:

```
buffer.put(0, (byte)'M').put((byte)'w');
```

This does an absolute put to replace the byte at location 0 with the hexadecimal value 0x4D, places 0x77 in the byte at the current position (which wasn't affected by the absolute put( )), and increments the position by one. The result is shown in Figure 2-4.

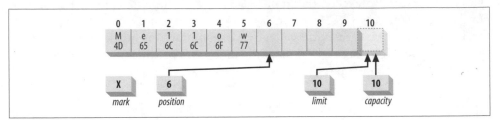

Figure 2-4. Buffer after modification

Flipping

We've filled the buffer, now we must prepare it for draining. We want to pass this buffer to a channel so the content can be written out. But if the channel performs a get( ) on the buffer now, it will fetch undefined data from beyond the good data we just inserted. If we set the position back to 0, the channel will start fetching at the right place, but how will it know when it has reached the end of the data we inserted? This is where the *limit* attribute comes in. The limit indicates the end of the active buffer content. We need to set the limit to the current position, then reset the position to 0. We can do so manually with code like this:

```
buffer.limit(buffer.position()).position(0);
```

But this *flipping* of buffers from fill to drain state was anticipated by the designers of the API; they provided a handy convenience method to do it for us:

```
buffer.flip();
```

The flip( ) method flips a buffer from a fill state, where data elements can be appended, to a drain state ready for elements to be read out. Following a flip, the buffer of Figure 2-4 would look like Figure 2-5.

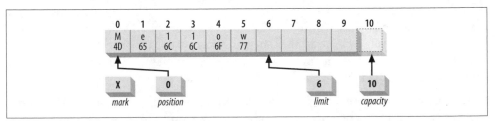

Figure 2-5. Buffer after being flipped

The rewind( ) method is similar to flip( ) but does not affect the limit. It only sets the position back to 0. You can use rewind( ) to go back and reread the data in a buffer that has already been flipped.

What if you flip a buffer twice? It effectively becomes zero-sized. Apply the same steps to the buffer of Figure 2-5; set the limit to the position and the position to 0. Both the limit and position become 0. Attempting get( ) on a buffer with position and limit of 0 results in a BufferUnderflowException. put( ) causes a BufferOverflowException.

Draining

If we pass the buffer of Figure 2-5 to a channel now, it will pull out the data we placed there, starting at the position and stopping at the limit. Slick, no?

By the same token, if you receive a buffer that was filled elsewhere, you'll probably need to flip it before retrieving the content. For example, if a channel read( ) operation has completed, and you want to look at the data placed in the buffer by the channel, you'll need to flip the buffer before calling get( ). The channel object invokes put( ) on the buffer to add data; puts and reads can be freely intermixed.

The boolean method hasRemaining( ) will tell you if you've reached the buffer's limit when draining. The following is a way to drain elements from a buffer to an array (in the section "Bulk Moves," we'll learn about more efficient ways to do bulk transfers):

```
for (int i = 0; buffer.hasRemaining( ), i++) {
        myByteArray [i] = buffer.get( );
}
```

Alternatively, the remaining( ) method will tell you the number of elements that remain from the current position to the limit. You can use a loop like this to drain the buffer of Figure 2-5:

```
int count = buffer.remaining( );

for (int i = 0; i < count, i++) {
        myByteArray [i] = buffer.get( );
}
```

If you have exclusive control of the buffer, this would be more efficient because the limit will not be checked (which requires invocation of an instance method on buffer) on every iteration of the loop. The first example above would allow for multiple threads to drain elements from the buffer concurrently.

 Buffers are not thread-safe. If you want to access a given buffer concurrently from multiple threads, you'll need to do your own synchronization (e.g., acquiring a lock on the buffer object) prior to accessing the buffer.

Once a buffer has been filled and drained, it can be reused. The clear( ) method resets a buffer to an empty state. It doesn't change any of the data elements of the buffer but simply sets the limit to the capacity and the position back to 0, as in Figure 2-2. This leaves the buffer ready to be filled again. See Example 2-1.

Example 2-1. Filling and draining buffers

```
package com.ronsoft.books.nio.buffers;

import java.nio.CharBuffer;

/**
 * Buffer fill/drain example.  This code uses the simplest
 * means of filling and draining a buffer: one element at
 * a time.
 * @author Ron Hitchens (ron@ronsoft.com)
 */
public class BufferFillDrain
{
    public static void main (String [] argv)
        throws Exception
    {
        CharBuffer buffer = CharBuffer.allocate (100);

        while (fillBuffer (buffer)) {
            buffer.flip( );
            drainBuffer (buffer);
            buffer.clear( );
        }
    }

    private static void drainBuffer (CharBuffer buffer)
    {
        while (buffer.hasRemaining( )) {
            System.out.print (buffer.get( ));
        }

        System.out.println ("");
    }

    private static boolean fillBuffer (CharBuffer buffer)
    {
        if (index >= strings.length) {
            return (false);
        }

        String string = strings [index++];

        for (int i = 0; i < string.length( ); i++) {
            buffer.put (string.charAt (i));
        }

        return (true);
    }

    private static int index = 0;

    private static String [] strings = {
        "A random string value",
```

Example 2-1. Filling and draining buffers (continued)

```
        "The product of an infinite number of monkeys",
        "Hey hey we're the Monkees",
        "Opening act for the Monkees: Jimi Hendrix",
        "'Scuse me while I kiss this fly",  // Sorry Jimi ;-)
        "Help Me!  Help Me!",
    };
}
```

Compacting

```
public abstract class ByteBuffer
        extends Buffer implements Comparable
{
        // This is a partial API listing

        public abstract ByteBuffer compact();
}
```

Occasionally, you may wish to drain some, but not all, of the data from a buffer, then resume filling it. To do this, the unread data elements need to be shifted down so that the first element is at index zero. While this could be inefficient if done repeatedly, it's occasionally necessary, and the API provides a method, compact( ), to do it for you. The buffer implementation can potentially copy the data much more efficiently than you could by using the get( ) and put( ) methods. So if you have a need to do this, use compact( ). Figure 2-6 shows a buffer from which we've drained some elements and that we now want to compact.

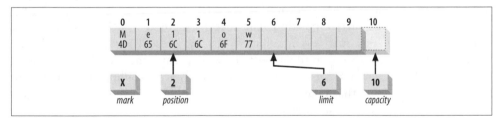

Figure 2-6. A partially drained buffer

Doing this:

```
    buffer.compact()
```

results in the buffer state shown in Figure 2-7.

Several things have happened here. You can see that data elements 2–5 were copied to locations 0–3. Locations 4 and 5 were unaffected but are now at or beyond the current position and therefore are "dead." They can be overwritten by subsequent calls to put( ). Also note that the position has been set to the number of data elements copied. That is, the buffer is now positioned to insert following the last "live" element in the buffer. And finally, the limit has been set to the capacity so the buffer

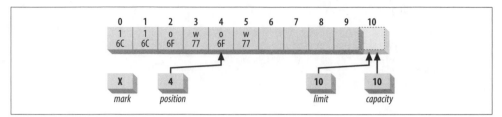

Figure 2-7. Buffer after compaction

can once again be filled fully. The effect of calling compact( ) is to drop the data elements already drained, preserve what hasn't been drained, and make the buffer ready to resume filling to capacity.

You can use a buffer in this way as a First In First Out (FIFO) queue. More efficient algorithms certainly exist (buffer shifting is not a very efficient way to do queuing), but compacting may be a convenient way to synchronize a buffer with logical blocks of data (packets) in a stream you are reading from a socket.

If you want to drain the buffer contents after compaction, the buffer will need to be flipped as discussed earlier. This is true whether you have subsequently added any new data elements to the buffer or not.

Marking

We've covered three of the four buffer attributes mentioned at the beginning of this section. The fourth, *mark*, allows a buffer to remember a position and return to it later. A buffer's mark is undefined until the mark( ) method is called, at which time the mark is set to the current position. The reset( ) method sets the position to the current mark. If the mark is undefined, calling reset( ) will result in an InvalidMarkException. Some buffer methods will discard the mark if one is set (rewind( ), clear( ), and flip( ) always discard the mark). Calling the versions of limit( ) or position( ) that take index arguments will discard the mark if the new value being set is less than the current mark.

 Be careful not to confuse reset( ) and clear( ). The clear( ) method makes a buffer empty, while reset( ) returns the position to a previously set mark.

Let's see how this works. Executing the following code on the buffer of Figure 2-5 results in the buffer state shown in Figure 2-8:

```
buffer.position(2).mark( ).position(4);
```

If this buffer were passed to a channel now, two bytes would be sent ("ow"), and the position would advance to 6. If we then call reset( ), the position would be set to the mark as shown in Figure 2-9. Passing the buffer to the channel again would result in four bytes ("llow") being sent.

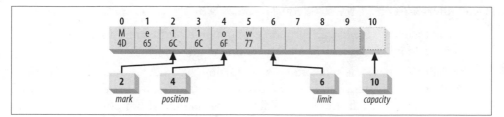

Figure 2-8. A buffer with a mark set

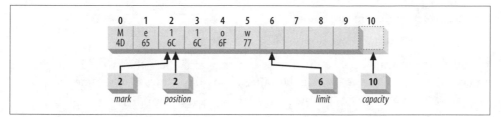

Figure 2-9. A buffer position reset to its mark

The output may not say anything sensible (owllow would be written down the channel), but you get the idea.

Comparing

It's occasionally necessary to compare the data contained in one buffer with that in another buffer. All buffers provide a custom equals( ) method for testing the equality of two buffers and a compareTo( ) method for comparing buffers:

```
public abstract class ByteBuffer
        extends Buffer implements Comparable
{
        // This is a partial API listing

        public boolean equals (Object ob)
        public int compareTo (Object ob)
}
```

Two buffers can be tested for equality with code like this:

```
if (buffer1.equals (buffer2)) {
        doSomething( );
}
```

The equals( ) method returns true if the remaining content of each buffer is identical; otherwise, it returns false. Because the test is for exact equality and is commutative. The names of the buffers in the previous listing could be reversed and produce the same result.

Two buffers are considered to be equal if and only if:

- Both objects are the same type. Buffers containing different data types are never equal, and no Buffer is ever equal to a non-Buffer object.
- Both buffers have the same number of remaining elements. The buffer capacities need not be the same, and the indexes of the data remaining in the buffers need not be the same. But the count of elements remaining (from position to limit) in each buffer must be the same.
- The sequence of remaining data elements, which would be returned from get( ), must be identical in each buffer.

If any of these conditions do not hold, false is returned.

Figure 2-10 illustrates two buffers with different attributes that would compare as equal. Figure 2-11 shows two similar buffers, possibly views of the same underlying buffer, which would test as unequal.

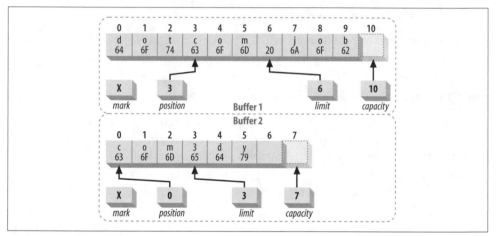

Figure 2-10. Two buffers considered to be equal

Buffers also support lexicographic comparisons with the compareTo( ) method. This method returns an integer that is negative, zero, or positive if the buffer argument is less than, equal to or greater than, respectively, the object instance on which compareTo( ) was invoked. These are the semantics of the java.lang.Comparable interface, which all typed buffers implement. This means that arrays of buffers can be sorted according to their content by invoking java.util.Arrays.sort( ).

Like equals( ), compareTo( ) does not allow comparisons between dissimilar objects. But compareTo( ) is more strict: it will throw ClassCastException if you pass in an object of the incorrect type, whereas equals( ) would simply return false.

Comparisons are performed on the remaining elements of each buffer, in the same way as they are for equals( ), until an inequality is found or the limit of either buffer

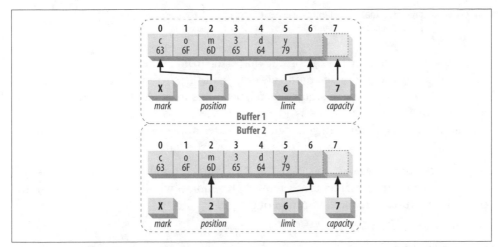

Figure 2-11. Two buffers considered to be unequal

is reached. If one buffer is exhausted before an inequality is found, the shorter buffer is considered to be less than the longer buffer. Unlike equals( ), compareTo( ) is not commutative: the order matters. In this example, a result less than 0 would indicate that buffer2 is less than buffer1, and the expression would evaluate to true.

```
if (buffer1.compareTo (buffer2) < 0) {
        doSomething( );
}
```

If the preceding code was applied to the buffers shown in Figure 2-10, the result would be 0, and the if statement would do nothing. The same test applied to the buffers of Figure 2-11 would return a positive number (to indicate that buffer2 is greater than buffer1), and the expression would also evaluate as false.

Bulk Moves

The design goal of buffers is to enable efficient data transfer. Moving data elements one at a time, such as the loops in Example 2-1, is not very efficient. As you can see in the following listing, the Buffer API provides methods to do bulk moves of data elements in or out of a buffer.

```
public abstract class CharBuffer
        extends Buffer implements CharSequence, Comparable
{
        // This is a partial API listing

        public CharBuffer get (char [] dst)
        public CharBuffer get (char [] dst, int offset, int length)

        public final CharBuffer put (char[] src)
        public CharBuffer put (char [] src, int offset, int length)
        public CharBuffer put (CharBuffer src)
```

```
            public final CharBuffer put (String src)
            public CharBuffer put (String src, int start, int end)
    }
```

There are two forms of get( ) for copying data from buffers to arrays. The first, which takes only an array as argument, drains a buffer to the given array. The second takes offset and length arguments to specify a subrange of the target array. The net effect of these bulk moves is identical to the loops discussed earlier but can potentially be much more efficient since the buffer implementation may take advantage of native code or other optimizations to move the data.

Bulk moves are always of a specified length. That is, you always request that a specific number of data elements be moved. It's not obvious when looking at the method signatures, but this invocation of get( ):

```
    buffer.get (myArray);
```

is equivalent to:

```
    buffer.get (myArray, 0, myArray.length);
```

 Bulk transfers are always of a fixed size. Omitting the length means that the *entire* array will be filled.

If the number of elements you ask for cannot be transferred, no data is transferred, the buffer state is left unchanged, and a BufferUnderflowException is thrown. So when you pass in an array and don't specify the length, you're asking for the entire array to be filled. If the buffer does not contain at least enough elements to completely fill the array, you'll get an exception. This means that if you want to transfer a small buffer into a large array, you need to explicitly specify the length of the data remaining in the buffer. The first example above will not, as you might conclude at first glance, copy the remaining data elements of the buffer into the bottom of the array. To drain a buffer into a larger array, do this:

```
    char [] bigArray = new char [1000];

    // Get count of chars remaining in the buffer
    int length = buffer.remaining( );

    // Buffer is known to contain < 1,000 chars
    buffer.get (bigArrray, 0, length);

    // Do something useful with the data
    processData (bigArray, length);
```

Note that it's necessary to query the buffer for the number of elements before calling get( ) (because we need to tell processData( ) the number of chars that were placed in bigArray). Calling get( ) advances the buffer's position, so calling remaining( )

afterwards returns 0. The bulk versions of get( ) return the buffer reference to facilitate invocation chaining, not a count of transferred data elements.

On the other hand, if the buffer holds more data than will fit in your array, you can iterate and pull it out in chunks with code like this:

```
char [] smallArray = new char [10];

while (buffer.hasRemaining( )) {
        int length = Math.min (buffer.remaining( ), smallArray.length);

        buffer.get (smallArray, 0, length);
        processData (smallArray, length);
}
```

The bulk versions of put( ) behave similarly but move data in the opposite direction, from arrays into buffers. They have similar semantics regarding the size of transfers:

```
buffer.put (myArray);
```

is equivalent to:

```
buffer.put (myArray, 0, myArray.length);
```

If the buffer has room to accept the data in the array (buffer.remaining( ) >= myArray.length), the data will be copied into the buffer starting at the current position, and the buffer position will be advanced by the number of data elements added. If there is not sufficient room in the buffer, no data will be transferred, and a BufferOverflowException will be thrown.

It's also possible to do bulk moves of data from one buffer to another by calling put( ) with a buffer reference as argument:

```
dstBuffer.put (srcBuffer);
```

This is equivalent to (assuming dstBuffer has sufficient space):

```
while (srcBuffer.hasRemaining( )) {
        dstBuffer.put (srcBuffer.get( ));
}
```

The positions of both buffers will be advanced by the number of data elements transferred. Range checks are done as they are for arrays. Specifically, if srcBuffer.remaining( ) is greater than dstBuffer.remaining( ), then no data will be transferred, and BufferOverflowException will be thrown. In case you're wondering, if you pass a buffer to itself, you'll receive a big, fat java.lang.IllegalArgumentException for your hubris.

I've been using CharBuffer for examples in this section, and so far, the discussion has also applied to other typed buffers, such as FloatBuffer, LongBuffer, etc. But the last two methods in the following API listing contain two bulk move methods unique to CharBuffer:

```
public abstract class CharBuffer
        extends Buffer implements CharSequence, Comparable
```

```
{
        // This is a partial API listing

        public final CharBuffer put (String src)
        public CharBuffer put (String src, int start, int end)
}
```

These take Strings as arguments and are similar to the bulk move methods that operate on char arrays. As all Java programmers know, Strings are not the same as arrays of chars. But Strings do contain sequences of chars, and we humans do tend to conceptualize them as char arrays (especially those of us who were or are C or C++ programmers). For these reasons, the CharBuffer class provides convenience methods to copy Strings into CharBuffers.

String moves are similar to char array moves, with the exception that subsequences are specified by the start and end-plus-one indexes (similar to String.subString( )) rather than the start index and length. So this:

```
buffer.put (myString);
```

is equivalent to:

```
buffer.put (myString, 0, myString.length( ));
```

And this is how you'd copy characters 5–8, a total of four characters, from myString into buffer:

```
buffer.put (myString, 5, 9);
```

A String bulk move is the equivalent of doing this:

```
for (int i = start; i < end; i++) }
        buffer.put (myString.charAt (i));
}
```

The same range checking is done for Strings as for char arrays. A BufferOverflowException is thrown if all the characters do not fit into the buffer.

Creating Buffers

As we saw in Figure 2-1, there are seven primary buffer classes, one for each of the nonboolean primitive data types in the Java language. (An eighth is shown there, MappedByteBuffer, which is a specialization of ByteBuffer used for memory mapped files. We'll discuss memory mapping in Chapter 3.) None of these classes can be instantiated directly. They are all abstract classes, but each contains static factory methods to create new instances of the appropriate class.

For this discussion, we'll use the CharBuffer class as an example, but the same applies to the other six primary buffer classes: IntBuffer, DoubleBuffer, ShortBuffer,

LongBuffer, FloatBuffer, and ByteBuffer. Here are the key methods for creating buffers, common to all of the buffer classes (substitute class names as appropriate):

```
public abstract class CharBuffer
        extends Buffer implements CharSequence, Comparable
{
        // This is a partial API listing

        public static CharBuffer allocate (int capacity)

        public static CharBuffer wrap (char [] array)
        public static CharBuffer wrap (char [] array, int offset, int length)

        public final boolean hasArray( )
        public final char [] array( )
        public final int arrayOffset( )
}
```

New buffers are created by either *allocation* or *wrapping*. Allocation creates a buffer object and allocates private space to hold capacity data elements. Wrapping creates a buffer object but does not allocate any space to hold the data elements. It uses the array you provide as backing storage to hold the data elements of the buffer.

To allocate a CharBuffer capable of holding 100 chars:

```
CharBuffer charBuffer = CharBuffer.allocate (100);
```

This implicitly allocates a char array from the heap to act as backing store for the 100 chars.

If you want to provide your own array to be used as the buffer's backing store, call the wrap( ) method:

```
char [] myArray = new char [100];
CharBuffer charbuffer = CharBuffer.wrap (myArray);
```

This constructs a new buffer object, but the data elements will live in the array. This implies that changes made to the buffer by invoking put( ) will be reflected in the array, and any changes made directly to the array will be visible to the buffer object. The version of wrap( ) that takes offset and length arguments will construct a buffer with the position and limit set according to the offset and length values you provide. Doing this:

```
CharBuffer charbuffer = CharBuffer.wrap (myArray, 12, 42);
```

creates a CharBuffer with a position of 12, a limit of 54, and a capacity of myArray. length.

This method does not, as you might expect, create a buffer that occupies only a subrange of the array. The buffer will have access to the full extent of the array; the offset and length arguments only set the initial state. Calling clear( ) on a buffer created this way and then filling it to its limit will overwrite all elements of the array.

The slice( ) method (discussed in the section "Duplicating Buffers") can produce a buffer that occupies only part of a backing array.

Buffers created by either allocate( ) or wrap( ) are always nondirect (direct buffers are discussed in the section "Direct Buffers"). Nondirect buffers have backing arrays, as we just discussed, and you can gain access to those arrays with the remaining API methods listed above. The boolean method hasArray( ) tells you if the buffer has an accessible backing array or not. If it returns true, the array( ) method returns a reference to the array storage used by the buffer object.

If hasArray( ) returns false, do not call array( ) or arrayOffset( ). You'll be rewarded with an UnsupportedOperationException if you do. If a buffer is read-only, its backing array is off-limits, even if an array was provided to wrap( ). Invoking array( ) or arrayOffset( ) will throw a ReadOnlyBufferException in such a case to prevent you from gaining access to and modifying the data content of the read-only buffer. If you have access to the backing array by other means, changes made to the array will be reflected in the read-only buffer. Read-only buffers are discussed in more detail in the section "Duplicating Buffers."

The final method, arrayOffset( ), returns the offset into the array where the buffer's data elements are stored. If you create a buffer with the three-argument version of wrap( ), arrayOffset( ) will always return 0 for that buffer, as we just discussed. However, if you slice a buffer backed by an array, the resulting buffer may have a nonzero array offset. The array offset and capacity of a buffer will tell you which elements of an array are used by a given buffer. Buffer slicing is discussed in the section "Duplicating Buffers."

Up to this point, the discussion in this section has applied to all buffer types. CharBuffer, which we've been using as an example, provides a couple of useful convenience methods not provided by the other buffer classes:

```
public abstract class CharBuffer
        extends Buffer implements CharSequence, Comparable
{
        // This is a partial API listing

        public static CharBuffer wrap (CharSequence csq)
        public static CharBuffer wrap (CharSequence csq, int start, int end)
}
```

These versions of wrap( ) create read-only view buffers whose backing store is the CharSequence object, or a subsequence of that object. (The CharSequence object is described in detail in Chapter 5.) CharSequence describes a readable sequence of characters. As of JDK 1.4, three standard classes implement CharSequence: String, StringBuffer, and CharBuffer. This version of wrap( ) can be useful to "bufferize" existing character data to access their content through the Buffer API. This can be handy for character set encoding (Chapter 6) and regular expression processing (Chapter 5).

```
CharBuffer charBuffer = CharBuffer.wrap ("Hello World");
```

The three-argument form takes start and end index positions describing a subsequence of the given CharSequence. This is a convenience pass-through to CharSequence.subsequence( ). The start argument is the first character in the sequence to use; end is the last position of the character plus one.

Duplicating Buffers

As we just discussed, buffer objects can be created that describe data elements stored externally in an array. But buffers are not limited to managing external data in arrays. They can also manage data externally in *other buffers*. When a buffer that manages data elements contained in another buffer is created, it's known as a view buffer. Most view buffers are views of ByteBuffers (see the section "View Buffers"). Before moving on to the specifics of byte buffers, we'll concentrate on the views that are common to all buffer types.

View buffers are always created by calling methods on an existing buffer instance. Using a factory method on an existing buffer instance means that the view object will be privy to internal implementation details of the original buffer. It will be able to access the data elements directly, whether they are stored in an array or by some other means, rather than going through the get( )/put( ) API of the original buffer object. If the original buffer is direct, views of that buffer will have the same efficiency advantages. Likewise for mapped buffers (discussed in Chapter 3).

In this section, we'll again use CharBuffer as an example, but the same operations can be done on any of the primary buffer types (see Figure 2-1).

```
public abstract class CharBuffer
        extends Buffer implements CharSequence, Comparable
{
        // This is a partial API listing

        public abstract CharBuffer duplicate( );
        public abstract CharBuffer asReadOnlyBuffer( );
        public abstract CharBuffer slice( );
}
```

The duplicate( ) method creates a new buffer that is just like the original. Both buffers share the data elements and have the same capacity, but each buffer will have its own position, limit, and mark. Changes made to data elements in one buffer will be reflected in the other. The duplicate buffer has the same view of the data as the original buffer. If the original buffer is read-only, or direct, the new buffer will inherit those attributes. Direct buffers are discussed in the section "Direct Buffers."

Duplicating a buffer creates a new Buffer object but does not make a copy of the data. Both the original buffer and the copy will act upon the same data elements.

The relationship between a buffer and its duplicate is illustrated in Figure 2-12. This results from code such as the following:

```
CharBuffer buffer = CharBuffer.allocate (8);
buffer.position (3).limit (6).mark().position (5);
CharBuffer dupeBuffer = buffer.duplicate();
buffer.clear();
```

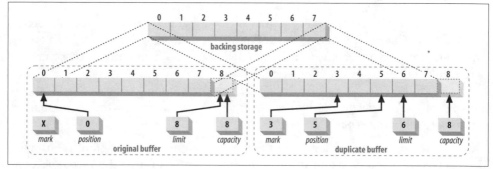

Figure 2-12. Duplicating a buffer

You can make a read-only view of a buffer with the asReadOnlyBuffer() method. This is the same as duplicate(), except that the new buffer will disallow put()s, and its isReadOnly() method will return true. Attempting a call to put() on the read-only buffer will throw a ReadOnlyBufferException.

 If a read-only buffer is sharing data elements with a writable buffer, or is backed by a wrapped array, changes made to the writable buffer or directly to the array will be reflected in all associated buffers, including the read-only buffer.

Slicing a buffer is similar to duplicating, but slice() creates a new buffer that starts at the original buffer's current position and whose capacity is the number of elements remaining in the original buffer (limit − position). The new buffer shares a subsequence of the data elements of the original buffer. The slice buffer will also inherit read-only and direct attributes. Figure 2-13 illustrates a slice buffer created with code similar to this:

```
CharBuffer buffer = CharBuffer.allocate (8);
buffer.position (3).limit (5);
CharBuffer sliceBuffer = buffer.slice();
```

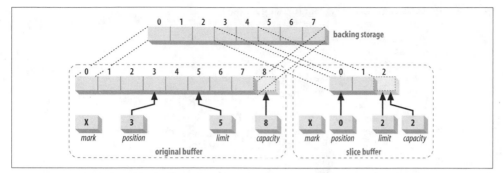

Figure 2-13. Creating a slice buffer

To create a buffer that maps to positions 12–20 (nine elements) of a preexisting array, code like this does the trick:

```
char [] myBuffer = new char [100];
CharBuffer cb = CharBuffer.wrap (myBuffer);
cb.position(12).limit(21);
CharBuffer sliced = cb.slice();
```

A more complete discussion of view buffers can be found in the section "View Buffers."

Byte Buffers

In this section, we'll take a closer look at byte buffers. There are buffer classes for all the primitive data types (except boolean), but byte buffers have characteristics not shared by the others. Bytes are the fundamental data unit used by the operating system and its I/O facilities. When moving data between the JVM and the operating system, it's necessary to break down the other data types into their constituent bytes. As we'll see in the following sections, the byte-oriented nature of system-level I/O can be felt throughout the design of buffers and the services with which they interact.

For reference, here is the complete API of `ByteBuffer`. Some of these methods have been discussed in previous sections and are simply type-specific versions. The new methods will be covered in this and following sections.

```
package java.nio;

public abstract class ByteBuffer extends Buffer
        implements Comparable
{
        public static ByteBuffer allocate (int capacity)
        public static ByteBuffer allocateDirect (int capacity)
        public abstract boolean isDirect();
        public static ByteBuffer wrap (byte[] array, int offset, int length)
        public static ByteBuffer wrap (byte[] array)
```

```
public abstract ByteBuffer duplicate();
public abstract ByteBuffer asReadOnlyBuffer();
public abstract ByteBuffer slice();
public final boolean hasArray()
public final byte [] array()
public final int arrayOffset()

public abstract byte get();
public abstract byte get (int index);
public ByteBuffer get (byte[] dst, int offset, int length)
public ByteBuffer get (byte[] dst, int offset, int length)

public abstract ByteBuffer put (byte b);
public abstract ByteBuffer put (int index, byte b);
public ByteBuffer put (ByteBuffer src)
public ByteBuffer put (byte[] src, int offset, int length)
public final ByteBuffer put (byte[] src)

public final ByteOrder order()
public final ByteBuffer order (ByteOrder bo)

public abstract CharBuffer asCharBuffer();
public abstract ShortBuffer asShortBuffer();
public abstract IntBuffer asIntBuffer();
public abstract LongBuffer asLongBuffer();
public abstract FloatBuffer asFloatBuffer();
public abstract DoubleBuffer asDoubleBuffer();

public abstract char getChar();
public abstract char getChar (int index);
public abstract ByteBuffer putChar (char value);
public abstract ByteBuffer putChar (int index, char value);

public abstract short getShort();
public abstract short getShort (int index);
public abstract ByteBuffer putShort (short value);
public abstract ByteBuffer putShort (int index, short value);

public abstract int getInt();
public abstract int getInt (int index);
public abstract ByteBuffer putInt (int value);
public abstract ByteBuffer putInt (int index, int value);

public abstract long getLong();
public abstract long getLong (int index);
public abstract ByteBuffer putLong (long value);
public abstract ByteBuffer putLong (int index, long value);

public abstract float getFloat();
public abstract float getFloat (int index);
public abstract ByteBuffer putFloat (float value);
public abstract ByteBuffer putFloat (int index, float value);
```

```
        public abstract double getDouble();
        public abstract double getDouble (int index);
        public abstract ByteBuffer putDouble (double value);
        public abstract ByteBuffer putDouble (int index, double value);

        public abstract ByteBuffer compact();
        public boolean equals (Object ob) {
        public int compareTo (Object ob) {
        public String toString()
        public int hashCode()
    }
```

Bytes Are Always Eight Bits, Right?

These days, bytes are almost universally recognized as being eight bits. But this wasn't always the case. In ages past, bytes ranged anywhere from 3 to 12 or more bits each, with the most common being 6 to 9 bits. The eight-bit byte was arrived at through a combination of practicality and market forces. It's practical because eight bits are enough to represent a usable character set (English characters anyway), eight is a power of two (which makes hardware design simpler), eight neatly holds two hexadecimal digits, and multiples of eight provide enough combined bits to store useful numeric values. The market force was IBM. The IBM 360 mainframe, first introduced in the 1960s, used eight-bit bytes. That pretty much settled the matter. For further background, consult the man himself, Bob Bemer of IBM, at *http://www.bobbemer.com/BYTE.HTM*.

Byte Ordering

The nonbyte primitive types, except for boolean,* are composed of several bytes grouped together. The data types and their sizes are summarized in Table 2-1.

Table 2-1. Primitive data types and sizes

Data type	Size (in bytes)
Byte	1
Char	2
Short	2
Int	4
Long	8

---

* Booleans represent one of two values: true or false. A byte can take on 256 unique values, so a boolean cannot be unambiguously mapped to one or several bytes. Bytes are the building blocks from which all buffers are constructed. The NIO architects determined that implementation of boolean buffers would be problematic, and the need for such a buffer type was debatable anyway.

Table 2-1. Primitive data types and sizes (continued)

Data type	Size (in bytes)
Float	4
Double	8

Each of the primitive data types is stored in memory as a contiguous sequence of bytes. For example, the 32-bit int value 0x037FB4C7 (decimal 58,700,999) might be packed into memory bytes as illustrated in Figure 2-14 (memory addresses increasing left to right). Notice the word "might" in the previous sentence. Although the size of a byte has been settled, the issue of *byte order* has not been universally agreed upon. The bytes representing an integer value might just as easily be organized in memory as shown in Figure 2-15.

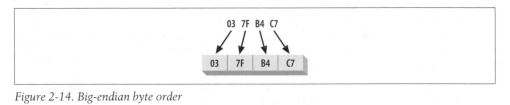

Figure 2-14. Big-endian byte order

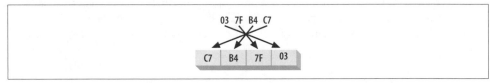

Figure 2-15. Little-endian byte order

The way multibyte numeric values are stored in memory is commonly referred to as *endian-ness*. If the numerically most-significant byte of the number, the *big end*, is at the lower address, then the system is *big-endian* (Figure 2-14). If the least-significant byte comes first, it's *little-endian* (Figure 2-15).

Endian-ness is rarely a choice for software designers; it's usually dictated by the hardware design. Both types of endian-ness, sometimes known as *byte sex*, are in wide-spread use today. There are good arguments for both approaches. Intel processors use the little-endian design. The Motorola CPU family, Sun Sparc, and PowerPC CPU architectures are all big-endian.

The question of byte order even transcends CPU hardware design. When the architects of the Internet were designing the Internet Protocol (IP) suite to interconnect all types of computers, they recognized the problem of exchanging numeric data between systems with differing internal byte orders. Therefore, the IPs define a notion of *network byte order*,* which is big-endian. All multibyte numeric values used within the protocol portions of IP packets must be converted between the local *host byte order* and the common network byte order.

In java.nio, byte order is encapsulated by the ByteOrder class:

```
package java.nio;

public final class ByteOrder
{
        public static final ByteOrder BIG_ENDIAN
        public static final ByteOrder LITTLE_ENDIAN

        public static ByteOrder nativeOrder( )
        public String toString( )
}
```

The ByteOrder class defines the constants that determine which byte order to use when storing or retrieving multibyte values from a buffer. The class acts as a type-safe enumeration. It defines two public fields that are preinitialized with instances of itself. Only these two instances of ByteOrder ever exist in the JVM, so they can be compared using the == operator. If you need to know the native byte order of the hardware platform the JVM is running on, invoke the nativeOrder( ) static class method. It will return one of the two defined constants. Calling toString( ) returns a String containing one of the two literal strings BIG_ENDIAN or LITTLE_ENDIAN.

Every buffer class has a current byte-order setting that can be queried by calling order( ):

```
public abstract class CharBuffer extends Buffer
        implements Comparable, CharSequence
{
        // This is a partial API listing

        public final ByteOrder order( )
}
```

This method returns one of the two constants from ByteOrder. For buffer classes other than ByteBuffer, the byte order is a read-only property and may take on different values depending on how the buffer was created. Except for ByteBuffer, buffers created by allocation or by wrapping an array will return the same value from order( ), as does ByteOrder.nativeOrder( ). This is because the elements contained in the buffer are directly accessed as primitive data within the JVM.

The ByteBuffer class is different: the default byte order is always ByteOrder.BIG_ENDIAN regardless of the native byte order of the system. Java's default byte order is big-endian, which allows things such as class files and serialized objects to work with any

---

* Internet terminology refers to bytes as *octets*. As mentioned in the sidebar, the size of a byte can be ambiguous. By using the term "octet," the IP specifications explicitly mandate that bytes consist of eight bits.

JVM. This can have performance implications if the native hardware byte order is little-endian. Accessing ByteBuffer content as other data types (to be discussed shortly) can potentially be much more efficient when using the native hardware byte order.

Hopefully, you're a little puzzled at this point as to why the ByteBuffer class would need a byte order setting at all. Bytes are bytes, right? Sure, but as you'll soon see in the section "Data Element Views," ByteBuffer objects possess a host of convenience methods for getting and putting the buffer content as other primitive data types. The way these methods encode or decode the bytes is dependent on the ByteBuffer's current byte-order setting.

The byte-order setting of a ByteBuffer can be changed at any time by invoking order( ) with either ByteOrder.BIG_ENDIAN or ByteOrder.LITTLE_ENDIAN as an argument:

```
public abstract class ByteBuffer extends Buffer
        implements Comparable
{
        // This is a partial API listing

        public final ByteOrder order( )
        public final ByteBuffer order (ByteOrder bo)
}
```

If a buffer was created as a view of a ByteBuffer object (see the section "View Buffers"), then the value returned by the order( ) method is the byte-order setting of the originating ByteBuffer at the time the view was created. The byte-order setting of the view cannot be changed after it's created and will not be affected if the original byte buffer's byte order is changed later.

Direct Buffers

The most significant way in which byte buffers are distinguished from other buffer types is that they can be the sources and/or targets of I/O performed by Channels. If you were to skip ahead to Chapter 3 (hey! hey!), you'd see that channels accept only ByteBuffers as arguments.

As we saw in Chapter 1, operating systems perform I/O operations on memory areas. These memory areas, as far as the operating system is concerned, are contiguous sequences of bytes. It's no surprise then that only byte buffers are eligible to participate in I/O operations. Also recall that the operating system will directly access the address space of the process, in this case the JVM process, to transfer the data. This means that memory areas that are targets of I/O operations must be contiguous sequences of bytes. In the JVM, an array of bytes may not be stored contiguously in memory, or the Garbage Collector could move it at any time. Arrays are objects in Java, and the way data is stored inside that object could vary from one JVM implementation to another.

For this reason, the notion of a *direct buffer* was introduced. Direct buffers are intended for interaction with channels and native I/O routines. They make a best effort to store the byte elements in a memory area that a channel can use for direct, or *raw*, access by using native code to tell the operating system to drain or fill the memory area directly.

Direct byte buffers are usually the best choice for I/O operations. By design, they support the most efficient I/O mechanism available to the JVM. Nondirect byte buffers can be passed to channels, but doing so may incur a performance penalty. It's usually not possible for a nondirect buffer to be the target of a native I/O operation. If you pass a nondirect ByteBuffer object to a channel for write, the channel may implicitly do the following on each call:

1. Create a temporary direct ByteBuffer object.
2. Copy the content of the nondirect buffer to the temporary buffer.
3. Perform the low-level I/O operation using the temporary buffer.
4. The temporary buffer object goes out of scope and is eventually garbage collected.

This can potentially result in buffer copying and object churn on every I/O, which are exactly the sorts of things we'd like to avoid. However, depending on the implementation, things may not be this bad. The runtime will likely cache and reuse direct buffers or perform other clever tricks to boost throughput. If you're simply creating a buffer for one-time use, the difference is not significant. On the other hand, if you will be using the buffer repeatedly in a high-performance scenario, you're better off allocating direct buffers and reusing them.

Direct buffers are optimal for I/O, but they may be more expensive to create than nondirect byte buffers. The memory used by direct buffers is allocated by calling through to native, operating system–specific code, bypassing the standard JVM heap. Setting up and tearing down direct buffers could be significantly more expensive than heap-resident buffers, depending on the host operating system and JVM implementation. The memory-storage areas of direct buffers are not subject to garbage collection because they are outside the standard JVM heap.

The performance tradeoffs of using direct versus nondirect buffers can vary widely by JVM, operating system, and code design. By allocating memory outside the heap, you may subject your application to additional forces of which the JVM is unaware. When bringing additional moving parts into play, make sure that you're achieving the desired effect. I recommend the old software maxim: first make it work, then make it fast. Don't worry too much about optimization up front; concentrate first on correctness. The JVM implementation may be able to perform buffer caching or other optimizations that will give you the performance you need without a lot of unnecessary effort on your part.[*]

A direct ByteBuffer is created by calling ByteBuffer.allocateDirect() with the desired capacity, just like the allocate() method we covered earlier. Note that wrapped buffers, those created with one of the wrap() methods, are always non-direct.

```
public abstract class ByteBuffer
        extends Buffer implements Comparable
{
        // This is a partial API listing

        public static ByteBuffer allocate (int capacity)
        public static ByteBuffer allocateDirect (int capacity)
        public abstract boolean isDirect();
}
```

All buffers provide a boolean method named isDirect() to test whether a particular buffer is direct. While ByteBuffer is the only type that can be allocated as direct, isDirect() could be true for nonbyte view buffers if the underlying buffer is a direct ByteBuffer. This leads us to...

View Buffers

As we've already discussed, I/O basically boils down to shuttling groups of bytes around. When doing high-volume I/O, odds are you'll be using ByteBuffers to read in files, receive data from network connections, etc. Once the data has arrived in your ByteBuffer, you'll need to look at it to decide what to do or manipulate it before sending it along. The ByteBuffer class provides a rich API for creating *view buffers*.

View buffers are created by a factory method on an existing buffer object instance. The view object maintains its own attributes, capacity, position, limit, and mark, but shares data elements with the original buffer. We saw the simple form of this in the section "Duplicating Buffers," in which buffers were duplicated and sliced. But ByteBuffer allows the creation of views to map the raw bytes of the byte buffer to other primitive data types. For example, the asLongBuffer() method creates a view buffer that will access groups of eight bytes from the ByteBuffer as longs.

Each of the factory methods in the following listing create a new buffer that is a view into the original ByteBuffer object. Invoking one of these methods will create a buffer of the corresponding type, which is a slice (see the section "Duplicating Buffers") of the underlying byte buffer corresponding to the byte buffer's current position and limit. The new buffer will have a capacity equal to the number of elements remaining in the byte buffer (as returned by remaining()) divided by the number of bytes comprising the view's primitive type (refer to Table 2-1). Any remaining bytes

---

[*] "We should forget about small efficiencies, say about 97% of the time: premature optimization is the root of all evil."—Donald Knuth

at the end of the slice will not be visible in the view. The first element of the view will begin at the position (as returned by position( )) of the ByteBuffer object at the time the view was created. View buffers with data elements that are aligned on natural modulo boundaries may be eligible for optimization by the implementation.

```java
public abstract class ByteBuffer
        extends Buffer implements Comparable
{
        // This is a partial API listing

        public abstract CharBuffer asCharBuffer( );
        public abstract ShortBuffer asShortBuffer( );
        public abstract IntBuffer asIntBuffer( );
        public abstract LongBuffer asLongBuffer( );
        public abstract FloatBuffer asFloatBuffer( );
        public abstract DoubleBuffer asDoubleBuffer( );
}
```

The following code creates a CharBuffer view of a ByteBuffer, as shown in Figure 2-16. (Example 2-2 puts this fragment into a larger context.)

```java
ByteBuffer byteBuffer = ByteBuffer.allocate (7).order (ByteOrder.BIG_ENDIAN);
CharBuffer charBuffer = byteBuffer.asCharBuffer( );
```

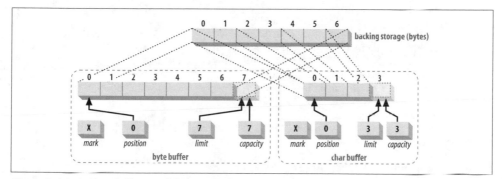

Figure 2-16. A CharBuffer view of a ByteBuffer

Example 2-2. Creating a char view of a ByteBuffer

```java
package com.ronsoft.books.nio.buffers;

import java.nio.Buffer;
import java.nio.ByteBuffer;
import java.nio.CharBuffer;
import java.nio.ByteOrder;

/**
 * Test asCharBuffer view.
 *
 * Created May 2002
 * @author Ron Hitchens (ron@ronsoft.com)
 */
```

Example 2-2. Creating a char view of a ByteBuffer (continued)

```java
public class BufferCharView
{
    public static void main (String [] argv)
        throws Exception
    {

        ByteBuffer byteBuffer =
            ByteBuffer.allocate (7).order (ByteOrder.BIG_ENDIAN);
        CharBuffer charBuffer = byteBuffer.asCharBuffer( );

        // Load the ByteBuffer with some bytes
        byteBuffer.put (0, (byte)0);
        byteBuffer.put (1, (byte)'H');
        byteBuffer.put (2, (byte)0);
        byteBuffer.put (3, (byte)'i');
        byteBuffer.put (4, (byte)0);
        byteBuffer.put (5, (byte)'!');
        byteBuffer.put (6, (byte)0);

        println (byteBuffer);
        println (charBuffer);
    }

    // Print info about a buffer
    private static void println (Buffer buffer)
    {
        System.out.println ("pos=" + buffer.position( )
            + ", limit=" + buffer.limit( )
            + ", capacity=" + buffer.capacity( )
            + ": '" + buffer.toString( ) + "'");
    }
}
pos=0, limit=7, capacity=7: 'java.nio.HeapByteBuffer[pos=0 lim=7 cap=7]'
pos=0, limit=3, capacity=3: 'Hi!'
```

Here's the output from executing `BufferCharView`:

```
pos=0, limit=7, capacity=7: 'java.nio.HeapByteBuffer[pos=0 lim=7 cap=7]'
pos=0, limit=3, capacity=3: 'Hi!
```

Once you've obtained the view buffer, you can create further subviews with `duplicate( )`, `slice( )`, and `asReadOnlyBuffer( )`, as discussed in the section "Duplicating Buffers."

Whenever a view buffer accesses the underlying bytes of a ByteBuffer, the bytes are packed to compose a data element according to the view buffer's byte-order setting. When a view buffer is created, it inherits the byte-order setting of the underlying ByteBuffer at the time the view is created. The byte-order setting of the view cannot be changed later. In Figure 2-16, you can see that two bytes of the underlying ByteBuffer map to each character of the CharBuffer. The ByteOrder setting of the CharBuffer determines how these byte pairs are combined to form chars. Refer to the section "Byte Ordering" for more details.

View buffers can potentially be much more efficient when derived from direct byte buffers. If the byte order of the view matches the native hardware byte order, the low-level code may be able to access the data values directly rather than going through the byte-packing and -unpacking process.

Data Element Views

The ByteBuffer class provides a lightweight mechanism to access groups of bytes as a multibyte data type. ByteBuffer contains accessor and mutator methods for each of the primitive data types:

```
public abstract class ByteBuffer
        extends Buffer implements Comparable
{
        public abstract char getChar( );
        public abstract char getChar (int index);
        public abstract short getShort( );
        public abstract short getShort (int index);
        public abstract int getInt( );
        public abstract int getInt (int index);
        public abstract long getLong( );
        public abstract long getLong (int index);
        public abstract float getFloat( );
        public abstract float getFloat (int index);
        public abstract double getDouble( );
        public abstract double getDouble (int index);

        public abstract ByteBuffer putChar (char value);
        public abstract ByteBuffer putChar (int index, char value);
        public abstract ByteBuffer putShort (short value);
        public abstract ByteBuffer putShort (int index, short value);
        public abstract ByteBuffer putInt (int value);
        public abstract ByteBuffer putInt (int index, int value);
        public abstract ByteBuffer putLong (long value);
        public abstract ByteBuffer putLong (int index, long value);
        public abstract ByteBuffer putFloat (float value);
        public abstract ByteBuffer putFloat (int index, float value);
        public abstract ByteBuffer putDouble (double value);
        public abstract ByteBuffer putDouble (int index, double value);
}
```

These methods access the bytes of the ByteBuffer, starting at the current position, as if a data element of that type were stored there. The bytes will be marshaled to or from the requested primitive data type according to the current byte-order setting in effect for the buffer. For example, if getInt( ) is called, the four bytes beginning at the current position would be packed into an int and returned as the method value. See the section "Byte Ordering."

Assume that a ByteBuffer named buffer is in the state shown in Figure 2-17.

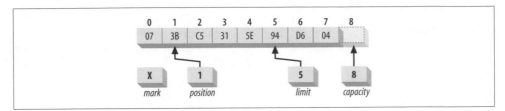

Figure 2-17. A ByteBuffer containing some data

This code:

```
int value = buffer.getInt( );
```

would return an int value composed of the byte values in locations 1–4 of the buffer. The actual value returned would depend on the current ByteOrder setting of the buffer. To be more specific:

```
int value = buffer.order (ByteOrder.BIG_ENDIAN).getInt( );
```

returns the numeric value 0x3BC5315E, while:

```
int value = buffer.order (ByteOrder.LITTLE_ENDIAN).getInt( );
```

returns the value 0x5E31C53B.

If the primitive data type you're trying to get requires more bytes than what remains in the buffer, a BufferUnderflowException will be thrown. For the buffer in Figure 2-17, this code would throw an exception because a long is eight bytes, and only five bytes remain in the buffer:

```
long value = buffer.getLong( );
```

The elements returned by these methods do not need to be aligned on any specific modulo boundary.* Data values will be fetched and assembled from the byte buffer beginning at the current position of the buffer, regardless of word alignment. This can be inefficient, but it allows for arbitrary placement of data in a byte stream. This can be useful for extracting numeric values from binary file data or packing data into platform-specific formats for export to external systems.

The put methods perform the inverse operation of the gets. Primitive data values will be broken into bytes according to the byte order of the buffer and stored. If insufficient space is available to store all the bytes, a BufferOverflowException will be thrown.

There are relative and absolute forms of each method. The relative forms advance the position by the number of bytes affected (see Table 2-1). The absolute versions leave the position unchanged.

---

* A modulo considers the remainder when dividing one number by another. Modulo boundaries are those points on a number line where the remainder for a particular divisor is zero. For example, any number evenly divisible by 4 is *modulo 4*: 4, 8, 12, 16, etc. Many CPU designs require modulo memory alignment of multi-byte numeric values.

Accessing Unsigned Data

The Java programming language does not provide direct support for unsigned numeric values (other than char). But there are many instances in which you may need to extract unsigned information from a data stream or file, or pack data to create file headers or other structured information with unsigned fields. The ByteBuffer API does not provide direct support for this, but it's not difficult to do. You just need to be careful about precision. The utility class in Example 2-3 may be useful when you must deal with unsigned data in buffers.

Example 2-3. Utility routines for getting/putting unsigned values

```
package com.ronsoft.books.nio.buffers;

import java.nio.ByteBuffer;

/**
 * Utility class to get and put unsigned values to a ByteBuffer object.
 * All methods here are static and take a ByteBuffer argument.
 * Since java does not provide unsigned primitive types, each unsigned
 * value read from the buffer is promoted up to the next bigger primitive
 * data type.  getUnsignedByte() returns a short, getUnsignedShort() returns
 * an int and getUnsignedInt() returns a long.  There is no getUnsignedLong()
 * since there is no primitive type to hold the value returned.  If needed,
 * methods returning BigInteger could be implemented.
 * Likewise, the put methods take a value larger than the type they will
 * be assigning.  putUnsignedByte takes a short argument, etc.
 *
 * @author Ron Hitchens (ron@ronsoft.com)
 */
public class Unsigned
{
    public static short getUnsignedByte (ByteBuffer bb)
    {
        return ((short)(bb.get() & 0xff));
    }

    public static void putUnsignedByte (ByteBuffer bb, int value)
    {
        bb.put ((byte)(value & 0xff));
    }

    public static short getUnsignedByte (ByteBuffer bb, int position)
    {
        return ((short)(bb.get (position) & (short)0xff));
    }

    public static void putUnsignedByte (ByteBuffer bb, int position,
        int value)
    {
```

```java
        bb.put (position, (byte)(value & 0xff));
    }

    // -------------------------------------------------------------

    public static int getUnsignedShort (ByteBuffer bb)
    {
        return (bb.getShort( ) & 0xffff);
    }

    public static void putUnsignedShort (ByteBuffer bb, int value)
    {
        bb.putShort ((short)(value & 0xffff));
    }

    public static int getUnsignedShort (ByteBuffer bb, int position)
    {
        return (bb.getShort (position) & 0xffff);
    }

    public static void putUnsignedShort (ByteBuffer bb, int position,
        int value)
    {
        bb.putShort (position, (short)(value & 0xffff));
    }

    // -------------------------------------------------------------

    public static long getUnsignedInt (ByteBuffer bb)
    {
        return ((long)bb.getInt( ) & 0xffffffffL);
    }

    public static void putUnsignedInt (ByteBuffer bb, long value)
    {
        bb.putInt ((int)(value & 0xffffffffL));
    }

    public static long getUnsignedInt (ByteBuffer bb, int position)
    {
        return ((long)bb.getInt (position) & 0xffffffffL);
    }

    public static void putUnsignedInt (ByteBuffer bb, int position,
        long value)
    {
        bb.putInt (position, (int)(value & 0xffffffffL));
    }
}
```

Memory-Mapped Buffers

Mapped buffers are byte buffers with data elements stored in a file and are accessed via *memory mapping*. Mapped buffers are always direct and can be created only from a `FileChannel` object. Usage of mapped buffers is similar to direct buffers, but `MappedByteBuffer` objects possess many special characteristics unique to file access. For this reason, I'm deferring discussion of mapped buffers to "Memory-Mapped Files" in Chapter 3, which also discusses file locking.

Summary

This chapter covered buffers, which live in the `java.nio` package. Buffer objects enable the advanced I/O capabilities covered in the remaining chapters. These key buffer topics were covered in this chapter:

Buffer attributes

>   Attributes that all buffers posses were covered in the section "Attributes." These attributes describe the current state of a buffer and affect how it behaves. In this section, we also learned how to manipulate the state of buffers and how to add and remove data elements.

Buffer creation

>   We learned how buffers are created in the section "Creating Buffers" and how to duplicate them in the section "Duplicating Buffers." There are many types of buffers. The way a buffer is created determines how and where it should be used.

Byte buffers

>   While buffers can be created for any primitive data type other than boolean, byte buffers have special features not shared by the other buffer types. Only byte buffers can be used with channels (discussed in Chapter 3), and byte buffers offer views of their content in terms of other data types. We also examined the issues related to byte ordering. `ByteBuffers` were discussed in the section "Byte Buffers."

This concludes our visit with the menagerie of buffers in `java.nio`. The next stop on the tour is `java.nio.channels` where you will encounter, not surprisingly, channels. Channels interact with byte buffers and unlock the door to high-performance I/O. Hop back on the bus, it's a short trip to our next stop.

CHAPTER 3
Channels

Brilliance! Sheer, unadulterated brilliance!
—Wile E. Coyote, Super Genius

Channels are the second major innovation of java.nio. They are not an extension or enhancement, but a new, first-class Java I/O paradigm. They provide direct connections to I/O services. A Channel is a conduit that transports data efficiently between byte buffers and the entity on the other end of the channel (usually a file or socket).

A good metaphor for a channel is a pneumatic tube, the type used at drive-up bank-teller windows. Your paycheck would be the information you're sending. The carrier would be like a buffer. You fill the buffer (place your paycheck in the carrier), "write" the buffer to the channel (drop the carrier into the tube), and the payload is carried to the I/O service (bank teller) on the other end of the channel.

The response would be the teller filling the buffer (placing your receipt in the carrier) and starting a channel transfer in the opposite direction (dropping the carrier back into the tube). The carrier arrives on your end of the channel (a filled buffer is ready for you to examine). You then flip the buffer (open the lid) and drain it (remove your receipt). You drive away and the next object (bank customer) is ready to repeat the process using the same carrier (Buffer) and tube (Channel) objects.

In most cases, channels have a one-to-one relationship with operating-system *file descriptors*, or *file handles*. Although channels are more generalized than file descriptors, most channels you will use on a regular basis are connected to open file descriptors. The channel classes provide the abstraction needed to maintain platform independence but still model the native I/O capabilities of modern operating systems.

Channels are gateways through which the native I/O services of the operating system can be accessed with a minimum of overhead, and buffers are the internal endpoints used by channels to send and receive data. (See Figure 3-1.)

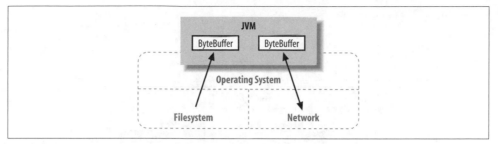

Figure 3-1. Channels act as conduits to I/O services

As you can see from the UML class diagram in Figure 3-2, the inheritance relationships of the channel classes are a bit more complicated than those of the buffer classes. The interrelationships are more complex, and there are some dependencies on classes defined in the java.nio.channels.spi subpackage. In this chapter, we'll make sense of this tangle. The channels SPI is summarized in Appendix B.

So without further ado, let's explore the exciting world of channels.

Channel Basics

First, let's take a closer look at the basic Channel interface. This is the full source of the Channel interface:

```
package java.nio.channels;

public interface Channel
{
        public boolean isOpen( );
        public void close( ) throws IOException;
}
```

Unlike buffers, the channel APIs are primarily specified by interfaces. Channel implementations vary radically between operating systems, so the channel APIs simply describe what can be done. Channel implementations often use native code, so this is only natural. The channel interfaces allow you to gain access to low-level I/O services in a controlled and portable way.

As you can see by the top-level Channel interface, there are only two operations common to all channels: checking to see if a channel is open (isOpen( )) and closing an open channel (close( )). Figure 3-2 shows that all the interesting stuff is in the classes that implement Channel and its subinterfaces.

The InterruptibleChannel interface is a marker that, when implemented by a channel, indicates that the channel is interruptible. Interruptible channels behave in specific ways when a thread accessing them is interrupted, which we will discuss in the section "Closing Channels." Most, but not all, channels are interruptible.

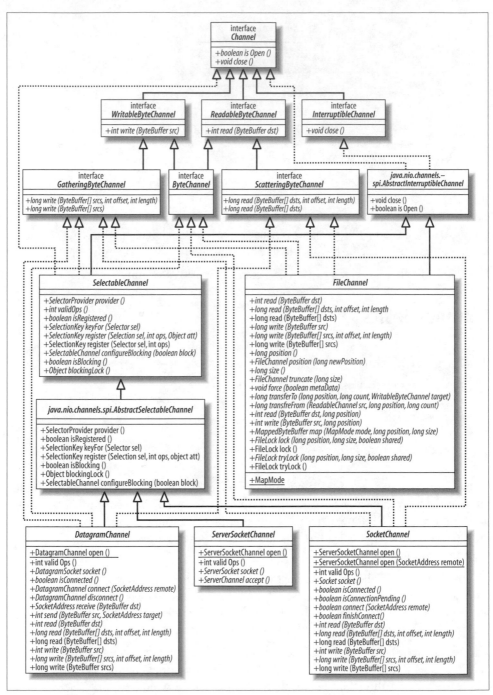

Figure 3-2. The channel family tree

The other interfaces extending Channel are the byte-oriented subinterfaces Writable-ByteChannel and ReadableByteChannel. This supports what we learned earlier: channels operate only on byte buffers. The structure of the hierarchy implies that channels for other data types could also extend from Channel. This is good class design, but nonbyte implementations are unlikely because operating systems do low-level I/O in terms of bytes.

You can see in Figure 3-2 that two of the classes in this family tree live in a different package, java.nio.channels.spi. These classes, AbstractInterruptibleChannel and AbstractSelectableChannel, provide the common methods needed by channel implementations that are interruptible or selectable, respectively. Although the interfaces describing channel behaviors are defined in the java.nio.channels package, the concrete implementations extend from classes in java.nio.channels.spi. This allows them access to protected methods that normal users of channels should never invoke.

As a user of channels, you can safely ignore the intermediate classes in the SPI package. The somewhat convoluted inheritance hierarchy is of interest only to those implementing new channels. The SPI package allows new channel implementations to be plugged into the JVM in a controlled and modular way. This means channels optimized for a particular operating system, filesystem, or application can be dropped in to maximize performance.

Opening Channels

Channels serve as conduits to I/O services. As we discussed in Chapter 1, I/O falls into two broad categories: file I/O and stream I/O. So it's no surprise that there are two types of channels: file and socket. If you refer to Figure 3-2, you'll see that there is one FileChannel class and three socket channel classes: SocketChannel, ServerSocketChannel, and DatagramChannel.

Channels can be created in several ways. The socket channels have factory methods to create new socket channels directly. But a FileChannel object can be obtained only by calling the getChannel( ) method on an open RandomAccessFile, FileInputStream, or FileOutputStream object. You cannot create a FileChannel object directly. File and socket channels are discussed detail in upcoming sections.

```
SocketChannel sc = SocketChannel.open( );
sc.connect (new InetSocketAddress ("somehost", someport));

ServerSocketChannel ssc = ServerSocketChannel.open( );
ssc.socket( ).bind (new InetSocketAddress (somelocalport));

DatagramChannel dc = DatagramChannel.open( );

RandomAccessFile raf = new RandomAccessFile ("somefile", "r");
FileChannel fc = raf.getChannel( );
```

As you'll see in the section "Socket Channels," the socket classes of java.net have new getChannel( ) methods as well. While these methods return a corresponding socket channel object, they are not sources of new channels as RandomAccessFile.getChannel( ) is. They return the channel associated with a socket if one already exists; they never create new channels.

Using Channels

As we learned in Chapter 2, channels transfer data to and from ByteBuffer objects.

Removing most of the clutter from Figure 3-2 yields the UML class diagram in Figure 3-3. The APIs of the subinterfaces are as follows:

```
public interface ReadableByteChannel
        extends Channel
{
        public int read (ByteBuffer dst) throws IOException;
}

public interface WritableByteChannel
        extends Channel
{
        public int write (ByteBuffer src) throws IOException;
}

public interface ByteChannel
        extends ReadableByteChannel, WritableByteChannel
{
}
```

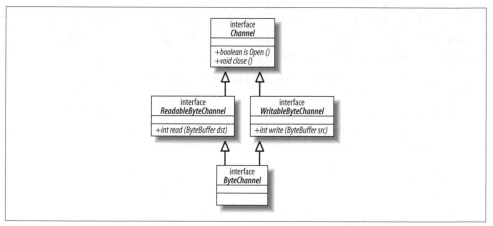

Figure 3-3. The ByteChannel interfaces

Channels can be *unidirectional* or *bidirectional*. A given channel class might implement ReadableByteChannel, which defines the read( ) method. Another might implement WritableByteChannel to provide write( ). A class implementing one or the other of these interfaces is unidirectional: it can transfer data in only one direction. If a class implements both interfaces, it is bidirectional and can transfer data in both directions.

Figure 3-3 shows an interface, ByteChannel, which extends both ReadableByteChannel and WritableByteChannel. ByteChannel doesn't declare any new API methods; it's a convenience interface that aggregates the multiple interfaces it inherits under a new name. By definition, a channel that implements ByteChannel implements both ReadableByteChannel and WritableByteChannel and is therefore bidirectional. This is syntactic sugar to simplify class definitions and make it easier to test channel objects with the instanceof operator.

This is good class design technique, and if you were writing your own Channel implementation, you would implement these interfaces as appropriate. But it turns out that they are not of much interest to someone using the standard channel classes of the java.nio.channels package. If you glance back at Figure 3-2, or skip ahead to the sections on file and socket channels, you'll see that each of the file and socket channels implement all three of these interfaces. In terms of class definition, this means that all file and socket channel objects are bidirectional. This is not a problem for sockets because they're always bidirectional, but it is an issue for files.

As you know, a given file can be opened with different permissions at different times. A FileChannel object obtained from the getChannel() method of a FileInputStream object is read-only but is bidirectional in terms of interface declarations because FileChannel implements ByteChannel. Invoking write() on such a channel will throw the unchecked NonWritableChannelException because FileInputStream always opens files with read-only permission.

It's important to keep in mind that a channel connects to a specific I/O service, and the capabilities of a given channel instance will be constrained by the characteristics of the service to which it's connected. A Channel instance connected to a read-only file cannot write, even though the class to which that channel instance belongs may have a write() method. It falls to the programmer to know how the channel was opened and not to attempt an operation the underlying I/O service won't allow.

```
// A ByteBuffer named buffer contains data to be written

FileInputStream input = new FileInputStream (fileName);
FileChannel channel = input.getChannel();

// This will compile but will throw an IOException
// because the underlying file is read-only
channel.write (buffer);
```

 Channel instances may not allow read( ) or write( ), depending on the access mode(s) of the underlying file handle.

The read( ) and write( ) methods of ByteChannel take ByteBuffer objects as arguments. Each returns the number of bytes transferred, which can be less than the number of bytes in the buffer, or even zero. The position of the buffer will have been advanced by the same amount. If a partial transfer was performed, the buffer can be resubmitted to the channel to continue transferring data where it left off. Repeat until the buffer's hasRemaining( ) method returns false. Example 3-1 shows how to copy data from one channel to another.

Example 3-1. Copying data between channels

```
package com.ronsoft.books.nio.channels;

import java.nio.ByteBuffer;
import java.nio.channels.ReadableByteChannel;
import java.nio.channels.WritableByteChannel;
import java.nio.channels.Channels;
import java.io.IOException;

/**
 * Test copying between channels.
 *
 * @author Ron Hitchens (ron@ronsoft.com)
 */
public class ChannelCopy
{
    /**
     * This code copies data from stdin to stdout.  Like the 'cat'
     * command, but without any useful options.
     */
    public static void main (String [] argv)
        throws IOException
    {
        ReadableByteChannel source = Channels.newChannel (System.in);
        WritableByteChannel dest = Channels.newChannel (System.out);

        channelCopy1 (source, dest);
        // alternatively, call channelCopy2 (source, dest);

        source.close( );
        dest.close( );
    }

    /**
     * Channel copy method 1.  This method copies data from the src
     * channel and writes it to the dest channel until EOF on src.
     * This implementation makes use of compact( ) on the temp buffer
     * to pack down the data if the buffer wasn't fully drained.  This
     * may result in data copying, but minimizes system calls.  It also
     * requires a cleanup loop to make sure all the data gets sent.
     */
    private static void channelCopy1 (ReadableByteChannel src,
        WritableByteChannel dest)
```

Example 3-1. Copying data between channels (continued)

```
        throws IOException
    {
        ByteBuffer buffer = ByteBuffer.allocateDirect (16 * 1024);

        while (src.read (buffer) != -1) {
            // Prepare the buffer to be drained
            buffer.flip( );

            // Write to the channel; may block
            dest.write (buffer);

            // If partial transfer, shift remainder down
            // If buffer is empty, same as doing clear( )
            buffer.compact( );
        }

        // EOF will leave buffer in fill state
        buffer.flip( );

        // Make sure that the buffer is fully drained
        while (buffer.hasRemaining( )) {
            dest.write (buffer);
        }
    }

    /**
     * Channel copy method 2.  This method performs the same copy, but
     * assures the temp buffer is empty before reading more data.  This
     * never requires data copying but may result in more systems calls.
     * No post-loop cleanup is needed because the buffer will be empty
     * when the loop is exited.
     */
    private static void channelCopy2 (ReadableByteChannel src,
        WritableByteChannel dest)
        throws IOException
    {
        ByteBuffer buffer = ByteBuffer.allocateDirect (16 * 1024);

        while (src.read (buffer) != -1) {
            // Prepare the buffer to be drained
            buffer.flip( );

            // Make sure that the buffer was fully drained
            while (buffer.hasRemaining( )) {
                dest.write (buffer);
            }

            // Make the buffer empty, ready for filling
            buffer.clear( );
        }
    }
}
```

Channels can operate in *blocking* or *nonblocking* modes. A channel in nonblocking mode never puts the invoking thread to sleep. The requested operation either completes immediately or returns a result indicating that nothing was done. Only stream-oriented channels, such as sockets and pipes, can be placed in nonblocking mode.

As you can see in Figure 3-2, the socket channel classes extend from SelectableChannel. Classes extending from SelectableChannel can be used with Selectors, which enable *readiness selection*. Combining nonblocking I/O with selectors allows your application to exploit *multiplexed I/O*. Selection and multiplexing are discussed in Chapter 4. The details of how to place sockets in nonblocking mode are covered in the section "Socket Channels."

Closing Channels

Unlike buffers, channels cannot be reused. An open channel represents a specific connection to a specific I/O service and encapsulates the state of that connection. When a channel is closed, that connection is lost, and the channel is no longer connected to anything.

```
package java.nio.channels;

public interface Channel
{
        public boolean isOpen( );
        public void close( ) throws IOException;
}
```

Calling a channel's close( ) method might cause the thread to block briefly* while the channel finalizes the closing of the underlying I/O service, even if the channel is in nonblocking mode. Blocking behavior when a channel is closed, if any, is highly operating system– and filesystem-dependent. It's harmless to call close( ) on a channel multiple times, but if the first thread has blocked in close( ), any additional threads calling close( ) block until the first thread has completed closing the channel. Subsequent calls to close( ) on the closed channel do nothing and return immediately.

The open state of a channel can be tested with the isOpen( ) method. If it returns true, the channel can be used. If false, the channel has been closed and can no longer be used. Attempting to read, write, or perform any other operation that requires the channel to be in an open state will result in a ClosedChannelException.

Channels introduce some new behaviors related to closing and interrupts. If a channel implements the InterruptibleChannel interface (see Figure 3-2), then it's subject to the following semantics. If a thread is blocked on a channel, and that thread is interrupted

---

* Socket channels could conceivably take a significant amount of time to close depending on the system's networking implementation. Some network protocol stacks may block a close while output is drained. Your mileage may vary.

(by another thread calling the blocked thread's `interrupt( )` method), the channel will be closed, and the blocked thread will be sent a `ClosedByInterruptException`.

Additionally, if a thread's *interrupt status* is set, and that thread attempts to access a channel, the channel will immediately be closed, and the same exception will be thrown. A thread's interrupt status is set when its `interrupt( )` method is called. A thread's current interrupt status can be tested with the `isInterrupted( )` method. The interrupt status of the current thread can be cleared by calling the static `Thread. interrupted( )` method.

> Don't confuse interrupting threads sleeping on `Channels` with those sleeping on `Selectors`. The former shuts down the channel; the latter does not. However, your thread's interrupt status will be set if it is interrupted while sleeping on a `Selector`. If that thread then touches a `Channel`, that channel will be closed. `Selectors` are discussed in Chapter 4.

It may seem rather draconian to shut down a channel just because a thread sleeping on that channel was interrupted. But this is an explicit design decision made by the NIO architects. Experience has shown that it's impossible to reliably handle interrupted I/O operations consistently across all operating systems. The requirement to provide deterministic channel behavior on all platforms led to the design choice of always closing channels when I/O operations are interrupted. This was deemed acceptable, because a thread is most often interrupted so it can be told to shut down. The `java.nio` package mandates this behavior to avoid the quagmire of operating-system peculiarities, which is especially treacherous in this area. This is a classic trade-off of features for robustness.

Interruptible channels are also *asynchronously closable*. A channel that implements `InterruptibleChannel` can be closed at any time, even if another thread is blocked waiting for an I/O to complete on that channel. When a channel is closed, any threads sleeping on that channel will be awakened and receive an `AsynchronousCloseException`. The channel will then be closed and will be no longer usable.

> The initial NIO release, JDK 1.4.0, contains several serious bugs related to interrupted channel operations and asynchronous closability. These problems are expected to be resolved in the 1.4.1 release. In 1.4.0, threads sleeping on a channel I/O operation may not be reliably awakened if they are interrupted or the channel closed by another thread. Be careful about depending on this behavior.

Channels that don't implement `InterruptibleChannel` are typically special-purpose channels without low-level, native-code implementations. These may be special-purpose channels that never block, wrappers around legacy streams, or writer classes for which these interruptible semantics cannot be implemented (see the section "The Channels Utility Class").

Scatter/Gather

Channels provide an important new capability known as *scatter/gather* (referred to in some circles as *vectored I/O*). Scatter/gather is a simple yet powerful concept (see "Scatter/gather" in Chapter 1). It refers to performing a single I/O operation across multiple buffers. For a write operation, data is *gathered* (drained) from several buffers in turn and sent along the channel. The buffers do not need to have the same capcity (and they usually don't). The effect is the same as if the content of all the buffers was concatenated into one large buffer before being sent. For reads, the data read from the channel is scattered to multiple buffers in sequence, filling each to its limit, until the data from the channel or the total buffer space is exhausted.

Most modern operating systems support native vectored I/O. When you request a scatter/gather operation on a channel, the request will be translated into appropriate native calls to fill or drain the buffers directly. This is a big win, because buffer copies and system calls are reduced or eliminated. Scatter/gather should be used with direct ByteBuffers to gain the greatest advantage from native I/O, especially if the buffers are long-lived.

Adding the scatter/gather interfaces to the UML class diagram of Figure 3-3 produces Figure 3-4. The following code illustrates how scatter is an extension of reading and gather is built on writing:

```
public interface ScatteringByteChannel
        extends ReadableByteChannel
{
        public long read (ByteBuffer [] dsts)
                throws IOException;

        public long read (ByteBuffer [] dsts, int offset, int length)
                throws IOException;
}


public interface GatheringByteChannel
        extends WritableByteChannel
{
        public long write(ByteBuffer[] srcs)
                throws IOException;

        public long write(ByteBuffer[] srcs, int offset, int length)
                throws IOException;
}
```

You can see that each interface adds two new methods that take an array of buffers as arguments. Also, each method provides a form that takes an offset and length.

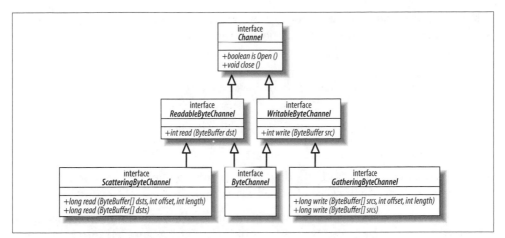

Figure 3-4. Scatter/gather interfaces

Let's understand first how to use the simple form. In the code below, let's assume that channel is connected to a socket that has 48 bytes ready to read:

```
ByteBuffer header = ByteBuffer.allocateDirect (10);
ByteBuffer body = ByteBuffer.allocateDirect (80);
ByteBuffer [] buffers = { header, body };

int bytesRead = channel.read (buffers);
```

Upon returning from read( ), bytesRead holds the value 48, the header buffer contains the first 10 bytes read from the channel, and body holds the following 38 bytes. The channel automatically scattered the data into the two buffers. The buffers have been filled (although in this case body has room for more) and will need to be flipped to make them ready for draining. In a case like this, we may not bother flipping the header buffer but access it randomly with absolute gets to check various header fields. The body buffer can be flipped and passed to the write( ) method of another channel to send it on its way. For example:

```
switch (header.getShort(0)) {
case TYPE_PING:
        break;

case TYPE_FILE:
        body.flip( );
        fileChannel.write (body);
        break;

default:
        logUnknownPacket (header.getShort(0), header.getLong(2), body);
        break;
}
```

Just as easily, we can assemble data in multiple buffers to be sent in one gather operation. Using the same buffers, we could put together and send packets on a socket channel like this:

```
body.clear( );
body.put("FOO".getBytes()).flip( );    // "FOO" as bytes

header.clear( );
header.putShort (TYPE_FILE).putLong (body.limit()).flip( );

long bytesWritten = channel.write (buffers);
```

This code sends a total of 13 bytes down the channel, gathering them from the buffers referenced by the `buffers` array passed to `write( )`.

Figure 3-5 is a graphical representation of a gathering write. Data is gathered from each of the buffers referenced by the array of buffers and assembled into a stream of bytes that are sent down the channel.

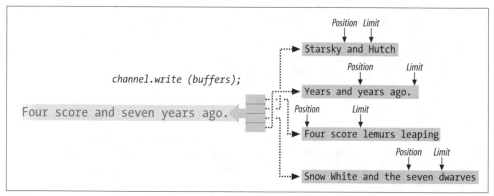

Figure 3-5. A gathering write using four buffers

Figure 3-6 shows a scattering read. Data arriving on the channel is scattered to the list of buffers, filling each in turn from its position to its limit. The position and limit values shown here are *before* the read operation commenced.

The versions of `read( )` and `write( )` that take `offset` and `length` arguments provide a way to use subsets of the buffers in an array of buffers. The `offset` value in this case refers to which buffer to begin using, not an offset into the data. The `length` argument indicates the number of buffers to use. For example, if we have a five-element array named `fiveBuffers` that has already been initialized with references to five buffers, the following code would write the content of the second, third, and fourth buffers:

```
int bytesRead = channel.write (fiveBuffers, 1, 3);
```

Scatter/gather can be an extraordinarily powerful tool when used properly. It allows you to delegate to the operating system the grunt work of separating out the data you read into multiple buckets, or assembling disparate chunks of data into a whole. This

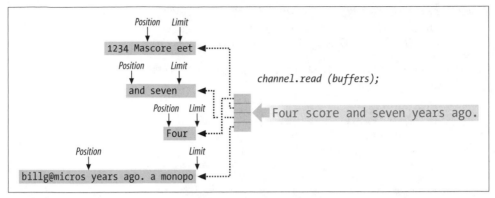

Figure 3-6. A scattering read using four buffers

can be a huge win because the operating system is highly optimized for this sort of thing. It saves you the work of moving things around, thereby avoiding buffer copies, and reduces the amount of code you need to write and debug. Since you are basically assembling data by providing references to data containers, the various chunks can be assembled in different ways by building multiple arrays of buffer references in different combinations, as Example 3-2 demonstrates.

Example 3-2. Collecting many buffers in a gathering write

```
package com.ronsoft.books.nio.channels;

import java.nio.ByteBuffer;
import java.nio.channels.GatheringByteChannel;
import java.io.FileOutputStream;
import java.util.Random;
import java.util.List;
import java.util.LinkedList;

/**
 * Demonstrate gathering write using many buffers.
 *
 * @author Ron Hitchens (ron@ronsoft.com)
 */
public class Marketing
{
    private static final String DEMOGRAPHIC = "blahblah.txt";

    // "Leverage frictionless methodologies"
    public static void main (String [] argv)
        throws Exception
    {
        int reps = 10;

        if (argv.length > 0) {
            reps = Integer.parseInt (argv [0]);
        }
```

Example 3-2. Collecting many buffers in a gathering write (continued)

```
    FileOutputStream fos = new FileOutputStream (DEMOGRAPHIC);
    GatheringByteChannel gatherChannel = fos.getChannel( );

    // Generate some brilliant marcom, er, repurposed content
    ByteBuffer [] bs = utterBS (reps);

    // Deliver the message to the waiting market
    while (gatherChannel.write (bs) > 0) {
        // Empty body
        // Loop until write( ) returns zero
    }

    System.out.println ("Mindshare paradigms synergized to "
        + DEMOGRAPHIC);

    fos.close( );
}

// ------------------------------------------------
// These are just representative; add your own

private static String [] col1 = {
    "Aggregate", "Enable", "Leverage",
    "Facilitate", "Synergize", "Repurpose",
    "Strategize", "Reinvent", "Harness"
};

private static String [] col2 = {
    "cross-platform", "best-of-breed", "frictionless",
    "ubiquitous", "extensible", "compelling",
    "mission-critical", "collaborative", "integrated"
};

private static String [] col3 = {
    "methodologies", "infomediaries", "platforms",
    "schemas", "mindshare", "paradigms",
    "functionalities", "web services", "infrastructures"
};

private static String newline = System.getProperty ("line.separator");

// The Marcom-atic 9000
private static ByteBuffer [] utterBS (int howMany)
    throws Exception
{
    List list = new LinkedList( );

    for (int i = 0; i < howMany; i++) {
        list.add (pickRandom (col1, " "));
        list.add (pickRandom (col2, " "));
        list.add (pickRandom (col3, newline));
    }
```

Example 3-2. Collecting many buffers in a gathering write (continued)

```
        ByteBuffer [] bufs = new ByteBuffer [list.size()];
        list.toArray (bufs);

        return (bufs);
    }

    // The communications director
    private static Random rand = new Random();

    // Pick one, make a buffer to hold it and the suffix, load it with
    // the byte equivalent of the strings (will not work properly for
    // non-Latin characters), then flip the loaded buffer so it's ready
    // to be drained
    private static ByteBuffer pickRandom (String [] strings, String suffix)
        throws Exception
    {
        String string = strings [rand.nextInt (strings.length)];
        int total = string.length() + suffix.length();
        ByteBuffer buf = ByteBuffer.allocate (total);

        buf.put (string.getBytes ("US-ASCII"));
        buf.put (suffix.getBytes ("US-ASCII"));
        buf.flip();

        return (buf);
    }
}
```

Here's the output from executing Marketing. While the output is meaningless, gathering writes allow us to generate it very efficiently!

```
Aggregate compelling methodologies
Harness collaborative platforms
Aggregate integrated schemas
Aggregate frictionless platforms
Enable integrated platforms
Leverage cross-platform functionalities
Harness extensible paradigms
Synergize compelling infomediaries
Repurpose cross-platform mindshare
Facilitate cross-platform infomediaries
```

File Channels

Up to this point, we've been discussing the channels generically, i.e., discussing those things common to all channel types. It's time to get specific. In this section, we discuss file channels (socket channels are covered in an upcoming section). As you can see in Figure 3-7, the FileChannel class can do normal read and write as well as scatter/gather. It also provides lots of new methods specific to files. Many of these methods are familiar file operations; others may be new to you. We'll discuss them all, right here, right now.

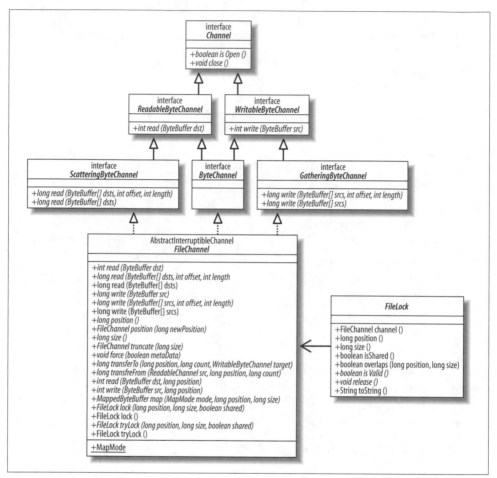

Figure 3-7. FileChannel family tree

File channels are always blocking and cannot be placed into nonblocking mode. Modern operating systems have sophisticated caching and prefetch algorithms that usually give local disk I/O very low latency. Network filesystems generally have higher latencies but often benefit from the same optimizations. The nonblocking paradigm of stream-oriented I/O doesn't make as much sense for file-oriented operations because of the fundamentally different nature of file I/O. For file I/O, the true winner is *asynchronous I/O*, which lets a process request one or more I/O operations from the operating system but does not wait for them to complete. The process is notified at a later time that the requested I/O has completed. Asynchronous I/O is an advanced capability not available on many operating systems. It is under consideration as a future NIO enhancement.

As mentioned in the section "Opening Channels," FileChannel objects cannot be created directly. A FileChannel instance can be obtained only by calling getChannel( ) on an open file object (RandomAccessFile, FileInputStream, or FileOutputStream).* Calling the getChannel( ) method returns a FileChannel object connected to the same file, with the same access permissions as the file object. You can then use the channel object to make use of the powerful FileChannel API:

```
package java.nio.channels;

public abstract class FileChannel
        extends AbstractChannel
        implements ByteChannel, GatheringByteChannel, ScatteringByteChannel
{
        // This is a partial API listing
        // All methods listed here can throw java.io.IOException

        public abstract int read (ByteBuffer dst, long position)
        public abstract int write (ByteBuffer src, long position)
        public abstract long size( )
        public abstract long position( )
        public abstract void position (long newPosition)
        public abstract void truncate (long size)
        public abstract void force (boolean metaData)

        public final FileLock lock( )
        public abstract FileLock lock (long position, long size, boolean shared)
        public final FileLock tryLock( )
        public abstract FileLock tryLock (long position, long size, boolean shared)

        public abstract MappedByteBuffer map (MapMode mode, long position, long size)

        public static class MapMode
        {
                public static final MapMode READ_ONLY
                public static final MapMode READ_WRITE
                public static final MapMode PRIVATE
        }

        public abstract long transferTo (long position, long count,
                WritableByteChannel target)
        public abstract long transferFrom (ReadableByteChannel src,
                long position, long count)
}
```

The previous listing shows the new API methods introduced by FileChannel. All of these can throw java.io.IOException, but the throws clause is not listed here.

---

* JSR 51 also specified the need for an expanded filesystem interface API. An implementation of that API didn't make it into the JDK 1.4 release but is expected to be in 1.5. Once the improved filesystem API is in place, it will probably become the preferred source of FileChannel objects.

Like most channels, `FileChannel` attempts to use native I/O services when possible. The `FileChannel` class itself is abstract; the actual object you get from `getChannel( )` is an instance of a concrete subclass that may implement some or all of these methods using native code.

`FileChannel` objects are thread-safe. Multiple threads can concurrently call methods on the same instance without causing any problems, but not all operations are multi-threaded. Operations that affect the channel's position or the file size are single-threaded. Threads attempting one of these operations will wait if another thread is already executing an operation that affects the channel position or file size. Concurrency behavior can also be affected by the underlying operating system or filesystem.

Like most I/O-related classes, `FileChannel` is an abstraction that reflects a concrete object external to the JVM. The `FileChannel` class guarantees that all instances within the same JVM will see a consistent view of a given file. But the JVM cannot make guarantees about factors beyond its control. The view of a file seen through a `FileChannel` instance may or may not be consistent with the view of that file seen by an external, non-Java processes. The semantics of concurrent file access by multiple processes is highly dependent on the underlying operating system and/or filesystem. Concurrent access to the same file by `FileChannel` objects running in different JVMs will, generally, be consistent with concurrent access between non-Java processes.

Accessing Files

Each `FileChannel` object has a one-to-one relationship with a file descriptor, so it comes as no surprise that the API methods listed here correspond closely to common file I/O system calls on your favorite POSIX-compliant operating system. The names may be different, but the usual suspects have been rounded up. You may also note the similarities to methods of the `RandomAccessFile` class from the `java.io` package. `RandomAccessFile` provides essentially the same abstraction. Until the advent of channels, this was how low-level file operations were performed. `FileChannel` models the same services, so its API is naturally similar.

For comparison, Table 3-1 lists the correspondences of `FileChannel`, `RandomAccessFile`, and POSIX I/O system calls.

Table 3-1. File I/O API comparison chart

FileChannel	RandomAccessFile	POSIX system call
`read( )`	`read( )`	`read( )`
`write( )`	`write( )`	`write( )`
`size( )`	`length( )`	`fstat( )`
`position( )`	`getFilePointer( )`	`lseek( )`
`position (long newPosition)`	`seek( )`	`lseek( )`

Table 3-1. File I/O API comparison chart (continued)

FileChannel	RandomAccessFile	POSIX system call
truncate( )	setLength( )	ftruncate( )
force( )	getFD( ).sync( )	fsync( )

Let's take a closer look at the basic file access methods (remember that each of these methods can throw java.io.IOException):

```
public abstract class FileChannel
        extends AbstractChannel
        implements ByteChannel, GatheringByteChannel, ScatteringByteChannel
{
        // This is a partial API listing

        public abstract long position( )
        public abstract void position (long newPosition)

        public abstract int read (ByteBuffer dst)
        public abstract int read (ByteBuffer dst, long position)
        public abstract int write (ByteBuffer src)
        public abstract int write (ByteBuffer src, long position)

        public abstract long size( )

        public abstract void truncate (long size)
        public abstract void force (boolean metaData)
}
```

Like the underlying file descriptor, each FileChannel object has a notion of *file position*. The position determines the location in the file where data will next be read or written. In this respect, the FileChannel class is similar to buffers, and (as we'll see in a later section) the MappedByteBuffer class makes it possible to access file data through the ByteBuffer API.

As you can see in the preceding listing, there are two forms of the position( ) method. The first, which takes no arguments, returns the current file position. The value returned is a long and represents the current byte position within the file.*

The second form of position( ) takes a long argument and sets the channel position to the given value. Attempting to set the position to a negative value will result in a java.lang.IllegalArgumentException, but it's OK to set the position beyond the end of the file. Doing so sets the position to the requested value but does not change the file size. If a read( ) is performed after setting the position beyond the current file size, the end-of-file condition is returned. Doing a write( ) with the position set beyond the file size will cause the file to grow to accommodate the new bytes writ-

---

* A signed long can represent a file size of 9,223,372,036,854,775,807 bytes. That's roughly 8.4 million terabytes, or enough data to fill about 90 million 100-GB disk drives from your local computer store.

ten. The behavior is identical to that for an absolute write( ) and may result in a file hole (see "What the Heck Is a File Hole?").

The FileChannel position is reflected from the underlying file descriptor, which is shared by the file object from which the channel reference was obtained. This means that updates made to the position by one object will be seen by the other:

```
RandomAccessFile randomAccessFile = new RandomAccessFile ("filename", "r");

// Set the file position
randomAccessFile.seek (1000);

// Create a channel from the file
FileChannel fileChannel = randomAccessFile.getChannel( );

// This will print "1000"
System.out.println ("file pos: " + fileChannel.position( ));

// Change the position using the RandomAccessFile object
randomAccessFile.seek (500);

// This will print "500"
System.out.println ("file pos: " + fileChannel.position( ));

// Change the position using the FileChannel object
fileChannel.position (200);

// This will print "200"
System.out.println ("file pos: " + randomAccessFile.getFilePointer( ));
```

Similar to the relative get( ) and put( ) methods of buffers, the file position is automatically updated as bytes are transferred by read( ) or write( ). If the position reaches the file size, as returned by the size( ) method, an end-of-file condition (-1) is returned by read( ). However, unlike buffers, if the position advances beyond the file size on write( ), the file expands to accommodate the new bytes.

Also like buffers, there are absolute forms of read( ) and write( ) that take a position argument. The absolute versions leave the current file position unchanged upon return. Absolute reads and writes may be more efficient because the state of the channel does not need to be updated; the request can pass straight through to native code. Even better, multiple threads can access the same file concurrently without interfering with each other. This is because each call is atomic and doesn't rely on any remembered state between invocations.

Attempting an absolute read beyond the end of the file, as returned by size( ), will return end-of-file. Doing an absolute write( ) at a position beyond the file size will cause the file to grow to accommodate the new bytes being written. The values of bytes in locations between the previous end-of-file position and the newly added bytes are unspecified by the FileChannel class but will in most cases reflect the

What the Heck Is a File Hole?

A file hole occurs when the space on disk allocated for a file is less than the file size. Most modern filesystems provide for sparsely populated files, allocating space on disk only for the data actually written (more properly, allocating only those filesystem pages to which data was written). If data is written to the file in noncontiguous locations, this can result in areas of the file that logically contain no data (holes). For example, the following code might produce a file like the one in Figure 3-8:

```java
package com.ronsoft.books.nio.channels;

import java.nio.ByteBuffer;
import java.nio.channels.FileChannel;
import java.io.File;
import java.io.RandomAccessFile;
import java.io.IOException;

/**
 * Create a file with holes in it
 *
 * @author Ron Hitchens (ron@ronsoft.com)
 */
public class FileHole
{
    public static void main (String [] argv)
        throws IOException
    {
        // Create a temp file, open for writing, and get a FileChannel
        File temp = File.createTempFile ("holy", null);
        RandomAccessFile file = new RandomAccessFile (temp, "rw");
        FileChannel channel = file.getChannel();
        // Create a working buffer
        ByteBuffer byteBuffer = ByteBuffer.allocateDirect (100);

        putData (0, byteBuffer, channel);
        putData (5000000, byteBuffer, channel);
        putData (50000, byteBuffer, channel);

        // Size will report the largest position written, but
        // there are two holes in this file.  This file will
        // not consume 5 MB on disk (unless the filesystem is
        // extremely brain-damaged)
        System.out.println ("Wrote temp file '" + temp.getPath()
            + "', size=" + channel.size());

        channel.close();
        file.close();
    }
```

—continued—

```
        private static void putData (int position, ByteBuffer buffer,
            FileChannel channel)
            throws IOException
    {

        String string = "*<-- location " + position;

        buffer.clear( );
        buffer.put (string.getBytes ("US-ASCII"));
        buffer.flip( );

        channel.position (position);
        channel.write (buffer);
    }
}
```

If the file is read sequentially, any holes appear to be filled with zeros but do not take up space on disk. A process reading this file would see 5,000,021 bytes, with most of them appearing to be zero. Try running the strings command on this file and see what you get. Try increasing the values to 50 or 100 MB and see what happens to your total disk-space consumption (shouldn't change) and the time it takes to scan the file sequentially (should change considerably).

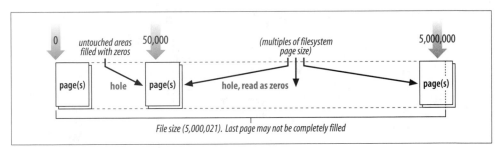

Figure 3-8. A disk file with two holes

underlying filesystem semantics. Depending on the operating-system and/or the file-system type, this may result in a hole in the file.

When it's necessary to reduce the size of a file, truncate( ) chops off any data beyond the new size you specify. If the current size is greater than the new size, all bytes beyond the new size are discarded. If the new size provided is greater than or equal to the current file size, the file is not modified. A side effect of truncate( ) in either case is that it sets the file position to the new size provided.

```
    public abstract class FileChannel
            extends AbstractChannel
            implements ByteChannel, GatheringByteChannel, ScatteringByteChannel
    {
            // This is a partial API listing
```

```
        public abstract void truncate (long size)
        public abstract void force (boolean metaData)
    }
```

The last method listed above is force( ). This method tells the channel to force any pending modifications made to the file out to disk. All modern filesystems cache data and defer disk updates to boost performance. Calling the force( ) method requests that all pending modifications to the file be synchronized to disk immediately.

If the file resides on a local filesystem, then upon returning from force( ), it's guaranteed that all modifications to the file since the channel was created (or the last call to force( )) have been written to disk. This is important for critical operations, such as transaction processing, to insure data integrity and reliable recovery. However, this guarantee of synchronization to permanent storage cannot be made if the file resides on a remote filesystem, such as NFS. The same may be true for other filesystems, depending on implementation. The JVM can't make promises the operating system or filesystem won't keep. If your application must maintain data integrity in the face of system failures, verify that the operating system and/or filesystem you're using are dependable in that regard.

 For applications in which confidence in data integrity are essential, verify the capabilities of the operating environment on which you plan to deploy.

The boolean argument to force( ) indicates whether metadata about the file should also be synchronized to disk before returning. Metadata represents things such as file ownership, access permissions, last modification time, etc. In most cases, this information is not critical for data recovery. Passing false to force( ) indicates that only the file data need be synchronized before returning. In most cases, synchronizing the metadata will require at least one additional low-level I/O operation by the operating system. Some high-volume transactional applications may gain a moderate performance increase without sacrificing data integrity by not requiring metadata updates on each call to force( ).

File Locking

Until 1.4, a feature sorely lacking from the Java I/O model was *file locking*. While most modern operating systems have long had file-locking capabilities of one form or another, file locks have not been available to Java programmers until the JDK 1.4 release. File locking is essential for integration with many non-Java applications. It can also be valuable for arbitrating access among multiple Java components of a large system.

As discussed in Chapter 1, locks can be shared or exclusive. The file-locking features described in this section depend heavily on the native operating-system implementation. Not all operating systems and filesystems support shared file locks. For those that don't, a request for a shared lock will be silently promoted to an exclusive-lock request. This guarantees correctness but may impact performance considerably. For example, employing only exclusive locks would serialize all the reader processes in Figure 1-7. Be sure you understand file-locking behavior on the operating system and filesystem(s) on which you plan to deploy; it could seriously affect your design choices.

Additionally, not all platforms implement basic file locking in the same way. File-locking semantics may vary between operating systems and even different filesystems on the same operating system. Some operating systems provide only advisory locking, some only exclusive locks, and some may provide both. You should always manage file locks as if they were advisory, which is the safest approach. But it's also wise to be aware of how locks are implemented in the underlying operating system. For example, if all locks are mandatory, the locks you obtain may impact other applications running on the same system if you don't release them in a timely manner.

An important caveat regarding the file-locking model implemented by `FileChannel` is that locks are applied *per file*, not per channel or per thread. This means that file locks are not appropriate for coordinating access between threads in the same JVM.

If one thread acquires an exclusive lock on a given file, and a second thread requests an exclusive lock for the same file region using an independently opened channel, the second thread will be granted access. If the two threads are running in different JVMs, the second thread would block, because locks are ultimately arbitrated by the operating system or filesystem almost always at the process rather than thread level. Locks are associated with a file, not with individual file handles or channels.

 Locks are associated with files, not channels. Use locks to coordinate with external processes, not between threads in the same JVM.

File locks are intended for arbitrating file access at the process level, such as between major application components or when integrating with components from other vendors. If you need to control concurrent access between multiple Java threads, you may need to implement your own, lightweight locking scheme. Memory-mapped files (described later in this chapter) may be an appropriate choice for that case.

Let's take a look at the `FileChannel` API methods related to file locking:

```
public abstract class FileChannel
        extends AbstractChannel
        implements ByteChannel, GatheringByteChannel, ScatteringByteChannel
{
        // This is a partial API listing

        public final FileLock lock( )
        public abstract FileLock lock (long position, long size, boolean shared)
```

```
                    public final FileLock tryLock( )
                    public abstract FileLock tryLock (long position, long size, boolean shared)
        }
```

This time, let's look first at the form of lock( ) that takes arguments. Locks are obtained on regions of files. Calling lock( ) with arguments specifies the beginning position within the file where the locked region should begin and the size of the region to lock. The third argument, shared, indicates whether you want the lock to be shared (true) or exclusive (false). To obtain a shared lock, you must have opened the file with read permission. Write permission is required for an exclusive lock. The position and size you provide must be nonnegative.

The lock region does not need to be constrained to the file size; a lock can extend beyond the end of the file. Therefore, it is possible to lock an area of a file before writing data there. It's also possible to lock a region that doesn't even overlap any of the file content, such as beyond the last byte of the file. If the file grows into that region, then your lock would cover that new area of the file. Conversely, if you lock a region of a file, and the file grows beyond your locked area, the new file content would not be protected by your lock.

The simple form of lock( ), which takes no arguments, is a convenience method for requesting an exclusive lock on an entire file, up to the maximum size it can attain. It's equivalent to:

```
    fileChannel.lock (0L, Long.MAX_VALUE, false);
```

The lock( ) method will block if the lock range you are requesting is valid, but it must wait for a preexisting lock to be released. If your thread is suspended in this situation, it's subject to interrupt semantics similar to those discussed in the section "Closing Channels." If the channel is closed by another thread, the suspended thread will resume and receive an AsynchronousCloseException. If the suspended thread is interrupted directly (by calling its interrupt( ) method), it will wake with a FileLockInterruptionException. This exception will also be thrown immediately if the thread's interrupt status is already set when lock( ) is invoked.

In the above API listing, the two methods named tryLock( ) are nonblocking variants of lock( ). They function the same as lock( ) but return null if the requested lock cannot be acquired immediately.

As you can see, lock( ) and tryLock( ) return a FileLock object. Here is the complete API of FileLock:

```
    public abstract class FileLock
    {
            public final FileChannel channel( )
            public final long position( )
            public final long size( )
            public final boolean isShared( )
            public final boolean overlaps (long position, long size)
            public abstract boolean isValid( );
```

```
        public abstract void release() throws IOException;
    }
```

The FileLock class encapsulates a locked file region. FileLock objects are created by FileChannel objects and are always associated with that specific channel instance. You can query a lock object to determine which channel created it by calling the channel() method.

A FileLock object is valid when created and remains so until its release() method is called, the channel it's associated with is closed, or the JVM shuts down. The validity of a lock can be tested by invoking its isValid() boolean method. A lock's validity may change over time, but its other properties—position, size, and exclusivity—are set at creation time and are immutable.

You can test a lock to determine if it is shared or exclusive by invoking isShared(). If shared locks are not supported by the underlying operating system or filesystem, this method will always return false, even if you passed true when requesting the lock. If your application depends on shared-locking behavior, test the returned lock to be sure you got the type you requested. FileLock objects are thread-safe; multiple threads may access a lock object concurrently.

Finally, a FileLock object can be queried to determine if it overlaps a given file region by calling its overlaps() method. This will let you quickly determine if a lock you hold intersects with a region of interest. A return of false does not guarantee that you can obtain a lock on the desired region. One or more locks may be held elsewhere in the JVM or by external processes. Use tryLock() to be sure.

Although a FileLock object is associated with a specific FileChannel instance, the lock it represents is associated with an underlying file, not the channel. This can cause conflicts, or possibly deadlocks, if you don't release a lock when you're finished with it. Carefully manage file locks to avoid such problems. Once you've successfully obtained a file lock, be sure to release it if subsequent errors occur on the channel. A code pattern similar to the following is recommended:

```
FileLock lock = fileChannel.lock()

try {
        <perform read/write/whatever on channel>
} catch (IOException) [
        <handle unexpected exception>
} finally {
        lock.release()
}
```

The code in Example 3-3 implements reader processes using shared locks and writers using exclusive locks, as illustrated in Figures 1-7 and 1-8. Because locks are associated with processes and not with Java threads, you will need to run multiple copies of this program. Start one writer and two or more readers to see how the different types of locks interact with each other.

Example 3-3. Shared- and exclusive-lock interaction

```
package com.ronsoft.books.nio.channels;

import java.nio.ByteBuffer;
import java.nio.IntBuffer;
import java.nio.channels.FileChannel;
import java.nio.channels.FileLock;
import java.io.RandomAccessFile;
import java.util.Random;

/**
 * Test locking with FileChannel.
 * Run one copy of this code with arguments "-w /tmp/locktest.dat"
 * and one or more copies with "-r /tmp/locktest.dat" to see the
 * interactions of exclusive and shared locks.  Note how too many
 * readers can starve out the writer.
 * Note: The filename you provide will be overwritten.  Substitute
 * an appropriate temp filename for your favorite OS.
 *
 * Created April, 2002
 * @author Ron Hitchens (ron@ronsoft.com)
 */
public class LockTest
{
    private static final int SIZEOF_INT = 4;
    private static final int INDEX_START = 0;
    private static final int INDEX_COUNT = 10;
    private static final int INDEX_SIZE = INDEX_COUNT * SIZEOF_INT;

    private ByteBuffer buffer = ByteBuffer.allocate (INDEX_SIZE);
    private IntBuffer indexBuffer = buffer.asIntBuffer();
    private Random rand = new Random( );

    public static void main (String [] argv)
        throws Exception
    {
        boolean writer = false;
        String filename;

        if (argv.length != 2) {
            System.out.println ("Usage: [ -r | -w ] filename");
            return;
        }

        writer = argv [0].equals ("-w");
        filename = argv [1];

        RandomAccessFile raf = new RandomAccessFile (filename,
            (writer) ? "rw" : "r");
        FileChannel fc = raf.getChannel();

        LockTest lockTest = new LockTest();
```

Example 3-3. Shared- and exclusive-lock interaction (continued)

```java
        if (writer) {
            lockTest.doUpdates (fc);
        } else {
            lockTest.doQueries (fc);
        }
    }

    // ---------------------------------------------------------------

    // Simulate a series of read-only queries while
    // holding a shared lock on the index area
    void doQueries (FileChannel fc)
        throws Exception
    {
        while (true) {
            println ("trying for shared lock...");
            FileLock lock = fc.lock (INDEX_START, INDEX_SIZE, true);
            int reps = rand.nextInt (60) + 20;

            for (int i = 0; i < reps; i++) {
                int n = rand.nextInt (INDEX_COUNT);
                int position = INDEX_START + (n * SIZEOF_INT);

                buffer.clear( );
                fc.read (buffer, position);

                int value = indexBuffer.get (n);

                println ("Index entry " + n + "=" + value);

                // Pretend to be doing some work
                Thread.sleep (100);
            }

            lock.release( );

            println ("<sleeping>");
            Thread.sleep (rand.nextInt (3000) + 500);
        }
    }

    // Simulate a series of updates to the index area
    // while holding an exclusive lock
    void doUpdates (FileChannel fc)
        throws Exception
    {
        while (true) {
            println ("trying for exclusive lock...");

            FileLock lock = fc.lock (INDEX_START,
                INDEX_SIZE, false);

            updateIndex (fc);
```

Example 3-3. Shared- and exclusive-lock interaction (continued)

```
                lock.release( );

                println ("<sleeping>");
                Thread.sleep (rand.nextInt (2000) + 500);
        }
    }

    // Write new values to the index slots
    private int idxval = 1;

    private void updateIndex (FileChannel fc)
        throws Exception
    {
        // "indexBuffer" is an int view of "buffer"
        indexBuffer.clear( );

        for (int i = 0; i < INDEX_COUNT; i++) {
            idxval++;
            println ("Updating index " + i + "=" + idxval);

            indexBuffer.put (idxval);

            // Pretend that this is really hard work
            Thread.sleep (500);
        }

        // leaves position and limit correct for whole buffer
        buffer.clear( );
        fc.write (buffer, INDEX_START);
    }

    // -----------------------------------------------------------------

    private int lastLineLen = 0;

    // Specialized println that repaints the current line
    private void println (String msg)
    {
        System.out.print ("\r ");
        System.out.print (msg);

        for (int i = msg.length( ); i < lastLineLen; i++) {
            System.out.print (" ");
        }

        System.out.print ("\r");
        System.out.flush( );
        lastLineLen = msg.length( );
    }
}
```

This code blithely ignores the advice I gave about using try/catch/finally to release locks. It's demo code; don't be so lazy in your real code.

Memory-Mapped Files

The new FileChannel class provides a method, map( ), that establishes a virtual memory mapping between an open file and a special type of ByteBuffer. (Memory-mapped files and how they interact with virtual memory were summarized in Chapter 1.) Calling map( ) on a FileChannel creates a virtual memory mapping backed by a disk file and wraps a MappedByteBuffer object around that virtual memory space. (See Figure 1-6.)

The MappedByteBuffer object returned from map( ) behaves like a memory-based buffer in most respects, but its data elements are stored in a file on disk. Calling get( ) will fetch data from the disk file, and this data reflects the current content of the file, even if the file has been modified by an external process since the mapping was established. The data visible through a file mapping is exactly the same as you would see by reading the file conventionally. Likewise, doing a put( ) to the mapped buffer will update the file on disk (assuming you have write permission), and your changes will be visible to other readers of the file.

Accessing a file through the memory-mapping mechanism can be far more efficient than reading or writing data by conventional means, even when using channels. No explicit system calls need to be made, which can be time-consuming. More importantly, the virtual memory system of the operating system automatically caches memory pages. These pages will be cached using system memory and will not consume space from the JVM's memory heap.

Once a memory page has been made valid (brought in from disk), it can be accessed again at full hardware speed without the need to make another system call to get the data. Large, structured files that contain indexes or other sections that are referenced or updated frequently can benefit tremendously from memory mapping. When combined with file locking to protect critical sections and control transactional atomicity, you begin to see how memory mapped buffers can be put to good use.

Let's take a look at how to use memory mapping:

```
public abstract class FileChannel
        extends AbstractChannel
        implements ByteChannel, GatheringByteChannel, ScatteringByteChannel
{
        // This is a partial API listing

        public abstract MappedByteBuffer map (MapMode mode, long position, long size)

        public static class MapMode
        {
```

```
        public static final MapMode READ_ONLY
        public static final MapMode READ_WRITE
        public static final MapMode PRIVATE
    }
}
```

As you can see, there is only one map( ) method to establish a file mapping. It takes a mode, a position and a size. The position and size arguments are the same as lock( )'s (discussed in the previous section). It's possible to create a MappedByteBuffer that represents a subrange of the bytes in a file. For example, to map bytes 100 through 299 (inclusive), do the following:

```
    buffer = fileChannel.map (FileChannel.MapMode.READ_ONLY, 100, 200);
```

To map an entire file:

```
    buffer = fileChannel.map (FileChannel.MapMode.READ_ONLY, 0, fileChannel.size( ));
```

Unlike ranges for file locks, mapped file ranges should not extend beyond the actual size of the file. If you request a mapping larger than the file, the file will be made larger to match the size of the mapping you request. If you pass Integer.MAX_VALUE for the size parameter, your file size would balloon to more than *2.1 gigabytes*. The map( ) method will try to do this even if you request a read-only mapping but will throw an IOException in most cases because the underlying file cannot be modified. This behavior is consistent with the behavior of file holes discussed earlier. See the section "Accessing Files" for details.

The FileChannel class defines constants to represent the mapping modes and uses the convention of a type-safe enumeration rather than numeric values to define these constants. The constants are static fields of an inner class defined inside FileChannel. Being object references, they can be type-checked at compile time, but you use them as you would a numeric constant.

Like conventional file handles, file mappings can be writable or read-only. The first two mapping modes, MapMode.READ_ONLY and MapMode.READ_WRITE, are fairly obvious. They indicate whether you want the mapping to be read-only or to allow modification of the mapped file. The requested mapping mode will be constrained by the access permissions of the FileChannel object on which map( ) is called. If the channel was opened as read-only, map( ) will throw a NonWritableChannelException if you ask for MapMode.READ_WRITE mode. NonReadableChannelException will be thrown if you request MapMode.READ_ONLY on a channel without read permission. It is permissible to request a MapMode.READ_ONLY mapping on a channel opened for read/write. The mutability of a MappedByteBuffer object can be checked by invoking isReadOnly( ) on it.

The third mode, MapMode.PRIVATE, indicates that you want a *copy-on-write* mapping. This means that any modifications you make via put( ) will result in a private copy of the data that only the MappedByteBuffer instance can see. No changes will be made to the underlying file, and any changes made will be lost when the buffer is garbage collected. Even though a copy-on-write mapping prevents any changes to the underlying file, you must have opened the file for read/write to set up a MapMode.PRIVATE mapping. This is necessary for the returned MappedByteBuffer object to allow put( )s.

Copy-on-write is a technique commonly used by operating systems to manage virtual address spaces when one process spawns another. Using copy-on-write allows the parent and child processes to share memory pages until one of them actually makes changes. The same advantages can accrue for multiple mappings of the same file (depending on underlying operating-system support, of course). If a large file is mapped by several MappedByteBuffer objects, each using MapMode.PRIVATE, then most of the file can be shared among all mappings.

Choosing the MapMode.PRIVATE mode does not insulate your buffer from changes made to the file by other means. Changes made to an area of the file will be reflected in a buffer created with this mode, unless the buffer has already modified the same area of the file. As described in Chapter 1, memory and filesystems are segmented into pages. When put( ) is invoked on a copy-on-write buffer, the affected page(s) is duplicated, and changes are made to the copy. The specific page size is implementation-dependent but will usually be the same as the underlying filesystem page size. If the buffer has not made changes to a given page, its content will reflect the corresponding location in the mapped file. Once a page has been copied as a result of a write, the copy will be used thereafter, and that page cannot be modified by other buffers or updates to the file. See Example 3-5 for code that illustrates this behavior.

You'll notice that there is no unmap( ) method. Once established, a mapping remains in effect until the MappedByteBuffer object is garbage collected. Unlike locks, mapped buffers are not tied to the channel that created them. Closing the associated FileChannel does not destroy the mapping; only disposal of the buffer object itself breaks the mapping. The NIO designers made this decision because destroying a mapping when a channel is closed raises security concerns, and solving the security problem would have introduced a performance problem. They recommend using phantom references (see java.lang.ref.PhantomReference) and a cleanup thread if you need to know positively when a mapping has been destroyed. Odds are that this will rarely be necessary.

A MemoryMappedBuffer directly reflects the disk file with which it is associated. If the file is structurally modified while the mapping is in effect, strange behavior can result (exact behaviors are, of course, operating system– and filesystem-dependent). A MemoryMappedBuffer has a fixed size, but the file it's mapped to is elastic. Specifically, if a file's size changes while the mapping is in effect, some or all of the buffer may become inaccessible, undefined data could be returned, or unchecked exceptions could be thrown. Be careful about how files are manipulated by other threads or external processes when they are memory-mapped.

All MappedByteBuffer objects are direct. This means that the memory space they occupy lives outside the JVM heap (and may not be counted in the JVM's memory footprint, depending on the operating system's virtual memory model).

Because they're `ByteBuffers`, `MappedByteBuffers` can be passed to the `read()` or `write()` method of a channel, such as a `SocketChannel`, to transfer data efficiently to or from the mapped file. When combined with scatter/gather, it becomes easy to compose data from memory buffers and mapped file content. See Example 3-4 for an example of composing HTTP responses this way. An even more efficient way of transferring file data to and from other channels is described in the section "Channel-to-Channel Transfers."

So far, we've been discussing mapped buffers as if they were just like other buffers, which is how you would use them most of the time. But `MappedByteBuffer` also defines a few unique methods of its own:

```
public abstract class MappedByteBuffer
        extends ByteBuffer
{
        // This is a partial API listing

        public final MappedByteBuffer load( )
        public final boolean isLoaded( )
        public final MappedByteBuffer force( )
}
```

When a virtual memory mapping is established to a file, it does not usually (depending on the operating system) cause any of the file data to be read in from disk. It's like opening a file: the file is located and a handle is established through which you can access the data when you're ready. For mapped buffers, the virtual memory system will cause chunks of the file to be brought in, on demand, as you touch them. This page validation, or *faulting-in*, takes time because one or more disk accesses are usually required to bring the data into memory. In some scenarios, you may want to bring all the pages into memory first to minimize buffer-access latency. If all the pages of the file are memory-resident, access speed will be identical to a memory-based buffer.

The `load()` method will attempt to touch the entire file so that all of it is memory-resident. As discussed in Chapter 1, a memory-mapped buffer establishes a virtual memory mapping to a file. This mapping enables the low-level virtual memory subsystem of the operating system to copy chunks of the file into memory on an as-needed basis. The in-memory, or validated, pages consume real memory and can squeeze out other, less recently used memory pages as they are brought into RAM.

Calling `load()` on a mapped buffer can be an expensive operation because it can generate a large number of page-ins, depending on the size of the mapped area of the file. There is, however, no guarantee that the file will be fully memory-resident upon return from `load()` because of the dynamic nature of demand paging. Results will vary by operating system, filesystem, available JVM memory, maximum JVM memory, file size relative to JVM and system memory, garbage-collector implementation, etc. Use load( ) with care; it may not yield the result you're hoping for. Its primary use is to pay the penalty of loading a file up front, so subsequent accesses are as fast as possible.

For applications in which near-realtime access is required, preloading is the way to go. But remember that there is no guarantee that all those pages will stay in memory, and you may suffer subsequent page-ins anyway. When and how memory pages are stolen is influenced by several factors, many of which are not controlled by the JVM. As of JDK 1.4, NIO does not provide an API for pinning pages in physical memory, although some operating systems support doing so.

For most applications, especially interactive or other event-driven applications, it's not worth paying the penalty upfront. It's better to amortize the page-in cost across actual accesses. Letting the operating system bring in pages on demand means that untouched pages never need be loaded. This can easily result in less total I/O activity than preloading the mapped file. The operating system has a sophisticated memory-management system in place. Let it do the job for you.

The isLoaded( ) method can be called to determine if a mapped file is fully memory-resident. If it returns true, odds are that the mapped buffer can be accessed with little or no latency. But again, there is no guarantee. Likewise, a return of false does not necessarily imply that access to the buffer will be slow or that the file isn't fully memory-resident. This method is a hint; the asynchronous nature of garbage collection, the underlying operating system, and the dynamics of the running system make it impossible to determine the exact state of all the mapped pages at any given point in time.

The last method listed above, force( ), is similar to the method of the same name in the FileChannel class (see the section "Accessing Files"). It forces any changes made to the mapped buffer to be flushed out to permanent disk storage. When updating a file through a MappedByteBuffer object, you should always use MappedByteBuffer.force( ) rather than FileChannel.force( ). The channel object may not be aware of all file updates made through the mapped buffer. MappedByteBuffer doesn't give you the option of not flushing file metadata—it's always flushed too. Note that the same considerations regarding nonlocal filesystems apply here as they do for FileChannel.force( ). (See the section "Accessing Files.")

If the mapping was established with MapMode.READ_ONLY or MAP_MODE.PRIVATE, then calling force( ) has no effect, since there will never be any changes to flush to disk (but doing so is harmless).

Example 3-4 illustrates the case of memory-mapped buffers and scatter/gather.

Example 3-4. Composing HTTP replies with mapped files and gathering writes

```
package com.ronsoft.books.nio.channels;

import java.nio.ByteBuffer;
import java.nio.MappedByteBuffer;
```

Example 3-4. Composing HTTP replies with mapped files and gathering writes (continued)

```java
import java.nio.channels.FileChannel;
import java.nio.channels.FileChannel.MapMode;
import java.nio.channels.GatheringByteChannel;
import java.io.FileInputStream;
import java.io.FileOutputStream;
import java.io.IOException;
import java.net.URLConnection;

/**
 * Dummy HTTP server using MappedByteBuffers.
 * Given a filename on the command line, pretend to be
 * a web server and generate an HTTP response containing
 * the file content preceded by appropriate headers.  The
 * data is sent with a gathering write.
 *
 * @author Ron Hitchens (ron@ronsoft.com)
 */
public class MappedHttp
{
    private static final String OUTPUT_FILE = "MappedHttp.out";

    private static final String LINE_SEP = "\r\n";
    private static final String SERVER_ID = "Server: Ronsoft Dummy Server";
    private static final String HTTP_HDR =
        "HTTP/1.0 200 OK" + LINE_SEP + SERVER_ID + LINE_SEP;
    private static final String HTTP_404_HDR =
        "HTTP/1.0 404 Not Found" + LINE_SEP + SERVER_ID + LINE_SEP;
    private static final String MSG_404 = "Could not open file: ";

    public static void main (String [] argv)
        throws Exception
    {
        if (argv.length < 1) {
            System.err.println ("Usage: filename");
            return;
        }

        String file = argv [0];
        ByteBuffer header = ByteBuffer.wrap (bytes (HTTP_HDR));
        ByteBuffer dynhdrs = ByteBuffer.allocate (128);
        ByteBuffer [] gather = { header, dynhdrs, null };
        String contentType = "unknown/unknown";
        long contentLength = -1;

        try {
            FileInputStream fis = new FileInputStream (file);
            FileChannel fc = fis.getChannel();
            MappedByteBuffer filedata =
                fc.map (MapMode.READ_ONLY, 0, fc.size());

            gather [2] = filedata;
```

```
                    contentLength = fc.size( );
                    contentType = URLConnection.guessContentTypeFromName (file);
            } catch (IOException e) {
                // file could not be opened; report problem
                ByteBuffer buf = ByteBuffer.allocate (128);
                String msg = MSG_404 + e + LINE_SEP;

                buf.put (bytes (msg));
                buf.flip( );

                // Use the HTTP error response
                gather [0] = ByteBuffer.wrap (bytes (HTTP_404_HDR));
                gather [2] = buf;

                contentLength = msg.length( );
                contentType = "text/plain";
            }

            StringBuffer sb = new StringBuffer( );
            sb.append ("Content-Length: " + contentLength);
            sb.append (LINE_SEP);
            sb.append ("Content-Type: ").append (contentType);
            sb.append (LINE_SEP).append (LINE_SEP);

            dynhdrs.put (bytes (sb.toString( )));
            dynhdrs.flip( );

            FileOutputStream fos = new FileOutputStream (OUTPUT_FILE);
            FileChannel out = fos.getChannel( );

            // All the buffers have been prepared; write 'em out
            while (out.write (gather) > 0) {
                // Empty body; loop until all buffers are empty
            }

            out.close( );

            System.out.println ("output written to " + OUTPUT_FILE);
        }

    // Convert a string to its constituent bytes
    // from the ASCII character set
    private static byte [] bytes (String string)
        throws Exception
    {
        return (string.getBytes ("US-ASCII"));
    }
}
```

Example 3-5 illustrates how the various modes of memory mapping interact. In particular, this code illustrates how copy-on-write is page-oriented. When a change is made by calling put( ) on a MappedByteBuffer object created with the MAP_MODE.PRIVATE mode, a copy of the affected page is made. This private copy not only holds local changes, it also insulates the buffer from external changes to that page. However, changes made to other areas of the mapped file will be seen.

Example 3-5. Three types of memory-mapped buffers

```java
package com.ronsoft.books.nio.channels;

import java.nio.ByteBuffer;
import java.nio.MappedByteBuffer;
import java.nio.channels.FileChannel;
import java.io.File;
import java.io.RandomAccessFile;

/**
 * Test behavior of Memory mapped buffer types.  Create a file, write
 * some data to it, then create three different types of mappings
 * to it.  Observe the effects of changes through the buffer APIs
 * and updating the file directly.  The data spans page boundaries
 * to illustrate the page-oriented nature of Copy-On-Write mappings.
 *
 * @author Ron Hitchens (ron@ronsoft.com)
 */
public class MapFile
{
    public static void main (String [] argv)
        throws Exception
    {
        // Create a temp file and get a channel connected to it
        File tempFile = File.createTempFile ("mmaptest", null);
        RandomAccessFile file = new RandomAccessFile (tempFile, "rw");
        FileChannel channel = file.getChannel();
        ByteBuffer temp = ByteBuffer.allocate (100);

        // Put something in the file, starting at location 0
        temp.put ("This is the file content".getBytes());
        temp.flip();
        channel.write (temp, 0);

        // Put something else in the file, starting at location 8192.
        // 8192 is 8 KB, almost certainly a different memory/FS page.
        // This may cause a file hole, depending on the
        // filesystem page size.
        temp.clear();
        temp.put ("This is more file content".getBytes());
        temp.flip();
        channel.write (temp, 8192);

        // Create three types of mappings to the same file
        MappedByteBuffer ro = channel.map (
            FileChannel.MapMode.READ_ONLY, 0, channel.size());
        MappedByteBuffer rw = channel.map (
            FileChannel.MapMode.READ_WRITE, 0, channel.size());
```

Example 3-5. Three types of memory-mapped buffers (continued)

```
MappedByteBuffer cow = channel.map (
    FileChannel.MapMode.PRIVATE, 0, channel.size( ));

// the buffer states before any modifications
System.out.println ("Begin");
showBuffers (ro, rw, cow);

// Modify the copy-on-write buffer
cow.position (8);
cow.put ("COW".getBytes( ));

System.out.println ("Change to COW buffer");
showBuffers (ro, rw, cow);

// Modify the read/write buffer
rw.position (9);
rw.put (" R/W ".getBytes( ));
rw.position (8194);
rw.put (" R/W ".getBytes( ));
rw.force( );

System.out.println ("Change to R/W buffer");
showBuffers (ro, rw, cow);

// Write to the file through the channel; hit both pages
temp.clear( );
temp.put ("Channel write ".getBytes( ));
temp.flip( );
channel.write (temp, 0);
temp.rewind( );
channel.write (temp, 8202);

System.out.println ("Write on channel");
showBuffers (ro, rw, cow);

// Modify the copy-on-write buffer again
cow.position (8207);
cow.put (" COW2 ".getBytes( ));

System.out.println ("Second change to COW buffer");
showBuffers (ro, rw, cow);

// Modify the read/write buffer
rw.position (0);
rw.put (" R/W2 ".getBytes( ));
rw.position (8210);
rw.put (" R/W2 ".getBytes( ));
rw.force( );

System.out.println ("Second change to R/W buffer");
showBuffers (ro, rw, cow);
```

Example 3-5. Three types of memory-mapped buffers (continued)

```
        // cleanup
        channel.close( );
        file.close( );
        tempFile.delete( );
    }

    // Show the current content of the three buffers
    public static void showBuffers (ByteBuffer ro, ByteBuffer rw,
        ByteBuffer cow)
        throws Exception
    {
        dumpBuffer ("R/O", ro);
        dumpBuffer ("R/W", rw);
        dumpBuffer ("COW", cow);
        System.out.println ("");
    }

    // Dump buffer content, counting and skipping nulls
    public static void dumpBuffer (String prefix, ByteBuffer buffer)
        throws Exception
    {
        System.out.print (prefix + ": '");

        int nulls = 0;
        int limit = buffer.limit( );

        for (int i = 0; i < limit; i++) {
            char c = (char) buffer.get (i);

            if (c == '\u0000') {
                nulls++;
                continue;
            }

            if (nulls != 0) {
                System.out.print ("|[" + nulls
                    + " nulls]|");
                nulls = 0;
            }

            System.out.print (c);
        }

        System.out.println ("'");
    }
}
```

Here's the output from running the preceding program:

```
Begin
R/O: 'This is the file content|[8168 nulls]|This is more file content'
R/W: 'This is the file content|[8168 nulls]|This is more file content'
COW: 'This is the file content|[8168 nulls]|This is more file content'
```

```
Change to COW buffer
R/O: 'This is the file content|[8168 nulls]|This is more file content'
R/W: 'This is the file content|[8168 nulls]|This is more file content'
COW: 'This is COW file content|[8168 nulls]|This is more file content'

Change to R/W buffer
R/O: 'This is t R/W le content|[8168 nulls]|Th R/W  more file content'
R/W: 'This is t R/W le content|[8168 nulls]|Th R/W  more file content'
COW: 'This is COW file content|[8168 nulls]|Th R/W  more file content'

Write on channel
R/O: 'Channel write le content|[8168 nulls]|Th R/W  moChannel write t'
R/W: 'Channel write le content|[8168 nulls]|Th R/W  moChannel write t'
COW: 'This is COW file content|[8168 nulls]|Th R/W  moChannel write t'

Second change to COW buffer
R/O: 'Channel write le content|[8168 nulls]|Th R/W  moChannel write t'
R/W: 'Channel write le content|[8168 nulls]|Th R/W  moChannel write t'
COW: 'This is COW file content|[8168 nulls]|Th R/W  moChann COW2 te t'

Second change to R/W buffer
R/O: ' R/W2 l write le content|[8168 nulls]|Th R/W  moChannel  R/W2 t'
R/W: ' R/W2 l write le content|[8168 nulls]|Th R/W  moChannel  R/W2 t'
COW: 'This is COW file content|[8168 nulls]|Th R/W  moChann COW2 te t'
```

Channel-to-Channel Transfers

Bulk transfers of file data from one place to another is so common that a couple of optimization methods have been added to the FileChannel class to make it even more efficient:

```
public abstract class FileChannel
        extends AbstractChannel
        implements ByteChannel, GatheringByteChannel, ScatteringByteChannel
{
        // This is a partial API listing

        public abstract long transferTo (long position, long count,
                WritableByteChannel target)

        public abstract long transferFrom (ReadableByteChannel src,
                long position, long count)
}
```

The transferTo( ) and transferFrom( ) methods allow you to cross-connect one channel to another, eliminating the need to pass data through an intermediate buffer. These methods exist only on the FileChannel class, so one of the channels involved in a channel-to-channel transfer must be a FileChannel. You can't do direct transfers between socket channels, but socket channels implement WritableByteChannel and ReadableByteChannel, so the content of a file can be transferred to a socket with transferTo( ), or data can be read from a socket directly into a file with transferFrom( ).

Direct channel transfers do not update the position associated with a FileChannel. The requested data transfer will begin where indicated by the position argument and will be at most count bytes. The number of bytes actually transferred is returned, which may be less than the number you requested.

For transferTo( ), where the source of the transfer is a file, if position + count is greater than the file size, the transfer will stop at the end of the file. If the target is a socket in nonblocking mode, the transfer may stop when its send queue is filled, possibly sending nothing if the output queue is already full. Likewise for transferFrom( ): if src is another FileChannel and its end-of-file is reached, the transfer will stop early. If src is a nonblocking socket, only the data currently queued will be transferred (which may be none). Sockets in blocking mode may also do partial transfers, depending on the operating system, because of the nondeterministic nature of network data transfer. Many socket implementations will provide what they currently have queued rather than waiting for the full amount you asked for.

Also, keep in mind that these methods may throw java.io.IOException if trouble is encountered during the transfer.

Channel-to-channel transfers can potentially be extremely fast, especially where the underlying operating system provides native support. Some operating systems can perform direct transfers without ever passing the data through user space. This can be a huge win for high-volume data transfer. (See Example 3-6.)

Example 3-6. File concatenation using channel transfer

```
package com.ronsoft.books.nio.channels;

import java.nio.channels.FileChannel;
import java.nio.channels.WritableByteChannel;
import java.nio.channels.Channels;
import java.io.FileInputStream;

/**
 * Test channel transfer.  This is a very simplistic concatenation
 * program.  It takes a list of file names as arguments, opens each
 * in turn and transfers (copies) their content to the given
 * WritableByteChannel (in this case, stdout).
 *
 * Created April 2002
 * @author Ron Hitchens (ron@ronsoft.com)
 */
public class ChannelTransfer
{
    public static void main (String [] argv)
        throws Exception
    {
```

Example 3-6. File concatenation using channel transfer (continued)

```
        if (argv.length == 0) {
            System.err.println ("Usage: filename ...");
            return;
        }

        catFiles (Channels.newChannel (System.out), argv);
    }

    // Concatenate the content of each of the named files to
    // the given channel.  A very dumb version of 'cat'.
    private static void catFiles (WritableByteChannel target,
        String [] files)
        throws Exception
    {
        for (int i = 0; i < files.length; i++) {
            FileInputStream fis = new FileInputStream (files [i]);
            FileChannel channel = fis.getChannel( );

            channel.transferTo (0, channel.size( ), target);

            channel.close( );
            fis.close( );
        }
    }
}
```

Socket Channels

Let's move on to the channel classes that model network sockets. Socket channels have different characteristics than file channels.

The new socket channels can operate in nonblocking mode and are selectable. These two capabilities enable tremendous scalability and flexibility in large applications, such as web servers and middleware components. As we'll see in this section, it's no longer necessary to dedicate a thread to each socket connection (and suffer the context-switching overhead of managing large numbers of threads). Using the new NIO classes, one or a few threads can manage hundreds or even thousands of active socket connections with little or no performance loss.

You can see in Figure 3-9 that all three of the socket channel classes (DatagramChannel, SocketChannel, and ServerSocketChannel) extend from AbstractSelectableChannel, which lives in the java.nio.channels.spi package. This means that it's possible to perform readiness selection of socket channels using a Selector object. Selection and multiplexed I/O are discussed in Chapter 4.

Notice that DatagramChannel and SocketChannel implement the interfaces that define read and write capabilities, but ServerSocketChannel does not. ServerSocketChannel

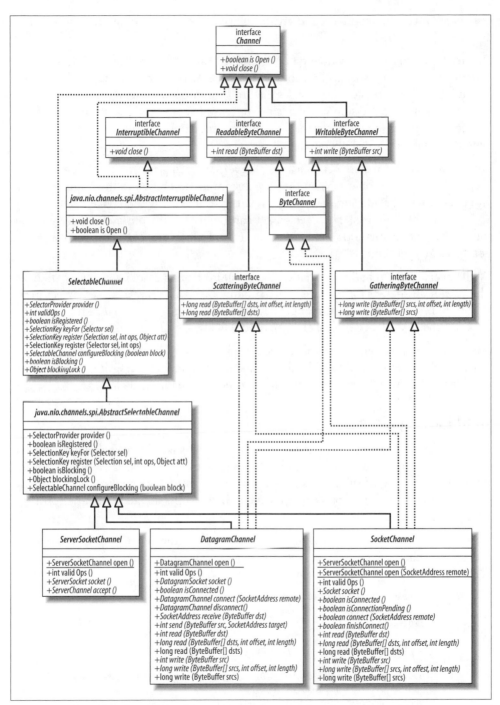

Figure 3-9. The socket channel family tree

listens for incoming connects and creates new SocketChannel objects. It never transfers any data itself.

Before discussing the individual types of socket channels, you should understand the relationship between sockets and socket channels. As described earlier, a channel is a conduit to an I/O service and provides methods for interacting with that service. In the case of sockets, the decision was made not to reimplement the socket protocol APIs in the corresponding channel classes. The preexisting socket channels in java.net are reused for most protocol operations.

All the socket channels (SocketChannel, ServerSocketChannel, and DatagramChannel) create a peer socket object when they are instantiated. These are the familiar classes from java.net (Socket, ServerSocket, and DatagramSocket), which have been updated to be aware of channels. The peer socket can be obtained from a channel by invoking its socket( ) method. Additionally, each of the java.net classes now has a getChannel( ) method.

While every socket channel (in java.nio.channels) has an associated java.net socket object, not all sockets have an associated channel. If you create a Socket object in the traditional way, by instantiating it directly, it will not have an associated SocketChannel, and its getChannel( ) method will always return null.

Socket channels delegate protocol operations to the peer socket object. In cases where socket methods seem to be duplicated in the channel class, there is some new or different behavior associated with the method on the channel class.

Nonblocking Mode

Socket channels can operate in nonblocking mode. This is a simple statement, but one with far-reaching implications. The blocking nature of traditional Java sockets has traditionally been one of the most significant limitations to Java application scalability. Nonblocking I/O is the basis upon which many sophisticated, high-performance applications are built.

To place a socket into nonblocking mode, we look to the common superclass of all the socket channel classes: SelectableChannel. The following methods are concerned with a channel's blocking mode:

```
public abstract class SelectableChannel
        extends AbstractChannel
        implements Channel
{
    // This is a partial API listing

    public abstract void configureBlocking (boolean block) throws IOException;
    public abstract boolean isBlocking( );
    public abstract Object blockingLock( );
}
```

Readiness selection is a mechanism by which a channel can be queried to determine if it's ready to perform an operation of interest, such as reading or writing. Nonblocking I/O and selectability are intimately linked. That's why the API methods for managing blocking mode are defined in the SelectableChannel superclass. The remainder of SelectableChannel's API will be discussed in Chapter 4.

Setting or resetting a channel's blocking mode is easy. Simply call configureBlocking( ) with true to place it in blocking mode, or false for nonblocking mode. It's as simple as that. You can determine which mode a socket channel is currently in by invoking isBlocking( ):

```
SocketChannel sc = SocketChannel.open( );

sc.configureBlocking (false);    // nonblocking
    ...
if ( ! sc.isBlocking( )) {
        doSomething (cs);
}
```

Nonblocking sockets are usually thought of for server-side use because they make it easier to manage many sockets simultaneously. But there can also be benefits to using one or a few sockets in nonblocking mode on the client side. For example, with nonblocking sockets, a GUI application can pay attention to user requests and carry on conversations with one or more servers simultaneously. Nonblocking mode is useful across a broad range of applications.

Occasionally, it's necessary to prevent changes to the blocking mode of a socket channel. The API provides the blockingLock( ) method, which returns an opaque object reference. The object returned is the one used internally by the channel implementation when it makes changes to the blocking mode. Only the thread holding the lock on this object will be able to change the channel's blocking mode. (An object lock is obtained by using the synchronized Java keyword. This is different than the lock( ) method discussed in the section "File Channels.") This can be handy to ensure that the blocking mode of a socket doesn't change during a critical section of code, or to change the mode temporarily without affecting any other threads.

```
Socket socket = null;
Object lockObj = serverChannel.blockingLock( );
// have a handle to the lock object, but haven't locked it yet

// may block here until lock is acquired
synchronize (lockObj)
{
        // This thread now owns the lock; mode can't be changed
        boolean prevState = serverChannel.isBlocking( );

        serverChannel.configureBlocking (false);
        socket = serverChannel.accept( );
        serverChannel.configureBlocking (prevState);
```

```
        }
        // lock is now released, mode is allowed to change

        if (socket != null) {
                doSomethingWithTheSocket (socket);
        }
```

ServerSocketChannel

Let's begin the discussion of the socket channels classes with the simplest: ServerSocketChannel. This is the complete API of ServerSocketChannel:

```
public abstract class ServerSocketChannel
        extends AbstractSelectableChannel
{
        public static ServerSocketChannel open( ) throws IOException
        public abstract ServerSocket socket( );
        public abstract ServerSocket accept( ) throws IOException;
        public final int validOps( )
}
```

The ServerSocketChannel class is a channel-based socket listener. It performs the same basic task as the familiar java.net.ServerSocket but adds channel semantics, including the ability to operate in nonblocking mode.

Create a new ServerSocketChannel object with the static open( ) factory method, which returns a channel associated with an unbound java.net.ServerSocket object. This peer ServerSocket can be obtained by invoking the socket( ) method on the returned ServerSocketChannel object. The ServerSocket objects created as peers of ServerSocketChannels are tied to the channel implementation. They are sockets whose associated SocketImpl knows about channels. Channels cannot be wrapped around arbitrary Socket objects.

Because ServerSocketChannel doesn't have a bind( ) method, it's necessary to fetch the peer socket and use it to bind to a port to begin listening for connections. Also use the peer ServerSocket API to set other socket options as needed.

```
ServerSocketChannel ssc = ServerSocketChannel.open( );
ServerSocket serverSocket = ssc.socket( );

// Listen on port 1234
serverSocket.bind (new InetSocketAddress (1234));
```

The ServerSocketChannel has an accept( ) method, as does its peer java.net. ServerSocket object. Once you've created a ServerSocketChannel and used the peer socket to bind it, you can then invoke accept( ) on either. If you choose to invoke accept( ) on the ServerSocket, it will behave the same as any other ServerSocket: always blocking and returning a java.net.Socket object. On the other hand, the accept( ) method of ServerSocketChannel returns objects of type SocketChannel and is capable of operating in nonblocking mode. If a security manager is in place, both methods perform the same security checks.

If invoked in nonblocking mode, ServerSocketChannel.accept( ) will immediately return null if no incoming connections are currently pending. This ability to check for connections without getting stuck is what enables scalability and reduces complexity. Selectability also comes into play. A ServerSocketChannel object can be registered with a Selector instance to enable notification when new connections arrive. Example 3-7 demonstrates how to use a nonblocking accept( ).

Example 3-7. A nonblocking accept( ) with ServerSocketChannel

```java
package com.ronsoft.books.nio.channels;

import java.nio.ByteBuffer;
import java.nio.channels.ServerSocketChannel;
import java.nio.channels.SocketChannel;
import java.net.InetSocketAddress;

/**
 * Test nonblocking accept( ) using ServerSocketChannel.
 * Start this program, then "telnet localhost 1234" to
 * connect to it.
 *
 * @author Ron Hitchens (ron@ronsoft.com)
 */
public class ChannelAccept
{
    public static final String GREETING = "Hello I must be going.\r\n";

    public static void main (String [] argv)
        throws Exception
    {
        int port = 1234;     // default

        if (argv.length > 0) {
            port = Integer.parseInt (argv [0]);
        }

        ByteBuffer buffer = ByteBuffer.wrap (GREETING.getBytes());
        ServerSocketChannel ssc = ServerSocketChannel.open();

        ssc.socket().bind (new InetSocketAddress (port));
        ssc.configureBlocking (false);

        while (true) {
            System.out.println ("Waiting for connections");

            SocketChannel sc = ssc.accept();

            if (sc == null) {
                // no connections, snooze a while
```

Example 3-7. A nonblocking accept( ) with ServerSocketChannel (continued)

```
                    Thread.sleep (2000);
            } else {
                System.out.println ("Incoming connection from: "
                    + sc.socket().getRemoteSocketAddress());

                buffer.rewind();
                sc.write (buffer);
                sc.close();
            }
        }
    }
}
```

The final method listed previously, validOps( ), is used with selectors. Selectors are discussed in detail in Chapter 4, and validOps( ) is covered in that discussion.

SocketChannel

Let's move on to SocketChannel, which is the most commonly used socket channel class:

```
public abstract class SocketChannel
        extends AbstractSelectableChannel
        implements ByteChannel, ScatteringByteChannel, GatheringByteChannel
{
        // This is a partial API listing

        public static SocketChannel open() throws IOException
        public static SocketChannel open (InetSocketAddress remote)
                throws IOException
        public abstract Socket socket();

        public abstract boolean connect (SocketAddress remote) throws IOException;
        public abstract boolean isConnectionPending();
        public abstract boolean finishConnect() throws IOException;
        public abstract boolean isConnected();

        public final int validOps()
}
```

The Socket and SocketChannel classes encapsulate point-to-point, ordered network connections similar to those provided by the familiar TCP/IP connections we all know and love. A SocketChannel acts as the client, initiating a connection to a listening server. It cannot receive until connected and then only from the address to which the connection was made. (As with ServerSocketChannel, discussion of the validOps( ) method will be deferred to Chapter 4 when we examine selectors. The common read/write methods are not listed here either; refer to the section "Using Channels" for details.)

Every SocketChannel object is created in tandem with a peer java.net.Socket object. The static open( ) method creates a new SocketChannel object. Invoking socket( ) on the new SocketChannel will return its peer Socket object. Calling getChannel( ) on that Socket returns the original SocketChannel.

 Although every SocketChannel object creates a peer Socket object, the reverse is not true. Socket objects created directly do not have associated SocketChannel objects, and their getChannel( ) methods return null.

A newly created SocketChannel is open but not connected. Attempting an I/O operation on an unconnected SocketChannel object will throw a NotYetConnectedException. The socket can be connected by calling connect( ) directly on the channel or by calling the connect( ) method on the associated Socket object. Once a socket channel is connected, it remains connected until it closes. You can test whether a particular SocketChannel is currently connected by invoking the boolean isConnected( ) method.

The second form of open( ), which takes an InetSocketAddress argument, is a convenience method that connects before returning. This:

```
SocketChannel socketChannel =
    SocketChannel.open (new InetSocketAddress ("somehost", somePort));
```

is equivalent to this:

```
SocketChannel socketChannel = SocketChannel.open( );
socketChannel.connect (new InetSocketAddress ("somehost", somePort));
```

If you choose to make the connection the traditional way—by invoking connect( ) on the peer Socket object—the traditional connection semantics apply. The thread will block until the connection is established, or until the supplied timeout expires. If you choose to make the connection by calling connect( ) directly on the channel, and the channel is in blocking mode (the default), the connection process is effectively the same.

There is no version of connect( ) on SocketChannel that lets you provide a timeout value. Instead, SocketChannel provides *concurrent connection* when connect( ) is invoked in nonblocking mode: it initiates a connection to the requested address then returns immediately. If the return value from connect( ) is true, the connection was established immediately (this may happen for local loopback connections). If the connection cannot be established immediately, connect( ) will return false, and connection establishment proceeds concurrently.

Stream-oriented sockets take time to set up because a packet dialog must take place between the two connecting systems to establish the state information needed to maintain the stream socket. Connecting to remote systems across the open Internet can be especially time-consuming. If a concurrent connection is underway on a SocketChannel, the isConnectPending( ) method returns true.

Call finishConnect( ) to complete the connection process. This method can be called safely at any time. One of the following will happen when invoking finishConnect( ) on a SocketChannel object in nonblocking mode:

- The connect( ) method has not yet been called. A NoConnectionPendingException is thrown.

- Connection establishment is underway but not yet complete. Nothing happens, and finishConnect( ) immediately returns false.

- The SocketChannel has been switched back to blocking mode since calling connect( ) in nonblocking mode. If necessary, the invoking thread blocks until connection establishment is complete. finishConnect( ) then returns true.

- Connection establishment has completed since the initial invocation of connect( ) or the last call to finishConnect( ). Internal state is updated in the SocketChannel object to complete the transition to connected state, and finishConnect( ) returns true. The SocketChannel object can then be used to transfer data.

- The connection is already established. Nothing happens, and finishConnect( ) returns true.

While in this intermediate connection-pending state, you should invoke only finishConnect( ), isConnectPending( ), or isConnected( ) on the channel. Once connection establishment has been successfully completed, isConnected( ) returns true.

```
InetSocketAddress addr = new InetSocketAddress (host, port);
SocketChannel sc = SocketChannel.open( );

sc.configureBlocking (false);
sc.connect (addr);

while ( ! sc.finishConnect()) {
    doSomethingElse( );
}

doSomethingWithChannel (sc);

sc.close( );
```

Example 3-8 illustrates runnable code that manages an asynchronous connection.

Example 3-8. Concurrent-connection establishment

```
package com.ronsoft.books.nio.channels;

import java.nio.channels.SocketChannel;
import java.net.InetSocketAddress;

/**
 * Demonstrate asynchronous connection of a SocketChannel.
```

Example 3-8. Concurrent-connection establishment (continued)

```
 * @author Ron Hitchens (ron@ronsoft.com)
 */
public class ConnectAsync
{
    public static void main (String [] argv)
        throws Exception
    {
        String host = "localhost";
        int port = 80;

        if (argv.length == 2) {
            host = argv [0];
            port = Integer.parseInt (argv [1]);
        }

        InetSocketAddress addr = new InetSocketAddress (host, port);
        SocketChannel sc = SocketChannel.open( );

        sc.configureBlocking (false);

        System.out.println ("initiating connection");

        sc.connect (addr);

        while ( ! sc.finishConnect( )) {
            doSomethingUseful( );
        }

        System.out.println ("connection established");

        // Do something with the connected socket
        // The SocketChannel is still nonblocking

        sc.close( );
    }

    private static void doSomethingUseful( )
    {
        System.out.println ("doing something useless");
    }
}
```

If an asynchronous-connection attempt fails, the next invocation of finishConnect( ) throws an appropriate checked exception to indicate the nature of the problem. The channel will then be closed and cannot be connected or used again.

The connection-related methods provide ways to poll a channel and determine its status while a connection is in progress. In Chapter 4, we'll see how to use Selectors to avoid polling and receive notification when an asynchronous connection has been established.

Socket channels are thread-safe. Multiple threads do not need to take special steps to protect against concurrent access, but only one read and one write operation will be in progress at any given time. Keep in mind that sockets are stream-oriented, not packet-oriented. They guarantee that the bytes sent will arrive in the same order but make no promises about maintaining groupings. A sender may write 20 bytes to a socket, and the receiver gets only 3 of those bytes when invoking read( ). The remaining 17 bytes may still be in transit. For this reason, it's rarely a good design choice to have multiple, noncooperating threads share the same side of a stream socket.

The connect( ) and finishConnect( ) methods are mutually synchronized, and any read or write calls will block while one of these operations is in progress, even in non-blocking mode. Test the connection state with isConnected( ) if there's any doubt or if you can't afford to let a read or write block on a channel in this circumstance.

DatagramChannel

The last of the socket channels is DatagramChannel. Like SocketChannel with Socket and ServerSocketChannel with ServerSocket, every DatagramChannel object has an associated DatagramSocket object. The naming pattern doesn't quite hold here: "DatagramSocketChannel" is a bit unwieldy, so "DatagramChannel" was chosen instead.

Just as SocketChannel models connection-oriented stream protocols such as TCP/IP, DatagramChannel models connectionless packet-oriented protocols such as UDP/IP:

```
public abstract class DatagramChannel
        extends AbstractSelectableChannel
        implements ByteChannel, ScatteringByteChannel, GatheringByteChannel
{
        // This is a partial API listing

        public static DatagramChannel open( ) throws IOException
        public abstract DatagramSocket socket( );

        public abstract DatagramChannel connect (SocketAddress remote)
                throws IOException;
        public abstract boolean isConnected( );
        public abstract DatagramChannel disconnect( ) throws IOException;

        public abstract SocketAddress receive (ByteBuffer dst) throws IOException;
        public abstract int send (ByteBuffer src, SocketAddress target)

        public abstract int read (ByteBuffer dst) throws IOException;
        public abstract long read (ByteBuffer [] dsts) throws IOException;
        public abstract long read (ByteBuffer [] dsts, int offset, int length)
                throws IOException;

        public abstract int write (ByteBuffer src) throws IOException;
        public abstract long write(ByteBuffer[] srcs) throws IOException;
        public abstract long write(ByteBuffer[] srcs, int offset, int length)
```

```
        throws IOException;
    }
```

The creation pattern is the same for DatagramChannel as for the other socket channels: invoke the static open( ) method to create a new instance. The new DatagramChannel will have a peer DatagramSocket object that can be obtained by calling the socket( ) method. DatagramChannel objects can act both as server (listener) and client (sender). If you want the newly created channel to listen, it must first be bound to a port or address/port combination. Binding is no different with DatagramChannel than it is for a conventional DatagramSocket; it's delegated to the API on the peer socket object:

```
    DatagramChannel channel = DatagramChannel.open( );
.   DatagramSocket socket = channel.socket( );

    socket.bind (new InetSocketAddress (portNumber));
```

DatagramChannels are connectionless. Each datagram is a self-contained entity, with its own destination address and a data payload independent of every other datagram's. Unlike stream-oriented sockets, a DatagramChannel can send individual datagrams to different destination addresses. Likewise, a DatagramChannel object can receive packets from any address. Each datagram arrives with information about where it came from (the source address).

A DatagramChannel that is not bound can still receive packets. When the underlying socket is created, a dynamically generated port number is assigned to it. Binding requests that the channel's associated port be set to a specific value (which may involve security checks or other validation). Whether the channel is bound or not, any packets sent will contain the DatagramChannel's source address, which includes the port number. Unbound DatagramChannels can receive packets addressed to their port, usually in response to a packet sent previously by that channel. Bound channels receive packets sent to the well-known port to which they've bound themselves. The actual sending or receiving of data is done by the send( ) and receive( ) methods:

```
    public abstract class DatagramChannel
            extends AbstractSelectableChannel
            implements ByteChannel, ScatteringByteChannel, GatheringByteChannel
    {
            // This is a partial API listing

            public abstract SocketAddress receive (ByteBuffer dst) throws IOException;
            public abstract int send (ByteBuffer src, SocketAddress target)
    }
```

The receive( ) method copies the data payload of the next incoming datagram into the provided ByteBuffer and returns a SocketAddress object to indicate where it came from. If the channel is in blocking mode, receive( ) may sleep indefinitely until a packet arrives. If nonblocking, it returns null if no packets are available. If the packet contains more data than will fit in your buffer, any excess will be silently discarded.

If the ByteBuffer you provide does not have sufficient remaining space to hold the packet you're receiving, any bytes that don't fit will be silently discarded.

Invoking send( ) sends the content of the given ByteBuffer object, from its current position to its limit, to the destination address and port described by the given SocketAddress object. If the DatagramChannel object is in blocking mode, the invoking thread may sleep until the datagram can be queued for transmission. If the channel is nonblocking, the return value will be either the number of bytes in the byte buffer or 0. Sending datagrams is an all-or-nothing proposition. If the transmit queue does not have sufficient room to hold the entire datagram, then nothing at all is sent.

If a security manager is installed, its checkConnect( ) method will be called on every invocation of send( ) or receive( ) to validate the destination address, unless the channel is in a connected state (discussed later in this section).

Note that datagram protocols are inherently unreliable; they make no delivery guarantees. A nonzero return value from send( ) does not indicate that the datagram arrived at its destination, only that it was successfully queued to the local networking layer for transmission. Additionally, transport protocols along the way may fragment the datagram. Ethernet, for example, cannot transport packets larger than about 1,500 bytes. If your datagram is large, it runs the risk of being broken into pieces, multiplying the chances of packet loss in transit. The datagram will be reassembled at the destination, and the receiver won't see the fragments, but if any fragments fail to arrive in a timely manner, the entire datagram will be discarded.

The DatagramChannel has a connect( ) method:

```
public abstract class DatagramChannel
        extends AbstractSelectableChannel
        implements ByteChannel, ScatteringByteChannel, GatheringByteChannel
{
        // This is a partial API listing

        public abstract DatagramChannel connect (SocketAddress remote)
                throws IOException;
        public abstract boolean isConnected();
        public abstract DatagramChannel disconnect( ) throws IOException;
}
```

The connection semantics of a DatagramChannel are different for datagram sockets than they are for stream sockets. Sometimes it's desirable to restrict the datagram conversation to two parties. Placing a DatagramChannel into a connected state causes datagrams to be ignored from any source address other than the one to which the channel is "connected." This can be helpful because the unwanted packets will be dropped by the networking layer, relieving your code of the effort required to receive, check, and discard them.

By the same token, when a DatagramChannel is connected, you cannot send to any destination address except the one given to the connect( ) method. Attempting to do so results in a SecurityException.

Connect a DatagramChannel by calling its connect( ) method with a SocketAddress object describing the address of the remote peer. If a security manager is installed, it's consulted to check permission. Thereafter, the security check overhead will not be incurred on each send/receive because packets to or from any other address are not allowed.

A scenario in which connected channels might be useful is a real-time, client/server game using UDP communication. Any given client will always be talking to the same server and wants to ignore packets from any other source. Placing the client's DatagramChannel instance in a connected state reduces the per-packet overhead (because security checks are not needed on each packet) and filters out bogus packets from cheating players. The server may want to do the same thing, but doing so requires a DatagramChannel object for each client.

Unlike stream sockets, the stateless nature of datagram sockets does not require a dialog with the remote system to set up connection state. There is no actual connection, just local state information that designates the allowed remote address. For this reason, there is no separate finishConnect( ) method on DatagramChannel. The connected state of a datagram channel can be tested with the isConnected( ) method.

Unlike SocketChannel, which must be connected to be useful and can connect only once, a DatagramChannel object can transition in and out of connected state any number of times. Each connection can be to a different remote address. Invoking disconnect( ) configures the channel so that it can once again receive from, or send to, any remote address as allowed by the security manager, if one is installed.

While a DatagramChannel is connected, it's not necessary to supply the destination address when sending, and the source address is known when receiving. This means that the conventional read( ) and write( ) methods can be used on a DatagramChannel while it's connected, including the scatter/gather versions to assemble or disassemble packet data:

```
public abstract class DatagramChannel
        extends AbstractSelectableChannel
        implements ByteChannel, ScatteringByteChannel, GatheringByteChannel
{
        // This is a partial API listing

        public abstract int read (ByteBuffer dst) throws IOException;
        public abstract long read (ByteBuffer [] dsts) throws IOException;
        public abstract long read (ByteBuffer [] dsts, int offset, int length)
                throws IOException;

        public abstract int write (ByteBuffer src) throws IOException;
        public abstract long write(ByteBuffer[] srcs) throws IOException;
```

```
        public abstract long write(ByteBuffer[] srcs, int offset, int length)
                throws IOException;
    }
```

The read( ) method returns the number of bytes read, which may be zero if the channel is in nonblocking mode. The return value of write( ) is consistent with send( ): either the number of bytes in your buffer(s) or 0 if the datagram cannot be sent (because the channel is nonblocking). Either can throw NotYetConnectedException if invoked while the DatagramChannel is not in a connected state.

Datagram channels are different beasts than stream sockets. Stream sockets are immensely useful because of their ordered, reliable data-transport characteristics. Most network connections are stream sockets (predominantly TCP/IP). But stream-oriented protocols such as TCP/IP necessarily incur significant overhead to maintain the stream semantics on top of the packet-oriented Internet infrastructure, and the stream metaphor does not apply to all situations. Datagram throughput can be higher than for stream protocols, and datagrams can do some things streams can't.

Here are some reasons to choose datagram sockets over stream sockets:

- Your application can tolerate lost or out-of-order data.
- You want to fire and forget and don't need to know if the packets you sent were received.
- Throughput is more important than reliability.
- You need to send to multiple receivers (multicast or broadcast) simultaneously.
- The packet metaphor fits the task at hand better than the stream metaphor.

If one or more of these characteristics apply to your application, then a datagram design may be appropriate.

Example 3-9 shows how to use a DatagramChannel to issue requests to time servers at multiple addresses. It then waits for the replies to arrive. For each reply that comes back, the remote time is compared to the local time. Because datagram delivery is not guaranteed, some responses may never arrive. Most Linux and Unix systems provide time service by default. There are also several public time servers on the Internet, such as *time.nist.gov*. Firewalls or your ISP may interfere with datagram delivery. Your mileage may vary.

Example 3-9. Time-service client using DatagramChannel

```
package com.ronsoft.books.nio.channels;

import java.nio.ByteBuffer;
import java.nio.ByteOrder;
import java.nio.channels.DatagramChannel;
import java.net.InetSocketAddress;
import java.util.Date;
import java.util.List;
```

Example 3-9. Time-service client using DatagramChannel (continued)

```java
import java.util.LinkedList;
import java.util.Iterator;

/**
 * Request time service, per RFC 868.  RFC 868
 * (http://www.ietf.org/rfc/rfc0868.txt) is a very simple time protocol
 * whereby one system can request the current time from another system.
 * Most Linux, BSD and Solaris systems provide RFC 868 time service
 * on port 37.  This simple program will inter-operate with those.
 * The National Institute of Standards and Technology (NIST) operates
 * a public time server at time.nist.gov.
 *
 * The RFC 868 protocol specifies a 32 bit unsigned value be sent,
 * representing the number of seconds since Jan 1, 1900.  The Java
 * epoch begins on Jan 1, 1970 (same as unix) so an adjustment is
 * made by adding or subtracting 2,208,988,800 as appropriate.  To
 * avoid shifting and masking, a four-byte slice of an
 * eight-byte buffer is used to send/recieve.  But getLong()
 * is done on the full eight bytes to get a long value.
 *
 * When run, this program will issue time requests to each hostname
 * given on the command line, then enter a loop to receive packets.
 * Note that some requests or replies may be lost, which means
 * this code could block forever.
 *
 * @author Ron Hitchens (ron@ronsoft.com)
 */
public class TimeClient
{
    private static final int DEFAULT_TIME_PORT = 37;
    private static final long DIFF_1900 = 2208988800L;

    protected int port = DEFAULT_TIME_PORT;
    protected List remoteHosts;
    protected DatagramChannel channel;

    public TimeClient (String [] argv) throws Exception
    {
        if (argv.length == 0) {
            throw new Exception ("Usage: [ -p port ] host ...");
        }

        parseArgs (argv);

        this.channel = DatagramChannel.open();
    }

    protected InetSocketAddress receivePacket (DatagramChannel channel,
        ByteBuffer buffer)
        throws Exception
    {
        buffer.clear();
```

Example 3-9. Time-service client using DatagramChannel (continued)

```
        // Receive an unsigned 32-bit, big-endian value
        return ((InetSocketAddress) channel.receive (buffer));
    }

    // Send time requests to all the supplied hosts
    protected void sendRequests()
        throws Exception
    {
        ByteBuffer buffer = ByteBuffer.allocate (1);
        Iterator it = remoteHosts.iterator();

        while (it.hasNext()) {
            InetSocketAddress sa = (InetSocketAddress) it.next();

            System.out.println ("Requesting time from "
                + sa.getHostName() + ":" + sa.getPort());

            // Make it empty (see RFC868)
            buffer.clear().flip();
            // Fire and forget
            channel.send (buffer, sa);
        }
    }

    // Receive any replies that arrive
    public void getReplies() throws Exception
    {
        // Allocate a buffer to hold a long value
        ByteBuffer longBuffer = ByteBuffer.allocate (8);

        // Assure big-endian (network) byte order
        longBuffer.order (ByteOrder.BIG_ENDIAN);
        // Zero the whole buffer to be sure
        longBuffer.putLong (0, 0);
        // Position to first byte of the low-order 32 bits
        longBuffer.position (4);

        // Slice the buffer; gives view of the low-order 32 bits
        ByteBuffer buffer = longBuffer.slice();
        int expect = remoteHosts.size();
        int replies = 0;

        System.out.println ("");
        System.out.println ("Waiting for replies...");

        while (true) {
            InetSocketAddress sa;

            sa = receivePacket (channel, buffer);
```

Example 3-9. Time-service client using DatagramChannel (continued)

```
            buffer.flip( );
            replies++;

            printTime (longBuffer.getLong (0), sa);

            if (replies == expect) {
                System.out.println ("All packets answered");

                break;
            }

            // Some replies haven't shown up yet
            System.out.println ("Received " + replies
                + " of " + expect + " replies");
        }
    }

    // Print info about a received time reply
    protected void printTime (long remote1900, InetSocketAddress sa)
    {
        // local time as seconds since Jan 1, 1970
        long local = System.currentTimeMillis( ) / 1000;
        // remote time as seconds since Jan 1, 1970
        long remote = remote1900 - DIFF_1900;
        Date remoteDate = new Date (remote * 1000);
        Date localDate = new Date (local * 1000);
        long skew = remote - local;

        System.out.println ("Reply from "
            + sa.getHostName() + ":" + sa.getPort( ));
        System.out.println ("  there: " + remoteDate);
        System.out.println ("   here: " + localDate);
        System.out.print ("    skew: ");

        if (skew == 0) {
            System.out.println ("none");
        } else if (skew > 0) {
            System.out.println (skew + " seconds ahead");
        } else {
            System.out.println ((-skew) + " seconds behind");
        }
    }

    protected void parseArgs (String [] argv)
    {
        remoteHosts = new LinkedList( );

        for (int i = 0; i < argv.length; i++) {
            String arg = argv [i];

            // Send client requests to the given port
            if (arg.equals ("-p")) {
```

Example 3-9. Time-service client using DatagramChannel (continued)

```
            i++;
            this.port = Integer.parseInt (argv [i]);
            continue;
        }

        // Create an address object for the hostname
        InetSocketAddress sa = new InetSocketAddress (arg, port);

        // Validate that it has an address
        if (sa.getAddress( ) == null) {
            System.out.println ("Cannot resolve address: "
                + arg);

            continue;
        }

        remoteHosts.add (sa);
    }
}

// --------------------------------------------------------------

public static void main (String [] argv)
    throws Exception
{
    TimeClient client = new TimeClient (argv);

    client.sendRequests( );
    client.getReplies( );
}
}
```

The program in Example 3-10 is an RFC 868 time server. This code answers requests from the client in Example 3-9 and shows how a DatagramChannel binds to a well-known port and then listens for requests from clients. This time server listens only for datagram (UDP) requests. The rdate command available on most Unix and Linux systems uses TCP to connect to an RFC 868 time service.

Example 3-10. DatagramChannel time server

```
package com.ronsoft.books.nio.channels;

import java.nio.ByteBuffer;
import java.nio.ByteOrder;
import java.nio.channels.DatagramChannel;
import java.net.SocketAddress;
import java.net.InetSocketAddress;
import java.net.SocketException;

/**
 * Provide RFC 868 time service (http://www.ietf.org/rfc/rfc0868.txt).
```

Example 3-10. DatagramChannel time server (continued)

```
 * This code implements an RFC 868 listener to provide time
 * service.  The defined port for time service is 37.  On most
 * unix systems, root privilege is required to bind to ports
 * below 1024.  You can either run this code as root or
 * provide another port number on the command line.  Use
 * "-p port#" with TimeClient if you choose an alternate port.
 *
 * Note: The familiar rdate command on unix will probably not work
 * with this server.  Most versions of rdate use TCP rather than UDP
 * to request the time.
 *
 * @author Ron Hitchens (ron@ronsoft.com)
 */
public class TimeServer
{
    private static final int DEFAULT_TIME_PORT = 37;
    private static final long DIFF_1900 = 2208988800L;

    protected DatagramChannel channel;

    public TimeServer (int port)
        throws Exception
    {
        this.channel = DatagramChannel.open( );
        this.channel.socket( ).bind (new InetSocketAddress (port));

        System.out.println ("Listening on port " + port
            + " for time requests");
    }

    public void listen( ) throws Exception
    {
        // Allocate a buffer to hold a long value
        ByteBuffer longBuffer = ByteBuffer.allocate (8);

        // Assure big-endian (network) byte order
        longBuffer.order (ByteOrder.BIG_ENDIAN);
        // Zero the whole buffer to be sure
        longBuffer.putLong (0, 0);
        // Position to first byte of the low-order 32 bits
        longBuffer.position (4);

        // Slice the buffer; gives view of the low-order 32 bits
        ByteBuffer buffer = longBuffer.slice( );

        while (true) {
            buffer.clear( );

            SocketAddress sa = this.channel.receive (buffer);

            if (sa == null) {
                continue;     // defensive programming
```

Example 3-10. DatagramChannel time server (continued)

```
        }
        // Ignore content of received datagram per RFC 868

        System.out.println ("Time request from " + sa);

        buffer.clear( );          // sets pos/limit correctly

        // Set 64-bit value; slice buffer sees low 32 bits
        longBuffer.putLong (0,
            (System.currentTimeMillis( ) / 1000) + DIFF_1900);

        this.channel.send (buffer, sa);
    }
}

// -------------------------------------------------------------

public static void main (String [] argv)
    throws Exception
{
    int port = DEFAULT_TIME_PORT;

    if (argv.length > 0) {
        port = Integer.parseInt (argv [0]);
    }

    try {
        TimeServer server = new TimeServer (port);

        server.listen( );
    } catch (SocketException e) {
        System.out.println ("Can't bind to port " + port
            + ", try a different one");

    }
    }
}
```

Pipes

The java.nio.channels package includes a class named Pipe. A *pipe*, in the general sense, is a conduit through which data can be passed in a single direction between two entities. The notion of a pipe has long been familiar to users of Unix (and Unix-like) operating systems. Pipes are used on Unix systems to connect the output of one process to the input of another. The Pipe class implements a pipe paradigm, but the pipes it creates are intraprocess (within the JVM process) rather than interprocess (between processes). See Figure 3-10.

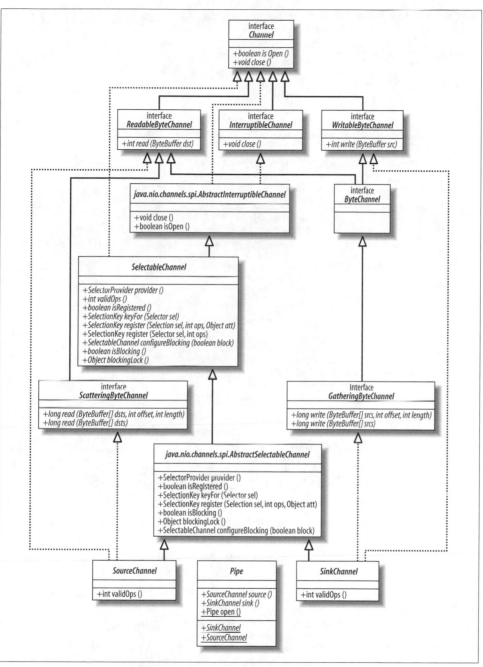

Figure 3-10. The Pipe family tree

The Pipe class creates a pair of Channel objects that provide a loopback mechanism. The two channels' far ends are connected so that whatever is written down the

SinkChannel appears on the SourceChannel. Figure 3-11 shows the class hierarchy for Pipe.

```
package java.nio.channels;

public abstract class Pipe
{
        public static Pipe open( ) throws IOException
        public abstract SourceChannel source( );
        public abstract SinkChannel sink( );

        public static abstract class SourceChannel
                extends AbstractSelectableChannel
                implements ReadableByteChannel, ScatteringByteChannel

        public static abstract class SinkChannel
                extends AbstractSelectableChannel
                implements WritableByteChannel, GatheringByteChannel
}
```

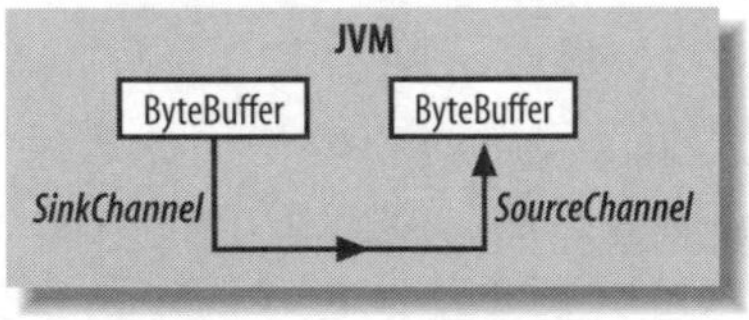

Figure 3-11. A pipe is a pair of looped channels

An instance of Pipe is created by invoking the Pipe.open( ) factory method with no arguments. The Pipe class defines two nested channel classes to implement the pipeline. These classes are Pipe.SourceChannel (the read end of the pipe) and Pipe.SinkChannel (the write end of the pipe). These Channel instances are created when the Pipe object is created and can be fetched by calling the source( ) and sink( ) methods, respectively, on the Pipe object.

At this point, you may be wondering what pipes are useful for. You can't use Pipe to set up a Unix-like pipe between operating system–level processes (you can use SocketChannel for that). The source and sink channels of Pipe provide functionality similar to java.io.PipedInputStream and java.io.PipedOutputStream but with full channel semantics. Notice that SinkChannel and SourceChannel both extend from AbstractSelectableChannel (and thus SelectableChannel), which means that pipe channels can be used with selectors (see Chapter 4).

Pipes can be used only to pass data within the same JVM. There are far more efficient ways of passing data between threads, but the advantage of using pipes is encapsulation. Producer and consumer threads can be written to the common Channel API. The same code can be used to write data to a file, socket, or pipe, depending on the type of channel it's given. Selectors can be used to check for data availability on pipes just as easily as on socket channels. This might allow a single consumer thread to efficiently collect data from multiple channels, in any combination of network connections or local worker threads, using a single Selector. The implications for scalability, redundancy, and reusability are significant.

Another useful application of Pipes is for testing. A unit-testing framework can connect a class to be tested to the write end of a pipe and check the data that comes out the read end. It can also set up the class being tested on the read end of the pipe and write controlled test data to it. Both scenarios can be very useful for regression testing.

The amount of data the pipeline holds is implementation-dependent. The only guarantee is that the bytes written to the SinkChannel will reappear on the SourceChannel in the same order. Example 3-11 demonstrates how pipes are used.

Example 3-11. Worker thread writing to a pipe

```
package com.ronsoft.books.nio.channels;

import java.nio.ByteBuffer;
import java.nio.channels.ReadableByteChannel;
import java.nio.channels.WritableByteChannel;
import java.nio.channels.Pipe;
import java.nio.channels.Channels;
import java.util.Random;

/**
 * Test Pipe objects using a worker thread.
 *
 * Created April, 2002
 * @author Ron Hitchens (ron@ronsoft.com)
 */
public class PipeTest
{
    public static void main (String [] argv)
        throws Exception
    {
        // Wrap a channel around stdout
        WritableByteChannel out = Channels.newChannel (System.out);
        // Start worker and get read end of channel
        ReadableByteChannel workerChannel = startWorker (10);
        ByteBuffer buffer = ByteBuffer.allocate (100);

        while (workerChannel.read (buffer) >= 0) {
            buffer.flip( );
            out.write (buffer);
            buffer.clear( );
        }
    }

    // This method could return a SocketChannel or
    // FileChannel instance just as easily
    private static ReadableByteChannel startWorker (int reps)
        throws Exception
```

Example 3-11. Worker thread writing to a pipe (continued)

```java
{
    Pipe pipe = Pipe.open( );
    Worker worker = new Worker (pipe.sink( ), reps);

    worker.start( );

    return (pipe.source( ));
}

// -----------------------------------------------------------------

/**
 * A worker thread object which writes data down a channel.
 * Note: this object knows nothing about Pipe, uses only a
 * generic WritableByteChannel.
 */
private static class Worker extends Thread
{
    WritableByteChannel channel;
    private int reps;

    Worker (WritableByteChannel channel, int reps)
    {
        this.channel = channel;
        this.reps = reps;
    }

    // Thread execution begins here
    public void run( )
    {
        ByteBuffer buffer = ByteBuffer.allocate (100);

        try {
            for (int i = 0; i < this.reps; i++) {
                doSomeWork (buffer);

                // channel may not take it all at once
                while (channel.write (buffer) > 0) {
                    // empty
                }
            }

            this.channel.close( );
        } catch (Exception e) {
            // easy way out; this is demo code
            e.printStackTrace( );
        }
    }

    private String [] products = {
        "No good deed goes unpunished",
        "To be, or what?",
```

Example 3-11. Worker thread writing to a pipe (continued)

```
            "No matter where you go, there you are",
            "Just say \"Yo\"",
            "My karma ran over my dogma"
        };

        private Random rand = new Random( );

        private void doSomeWork (ByteBuffer buffer)
        {
            int product = rand.nextInt (products.length);

            buffer.clear( );
            buffer.put (products [product].getBytes( ));
            buffer.put ("\r\n".getBytes( ));
            buffer.flip( );
        }
    }
}
```

The Channels Utility Class

NIO channels provide a new, stream-like I/O metaphor, but the familiar byte stream and character reader/writer classes are still around and widely used. Channels may eventually be retrofitted into the java.io classes (an implementation detail), but the APIs presented by java.io streams and reader/writers will not be going away anytime soon (nor should they).

A utility class, with the slightly repetitive name of java.nio.channels.Channels, defines several static factory methods to make it easier for channels to interconnect with streams and readers/writers. Table 3-2 summarizes these methods.

Table 3-2. Summary of java.nio.channels.Channels utility methods

Method	Returns	Description
newChannel (InputStream in)	ReadableByteChannel	Returns a channel that will read bytes from the provided input stream.
newChannel (OutputStream out)	WritableByteChannel	Returns a channel that will write bytes to the provided output stream.
newInputStream (ReadableByteChannel ch)	InputStream	Returns a stream that will read bytes from the provided channel.
newOutputStream (WritableByteChannel ch)	OutputStream	Returns a stream that will write bytes to the given channel.

Method	Returns	Description
newReader (ReadableByteChannel ch, CharsetDecoder dec, int minBufferCap)	Reader	Returns a reader that will read bytes from the provided channel and decode them according to the given CharsetDecoder. Charset encoding/decoding is discussed in Chapter 6.
newReader (ReadableByteChannel ch, String csName)	Reader	Returns a reader that will read bytes from the provided channel and decode them into characters according to the given charset name.
newWriter (WritableByteChannel ch, CharsetEncoder dec, int minBufferCap)	Writer	Returns a writer that will encode characters with the provided CharsetEncoder object and write them to the given channel.
newWriter (WritableByteChannel ch, String csName)	Writer	Returns a writer that will encode characters according to the provided charset name and write them to the given channel.

Recall that conventional streams transfer bytes and that readers and writers work with character data. The first four rows of Table 3-2 describe methods for interconnecting streams and channels. Since both operate on byte streams, these four methods do straightforward wrapping of streams around channels and vice versa.

Readers and writers operate on characters, which in the Java world are not at all the same as bytes. To hook up a channel (which knows only about bytes) to a reader or writer requires an intermediate conversion to handle the byte/char impedance mismatch. The factory methods described in the second half of Table 3-2 use character set encoders and decoders for this purpose. Charsets and character set transcoding are discussed in detail in Chapter 6.

The wrapper Channel objects returned by these methods may or may not implement the InterruptibleChannel interface. Also, they might not extend from SelectableChannel. Therefore, it may not be possible to use these wrapper channels interchangeably with the other channel types defined in the java.nio.channels package. The specifics are implementation-dependent. If your application relies on these semantics, test the returned channel object with the instanceof operator.

Summary

We covered a lot of ground in this chapter. Channels make up the infrastructure, or the plumbing, which carries data between ByteBuffers and I/O services of the operating system (or whatever the channel is connected to). The key concepts discussed in this chapter were:

Basic channel operations
> In the section "Channel Basics," we learned the basic operations of channels. These included how to open a channel using the API calls common to all channels and how to close a channel when finished.

Scatter/gather channels
> The topic of scatter/gather I/O using channels was introduced in the section "Scatter/Gather." Vectored I/O enables you to perform one I/O operation across multiple buffers automatically.

File channels
> The multifaceted FileChannel class was discussed in the section "File Channels." This powerful new channel provides access to advanced file operations not previously available to Java programs. Among these new capabilities are file locking, memory-mapped files, and channel-to-channel transfers.

Socket channels
> The several types of socket channels were covered in the section "Socket Channels." Also discussed was nonblocking mode, an important new feature supported by socket channels.

Pipes
> In the section "Pipes," we looked at the Pipe class, a useful new loopback mechanism using specialized channel implementations.

Channels utility class
> The Channels class contains utility methods that provide for cross-connecting channels with conventional byte streams and character reader/writer objects. See the section "The Channels Utility Class."

There are many channels on your NIO dial, and we've surfed them all. The material in this chapter was a lot to absorb. Channels are the key abstraction of NIO. Now that we understand what channels are and how to use them effectively to access the I/O services of the native operating system, it's time to move on to the next major innovation of NIO. In the next chapter, we'll learn how to manage many of these powerful new channels easily and efficiently.

Take a bathroom break, visit the gift shop, and then please reboard the bus. Next stop: selectors.

CHAPTER 4

Selectors

Life is a series of rude awakenings.
—R. Van Winkle

In this chapter, we'll explore selectors. Selectors provide the ability to do *readiness selection*, which enables *multiplexed I/O*. As described in Chapter 1, readiness selection and multiplexing make it possible for a single thread to efficiently manage many I/O channels simultaneously. C/C++ coders have had the POSIX select( ) and/or poll( ) system calls in their toolbox for many years. Most other operating systems provide similar functionality. But readiness selection was never available to Java programmers until JDK 1.4. Programmers whose primary body of experience is in the Java environment may not have encountered this I/O model before.

For an illustration of readiness selection, let's return to the drive-through bank example of Chapter 3. Imagine a bank with three drive-through lanes. In the traditional (nonselector) scenario, imagine that each drive-through lane has a pneumatic tube that runs to its own teller station inside the bank, and each station is walled off from the others. This means that each tube (channel) requires a dedicated teller (worker thread). This approach doesn't scale well and is wasteful. For each new tube (channel) added, a new teller is required, along with associated overhead such as tables, chairs, paper clips (memory, CPU cycles, context switching), etc. And when things are slow, these resources (which have associated costs) tend to sit idle.

Now imagine a different scenario in which each pneumatic tube (channel) is connected to a single teller station inside the bank. The station has three slots where the carriers (data buffers) arrive, each with an indicator (selection key) that lights up when the carrier is in the slot. Also imagine that the teller (worker thread) has a sick cat and spends as much time as possible reading *Do It Yourself Taxidermy*.* At the end of each paragraph, the teller glances up at the indicator lights (invokes select( )) to determine if any of the channels are ready (readiness selection). The teller (worker

---

* Not currently in the O'Reilly catalog.

thread) can perform another task while the drive-through lanes (channels) are idle yet still respond to them in a timely manner when they require attention.

While this analogy is not exact, it illustrates the paradigm of quickly checking to see if attention is required by any of a set of resources, without being forced to wait if something isn't ready to go. This ability to check and continue is key to scalability. A single thread can monitor large numbers of channels with readiness selection. The Selector and related classes provide the APIs to do readiness selection on channels.

Selector Basics

Getting a handle on the topics discussed in this chapter will be somewhat tougher than understanding the relatively straightforward buffer and channel classes. It's trickier, because there are three main classes, all of which come into play at the same time. If you find yourself confused, back up and take another run at it. Once you see how the pieces fit together and their individual roles, it should all make sense.

We'll begin with the executive summary, then break down the details. You register one or more previously created selectable channels with a selector object. A key that represents the relationship between one channel and one selector is returned. Selection keys remember what you are interested in for each channel. They also track the operations of interest that their channel is currently ready to perform. When you invoke select( ) on a selector object, the associated keys are updated by checking all the channels registered with that selector. You can obtain a set of the keys whose channels were found to be ready at that point. By iterating over these keys, you can service each channel that has become ready since the last time you invoked select( ).

That's the 30,000-foot view. Now let's swoop in low and see what happens at ground level (or below).

At this point, you may want to skip ahead to Example 4-1 and take a quick look at the code. Between here and there, you'll learn the specifics of how these new classes work, but armed with just the high-level information in the preceding paragraph, you should be able to see how the selection model works in practice.

At the most fundamental level, selectors provide the capability to ask a channel if it's ready to perform an I/O operation of interest to you. For example, a SocketChannel object could be asked if it has any bytes ready to read, or we may want to know if a ServerSocketChannel has any incoming connections ready to accept.

Selectors provide this service when used in conjunction with SelectableChannel objects, but there's more to the story than that. The real power of readiness selection is that a potentially large number of channels can be checked for readiness simultaneously. The caller can easily determine which of several channels are ready to go. Optionally, the invoking thread can ask to be put to sleep until one or more of the channels registered with the Selector is ready, or it can periodically poll the selector to see if anything has become ready since the last check. If you think of a web server, which must manage large numbers of concurrent connections, it's easy to imagine how these capabilities can be put to good use.

At first blush, it may seem possible to emulate readiness selection with nonblocking mode alone, but it really isn't. Nonblocking mode will either do what you request or indicate that it can't. This is semantically different from determining if it's *possible* to do a certain type of operation. For example, if you attempt a nonblocking read and it succeeds, you not only discovered that a read( ) is possible, you also read some data. You must then do something with that data.

This effectively prevents you from separating the code that checks for readiness from the code that processes the data, at least without significant complexity. And even if it was possible simply to ask each channel if it's ready, this would still be problematic because your code, or some code in a library package, would need to iterate through all the candidate channels and check each in turn. This would result in at least one system call per channel to test its readiness, which could be expensive, but the main problem is that the check would not be atomic. A channel early in the list could become ready after it's been checked, but you wouldn't know it until the next time you poll. Worst of all, you'd have no choice but to continually poll the list. You wouldn't have a way of being notified when a channel you're interested in becomes ready.

This is why the traditional Java solution to monitoring multiple sockets has been to create a thread for each and allow the thread to block in a read( ) until data is available. This effectively makes each blocked thread a socket monitor and the JVM's thread scheduler becomes the notification mechanism. Neither was designed for these purposes. The complexity and performance cost of managing all these threads, for the programmer and for the JVM, quickly get out of hand as the number of threads grows.

True readiness selection must be done by the operating system. One of the most important functions performed by an operating system is to handle I/O requests and notify processes when their data is ready. So it only makes sense to delegate this function down to the operating system. The Selector class provides the abstraction by which Java code can request readiness selection service from the underlying operating system in a portable way.

Let's take a look at the specific classes that deal with readiness selection in the java.nio.channels package.

The Selector, SelectableChannel, and SelectionKey Classes

At this point, you may be confused about how all this selection stuff works in Java. Let's identify the moving parts and how they interact. The UML diagram in Figure 4-1 makes the situation look more complicated than it really is. Refer to

Figure 4-2 and you'll see that there are really only three pertinent class APIs when doing readiness selection:

Selector

The Selector class manages information about a set of registered channels and their readiness states. Channels are registered with selectors, and a selector can be asked to update the readiness states of the channels currently registered with it. When doing so, the invoking thread can optionally indicate that it would prefer to be suspended until one of the registered channels is ready.

SelectableChannel

This abstract class provides the common methods needed to implement channel selectability. It's the superclass of all channel classes that support readiness selection. FileChannel objects are not selectable because they don't extend from SelectableChannel (see Figure 4-2). All the socket channel classes are selectable, as well as the channels obtained from a Pipe object. SelectableChannel objects can be registered with Selector objects, along with an indication of which operations on that channel are of interest for that selector. A channel can be registered with multiple selectors, but only once per selector.

SelectionKey

A SelectionKey encapsulates the registration relationship between a specific channel and a specific selector. A SelectionKey object is returned from SelectableChannel.register( ) and serves as a token representing the registration. SelectionKey objects contain two bit sets (encoded as integers) indicating which channel operations the registrant has an interest in and which operations the channel is ready to perform.

Let's take a look at the relevant API methods of SelectableChannel:

```
public abstract class SelectableChannel
        extends AbstractChannel
        implements Channel
{
        // This is a partial API listing

        public abstract SelectionKey register (Selector sel, int ops)
                throws ClosedChannelException;
        public abstract SelectionKey register (Selector sel, int ops, Object att)
                throws ClosedChannelException;

        public abstract boolean isRegistered( );
        public abstract SelectionKey keyFor (Selector sel);
        public abstract int validOps( );

        public abstract void configureBlocking (boolean block)
                throws IOException;
        public abstract boolean isBlocking( );
        public abstract Object blockingLock( );
}
```

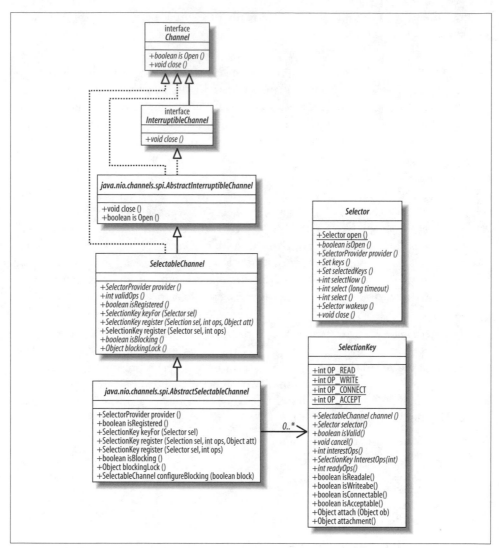

Figure 4-1. Selection class family tree

Nonblocking and multiplexing go hand-in-hand—so much so that the architects of java.nio placed the APIs for both in the same class.

We've already discussed how to configure and check a channel's blocking mode with the last three methods of SelectableChannel, which are listed above. (Refer to "Nonblocking Mode" in Chapter 3 for a detailed discussion.) A channel must first be placed in nonblocking mode (by calling configureBlocking(false)) before it can be registered with a selector.

Invoking the selectable channel's register() method registers it with a selector. If you attempt to register a channel that is in blocking mode, register() will throw an

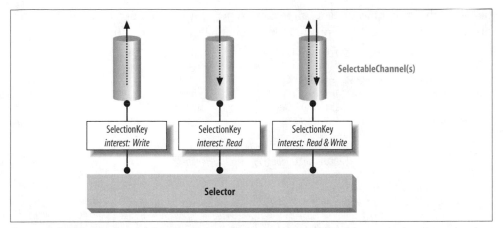

Figure 4-2. Relationships of the selection classes

unchecked IllegalBlockingModeException. Also, a channel cannot be returned to blocking mode while registered. Attempting to do so will throw IllegalBlocking-ModeException from the configureBlocking( ) method.

And, of course, attempting to register a SelectableChannel instance that has been closed will throw ClosedChannelException, as indicated by the method signature.

Before we take a closer look at register( ) and the other methods of SelectableChannel, let's look at the API of the Selector class so we can better understand the relationship:

```
public abstract class Selector
{
        public static Selector open( ) throws IOException
        public abstract boolean isOpen( );
        public abstract void close( ) throws IOException;
        public abstract SelectionProvider provider( );

        public abstract int select( ) throws IOException;
        public abstract int select (long timeout) throws IOException;
        public abstract int selectNow( ) throws IOException;
        public abstract void wakeup( );

        public abstract Set keys( );
        public abstract Set selectedKeys( );
}
```

Although the register( ) method is defined on the SelectableChannel class, channels are registered with selectors, not the other way around. A selector maintains a set of channels to monitor. A given channel can be registered with more than one selector and has no idea which Selector objects it's currently registered with. The choice to put the register( ) method in SelectableChannel rather than in Selector was somewhat arbitrary. It returns a SelectionKey object that encapsulates a relationship between the two objects. The important thing is to remember that the `Selector` object controls the selection process for the channels registered with it.

```
public abstract class SelectionKey
{
    public static final int OP_READ
    public static final int OP_WRITE
    public static final int OP_CONNECT
    public static final int OP_ACCEPT

    public abstract SelectableChannel channel();
    public abstract Selector selector();

    public abstract void cancel();
    public abstract boolean isValid();

    public abstract int interestOps();
    public abstract void interestOps (int ops);
    public abstract int readyOps();

    public final boolean isReadable()
    public final boolean isWritable()
    public final boolean isConnectable()
    public final boolean isAcceptable()

    public final Object attach (Object ob)
    public final Object attachment()
}
```

 Selectors are the managing objects, not the selectable channel objects. The `Selector` object performs readiness selection of channels registered with it and manages selection keys.

The interpretation of a key's interest and readiness sets is channel-specific. Each channel implementation typically defines its own specialized `SelectionKey` class, constructs it within the `register()` method, and passes it to the provided `Selector` object.

In the following sections, we'll cover all the methods of these three classes in more detail.

Setting Up Selectors

At this point, you may still be confused. You see a bunch of methods in the three preceding listings and can't tell what they do or what they mean. Before drilling into the details of all this, let's take a look at a typical usage example. It should help to put things into context.

To set up a `Selector` to monitor three `Socket` channels, you'd do something like this (refer to Figure 4-2):

```
Selector selector = Selector.open();

channel1.register (selector, SelectionKey.OP_READ);
channel2.register (selector, SelectionKey.OP_WRITE);
channel3.register (selector, SelectionKey.OP_READ | SelectionKey.OP_WRITE);

// Wait up to 10 seconds for a channel to become ready
readyCount = selector.select (10000);
```

This code creates a new selector, then registers three (preexisting) socket channels with that selector, each with a different set of interests. The select( ) method is then called to put the thread to sleep until one of these interesting things happens or the 10-second timer expires.

Now let's start looking at the Selector API in detail:

```
public abstract class Selector
{
        // This is a partial API listing

        public static Selector open() throws IOException
        public abstract boolean isOpen();
        public abstract void close() throws IOException;
        public abstract SelectionProvider provider();
}
```

Selector objects are instantiated by calling the static factory method open( ). Selectors are not primary I/O objects like channels or streams: data never passes through them. The open( ) class method interfaces to the SPI to request a new instance from the default SelectorProvider object. It's also possible to create a new Selector instance by calling the openSelector( ) method of a custom SelectorProvider object. You can determine which SelectorProvider object created a given Selector instance by calling its provider( ) method. In most cases, you do not need to be concerned about the SPI; just call open( ) to create a new Selector object. For those rare circumstances when you must deal with it, the channel SPI package is summarized in Appendix B.

Continuing the convention of treating a Selector as an I/O object: when you're finished with it, call close( ) to release any resources it may be holding and to invalidate any associated selection keys. Once a Selector has been closed, attempting to invoke most methods on it will result in a ClosedSelectorException. Note that ClosedSelectorException is an unchecked (runtime) exception. You can test a Selector to determine if it's currently open with the isOpen( ) method.

We'll finish with the Selector API in a bit, but right now let's take a look at registering channels with selectors. Here's an abbreviated version of the SelectableChannel API from earlier in this chapter:

```
public abstract class SelectableChannel
        extends AbstractChannel
        implements Channel
```

```
{
        // This is a partial API listing

        public abstract SelectionKey register (Selector sel, int ops)
                throws ClosedChannelException;
        public abstract SelectionKey register (Selector sel, int ops, Object att)
                throws ClosedChannelException;

        public abstract boolean isRegistered( );
        public abstract SelectionKey keyFor (Selector sel);
        public abstract int validOps( );
}
```

As mentioned earlier, the register( ) method lives in the SelectableChannel class, although channels are actually registered with selectors. You can see that register( ) takes a Selector object as an argument, as well as an integer parameter named ops. This second argument represents the *operation interest set* for which the channel is being registered. This is a bit mask that represents the I/O operations that the selector should test for when checking the readiness of that channel. The specific operation bits are defined as public static fields in the SelectionKey class.

As of JDK 1.4, there are four defined selectable operations: read, write, connect, and accept. Not all operations are supported on all selectable channels. A SocketChannel cannot do an accept, for example. Attempting to register interest in an unsupported operation will result in the unchecked IllegalArgumentException being thrown. You can discover the set of operations a particular channel object supports by calling its validOps( ) method. We saw this method on the socket channel classes discussed in Chapter 3.

Selectors contain sets of channels currently registered with them. Only one registration of a given channel with a given selector can be in effect at any given time. However, it is permissible to register a given channel with a given selector more than once. Doing so returns the same SelectionKey object after updating its operation interest set to the given value. In effect, subsequent registrations simply update the key associated with the preexisting registration (see the section "Using Selection Keys").

An exceptional situation is when you attempt to reregister a channel with a selector for which the associated key has been cancelled, but the channel is still registered. Channels are not immediately deregistered when the associated key is cancelled. They remain registered until the next selection operation occurs (see the section "Using Selectors"). In this case, the unchecked CancelledKeyException will be thrown. Test the state of the SelectionKey object if there is a chance the key may have been cancelled.

In the previous listing, you'll notice a second version of register( ) that takes a generic object argument. This is a convenience method that passes the object reference you provide to the attach( ) method of the new selection key before returning it to you. We'll take a closer look at the API for SelectionKey in the next section.

A single channel object can be registered with multiple selectors. A channel can be queried to see if it is currently registered with any selectors by calling the isRegistered( ) method. This method does not provide information about which selectors the channel is registered with, only that it is registered with at least one. Additionally, there can be a delay between the time a registration key is cancelled and the time a channel is deregistered. This method is a hint, not a definitive answer.

Each registration of a channel with a selector is encapsulated by a SelectionKey object. The keyFor( ) method returns the key associated with this channel and the given selector. If the channel is currently registered with the given selector, the associated key is returned. If no current registration relationship exists for this channel with the given selector, null is returned.

Using Selection Keys

Let's look again at the API of the SelectionKey class:

```
package java.nio.channels;

public abstract class SelectionKey
{
        public static final int OP_READ
        public static final int OP_WRITE
        public static final int OP_CONNECT
        public static final int OP_ACCEPT

        public abstract SelectableChannel channel( );
        public abstract Selector selector( );

        public abstract void cancel( );
        public abstract boolean isValid( );

        public abstract int interestOps( );
        public abstract void interestOps (int ops);
        public abstract int readyOps( );

        public final boolean isReadable( )
        public final boolean isWritable( )
        public final boolean isConnectable( )
        public final boolean isAcceptable( )

        public final Object attach (Object ob)
        public final Object attachment( )
}
```

As mentioned earlier, a key represents the registration of a particular channel object with a particular selector object. You can see that relationship reflected in the first two methods above. The channel( ) method returns the SelectableChannel object associated with the key, and selector( ) returns the associated Selector object. Nothing surprising there.

Key objects represent a specific registration relationship. When it's time to terminate that relationship, call the cancel( ) method on the SelectionKey object. A key can be checked to see if it still represents a valid registration by calling its isValid( ) method. When a key is cancelled, it's placed in the cancelled set of the associated selector. The registration is not immediately terminated, but the key is immediately invalidated (see the section "Using Selectors"). Upon the next invocation of select( ) (or upon completion of an in-progress select( ) invocation), any cancelled keys will be cleared from the cancelled key set, and the corresponding deregistrations will be completed. The channel can be reregistered, and a new SelectionKey object will be returned.

When a channel is closed, all keys associated with it are automatically cancelled (remember, a channel can be registered with many selectors). When a selector is closed, all channels registered with that selector are deregistered, and the associated keys are invalidated (cancelled). Once a key has been invalidated, calling any of its methods related to selection will throw a CancelledKeyException.

A SelectionKey object contains two sets encoded as integer bit masks: one for those operations of interest to the channel/selector combination (the *interest* set) and one representing operations the channel is currently ready to perform (the *ready* set). The current interest set can be retrieved from the key object by invoking its interestOps( ) method. Initially, this will be the value passed in when the channel was registered. This interest set will never be changed by the selector, but you can change it by calling interestOps( ) with a new bit mask argument. The interest set can also be modified by reregistering the channel with the selector (which is effectively a roundabout way of invoking interestOps( )), as described in the section "Setting Up Selectors." Changes made to the interest set of a key while a select( ) is in progress on the associated Selector will not affect that selection operation. Any changes will be seen on the next invocation of select( ).

The set of operations that are ready on the channel associated with a key can be retrieved by calling the key's readyOps( ) method. The ready set is a subset of the interest set and represents those operations from the interest set which were determined to be ready on the channel by the last invocation of select( ). For example, the following code tests to see if the channel associated with a key is ready for reading. If so, it reads data from it into a buffer and sends it along to a consumer method.

```
if ((key.readyOps( ) & SelectionKey.OP_READ) != 0)
{
        myBuffer.clear( );
        key.channel( ).read (myBuffer);
        doSomethingWithBuffer (myBuffer.flip( ));
}
```

As noted earlier, there are currently four channel operations that can be tested for readiness. You can check these by testing the bit mask as shown in the code above, but the SelectionKey class defines four boolean convenience methods to test the bits for you: isReadable( ), isWritable( ), isConnectable( ), and isAcceptable( ). Each of these is equivalent to checking the result of readyOps( ) against the appropriate operation bit value. For example:

```
if (key.isWritable( ))
```

is equivalent to:

```
if ((key.readyOps( ) & SelectionKey.OP_WRITE) != 0)
```

All four of these methods are safe to call on any SelectionKey object. Recall that a channel cannot be registered for interest in an operation it doesn't support. Since an unsupported operation will never be in a channel's interest set, it can never appear in its ready set. Therefore, calling one of these methods for an unsupported operation will always return false because that operation will never be ready on that channel.

It's important to note that the readiness indication associated with a selection key as returned by readyOps( ) is a hint, not an iron-clad guarantee. The state of the underlying channel can change at any time. Other threads may perform operations on the channel that affect its readiness state. And, as always, operating system–specific idiosyncrasies may come into play.

 The ready set contained by a SelectionKey object is as of the time the selector last checked the states of the registered channels. The readiness of individual channels could have changed in the meantime.

You may have noticed from the SelectionKey API that although there is a way to get the operation ready set, there is no API method to set or reset the members of that set. You cannot, in fact, directly modify a key's ready set. In the next section, which describes the selection process, we'll see how selectors and keys interact to provide up-to-date readiness indication.

Let's examine the remaining two methods of the SelectionKey API:

```
public abstract class SelectionKey
{
        // This is a partial API listing

        public final Object attach (Object ob)
        public final Object attachment( )
}
```

These two methods allow you to place an *attachment* on a key and retrieve it later. This is a convenience that allows you to associate an arbitrary object with a key. This object can be a reference to anything meaningful to you, such as a business object, session handle, another channel, etc. This allows you to iterate through the keys associated with a selector, using the attached object handle on each as a reference to retrieve the associated context.

The attach( ) method stores the provided object reference in the key object. The SelectionKey class does not use the object except to store it. Any previous attachment reference stored in the key will be replaced. The null value may be given to clear the attachment. The attachment handle associated with a key can be fetched by calling the attachment( ) method. This method could return null if no attachment was set or if null was explicitly given.

 If the selection key is long-lived, but the object you attach should not be, remember to clear the attachment when you're done. Otherwise, your attached object will not be garbage collected, and you may have a memory leak.

An overloaded version of the register( ) method on the SelectableChannel class takes an Object argument. This is a convenience that lets you attach an object to the new key during registration. This:

```
SelectionKey key = channel.register (selector, SelectionKey.OP_READ, myObject);
```

is equivalent to this:

```
SelectionKey key = channel.register (selector, SelectionKey.OP_READ);
key.attach (myObject);
```

One last thing to note about the SelectionKey class relates to concurrency. Generally, SelectionKey objects are thread-safe, but it's important to know that operations that modify the interest set are synchronized by Selector objects. This could cause calls to the interestOps( ) method to block for an indeterminate amount of time. The specific locking policy used by a selector, such as whether the locks are held throughout the selection process, is implementation-dependent. Luckily, this multiplexing capability is specifically designed to enable a single thread to manage many channels. Using selectors by multiple threads should be an issue in only the most complex of applications. Frankly, if you're sharing selectors among many threads and encountering synchronization issues, your design probably needs a rethink.

We've covered the API for the SelectionKey class, but we're not finished with selection keys—not by a long shot. Let's take a look at how to manage keys when using them with selectors.

Using Selectors

Now that we have a pretty good handle on the various classes and how they relate to one another, let's take a closer look at the Selector class, the heart of readiness selection. Here is the abbreviated API of the Selector class we saw earlier. In the section "Setting Up Selectors," we saw how to create new selectors, so those methods have been left out:

```
public abstract class Selector
{
        // This is a partial API listing

        public abstract Set keys();
        public abstract Set selectedKeys();

        public abstract int select() throws IOException;
        public abstract int select (long timeout) throws IOException;
        public abstract int selectNow() throws IOException;

        public abstract void wakeup();
}
```

The Selection Process

Before getting into the details of the API, you should know a little about the inner workings of Selector. As previously discussed, a selector maintains a set of registered channels, and each of these registrations is encapsulated in a SelectionKey object. Each Selector object maintains three sets of keys:

Registered key set
> The set of currently registered keys associated with the selector. Not every registered key is necessarily still valid. This set is returned by the keys() method and may be empty. The registered key set is not directly modifiable; attempting to do so yields a java.lang.UnsupportedOperationException.

Selected key set
> A subset of the registered key set. Each member of this set is a key whose associated channel was determined by the selector (during a prior selection operation) to be ready for at least one of the operations in the key's interest set. This set is returned by the selectedKeys() method (and may be empty).

> Don't confuse the selected key set with the ready set. This is a set of keys, each with an associated channel that is ready for at least one operation. Each key has an embedded ready set that indicates the set of operations the associated channel is ready to perform.

> Keys can be directly removed from this set, but not added. Attempting to add to the selected key set throws java.lang.UnsupportedOperationException.

Cancelled key set
> A subset of the registered key set, this set contains keys whose cancel() methods have been called (the key has been invalidated), but they have not been deregistered. This set is private to the selector object and cannot be accessed directly.

All three of these sets are empty in a newly instantiated `Selector` object.

The core of the `Selector` class is the *selection* process. You've seen several references to it already—now it's time to explain it. Essentially, selectors are a wrapper for a native call to `select( )`, `poll( )`, or a similar operating system–specific system call. But the `Selector` does more than a simple pass-through to native code. It applies a specific process on each selection operation. An understanding of this process is essential to properly managing keys and the state information they represent.

A selection operation is performed by a selector when one of the three forms of `select( )` is invoked. Whichever is called, the following three steps are performed:

1. The cancelled key set is checked. If it's nonempty, each key in the cancelled set is removed from the other two sets, and the channel associated with the cancelled key is deregistered. When this step is complete, the cancelled key set is empty.

2. The operation interest sets of each key in the registered key set are examined. Changes made to the interest sets after they've been examined in this step will not be seen during the remainder of the selection operation.

   Once readiness criteria have been determined, the underlying operating system is queried to determine the actual readiness state of each channel for its operations of interest. Depending on the specific `select( )` method called, the thread may block at this point if no channels are currently ready, possibly with a time-out value.

   Upon completion of the system calls, which may have caused the invoking thread to be put to sleep for a while, the current readiness status of each channel will have been determined. Nothing further happens to any channel not found to be currently ready. For each channel that the operating system indicates is ready for at least one of the operations in its interest set, one of the following two things happens:

   a. If the key for the channel is not already in the selected key set, the key's ready set is cleared, and the bits representing the operations determined to be currently ready on the channel are set.

   b. Otherwise, the key is already in the selected key set. The key's ready set is updated by setting bits representing the operations found to be currently ready. Any previously set bits representing operations that are no longer ready are not cleared. In fact, no bits are cleared. The ready set as determined by the operating system is bitwise-disjoined into the previous ready set.[*] Once a key has been placed in the selected key set of the selector, its ready set is cumulative. Bits are set but never cleared.

3. Step 2 can potentially take a long time, especially if the invoking thread sleeps. Keys associated with this selector could have been cancelled in the meantime.

---

[*] A fancy way of saying the bits are logically ORed together.

When Step 2 completes, the actions taken in Step 1 are repeated to complete deregistration of any channels whose keys were cancelled while the selection operation was in progress.

4. The value returned by the select operation is the number of keys whose operation ready sets were modified in Step 2, not the total number of channels in the selection key set. The return value is not a count of ready channels, but the number of channels that became ready since the last invocation of select( ). A channel ready on a previous call and still ready on this call won't be counted, nor will a channel that was ready on a previous call but is no longer ready. These channels could still be in the selection key set but *will not* be counted in the return value. The return value could be 0.

Using the internal cancelled key set to defer deregistration is an optimization to prevent threads from blocking when they cancel a key and to prevent collisions with in-progress selection operations. Deregistering a channel is a potentially expensive operation that may require deallocation of resources (remember that keys are channel-specific and may have complex interactions with their associated channel objects). Cleaning up cancelled keys and deregistering channels immediately before or after a selection operation eliminates the potentially thorny problem of deregistering channels while they're in the middle of selection. This is another good example of compromise in favor of robustness.

The Selector class's select( ) method comes in three different forms:

```
public abstract class Selector
{
        // This is a partial API listing

        public abstract int select( ) throws IOException;
        public abstract int select (long timeout) throws IOException;
        public abstract int selectNow( ) throws IOException;

        public abstract void wakeup( );
}
```

The three forms of select differ only in whether they block if none of the registered channels are currently ready. The simplest form takes no argument and is invoked like this:

```
int n = selector.select( );
```

This call blocks indefinitely if no channels are ready. As soon as at least one of the registered channels is ready, the selection key set of the selector is updated, and the ready sets for each ready channel will be updated. The return value will be the number of channels determined to be ready. Normally, this method returns a nonzero value since it blocks until a channel is ready. But it can return 0 if the wakeup( ) method of the selector is invoked by another thread.

Sometimes you want to limit the amount of time a thread will wait for a channel to become ready. For those situations, an overloaded form of select( ) that takes a timeout argument is available:

```
int n = selector.select (10000);
```

This call behaves exactly the same as the previous example, except that it returns a value of 0 if no channels have become ready within the timeout period you provide (specified in milliseconds). If one or more channels become ready before the time limit expires, the status of the keys will be updated, and the method will return at that point. Specifying a timeout value of 0 indicates to wait indefinitely and is identical in all respects to the no-argument version of select( ).

The third and final form of selection is totally nonblocking:

```
int n = selector.selectNow( );
```

The selectNow( ) method performs the readiness selection process but will never block. If no channels are currently ready, it immediately returns 0.

Stopping the Selection Process

The last of the Selector API methods, wakeup( ), provides the capability to gracefully break out a thread from a blocked select( ) invocation:

```
public abstract class Selector
{
        // This is a partial API listing

        public abstract void wakeup( );
}
```

There are three ways to wake up a thread sleeping in select( ):

Call wakeup( )

Calling wakeup( ) on a Selector object causes the first selection operation on that selector that has not yet returned to return immediately. If no selection is currently underway, then the next invocation of one of the select( ) methods will return immediately. Subsequent selection operations will behave normally. Invoking wakeup( ) multiple times between selection operations is no different than invoking it once.

Sometimes this deferred wakeup behavior may not be what you want. You may want to wake only a sleeping thread but allow subsequent selections to proceed normally. You can work around this problem by invoking selectNow( ) after calling wakeup( ). However, if you structure your code to pay attention to the return codes and process the selection set properly, it shouldn't make any difference if the next select( ) returns immediately with nothing ready. You should be prepared for this eventuality anyway.

Call close( )

If a selector's close( ) method is called, any thread blocked in a selection operation will be awakened as if the wakeup( ) method had been called. Channels associated with the selector will then be deregistered and the keys cancelled.

Call interrupt( )

If the sleeping thread's interrupt( ) method is called, its *interrupt status* is set. If the awakened thread then attempts an I/O operation on a channel, the channel is closed immediately, and the thread catches an exception. This is because of the interruption semantics of channels discussed in Chapter 3. Use wakeup( ) to gracefully awaken a thread sleeping in select( ). Take steps to clear the interrupt status if you want a sleeping thread to continue after being directly interrupted (see the documentation for Thread.interrupted( )).

The Selector object catches the InterruptedException exception and call wakeup( ).

Note that none of these methods automatically close any of the channels involved. Interrupting a selector is not the same as interrupting a channel (see "Closing Channels" in Chapter 3). Selection does not change the state of any of the channels involved, it only tests their state. There is no ambiguity regarding channel state when a thread sleeping in a selector is interrupted.

Managing Selection Keys

Now that we understand how the various pieces of the puzzle fit together, it's time see how they interoperate in normal use. To use the information provided by selectors and keys effectively, it's important to properly manage the keys.

Selections are cumulative. Once a selector adds a key to the selected key set, it never removes it. And once a key is in the selected key set, ready indications in the ready set of that key are set but never cleared. At first blush, this seems troublesome because a selection operation may not give a true representation of the current state of the registered channels. This is an intentional design decision. It provides a great deal of flexibility but assigns responsibility to the programmer to properly manage the keys to ensure that the state information they represent does not become stale.

The secret to using selectors properly is to understand the role of the selected key set maintained by the selector. (See the section "The Selection Process," specifically Step 2 of the selection process.) The important part is what happens when a key is *not* already in the selected set. When at least one operation of interest becomes ready on the channel, the ready set of the key is cleared, and the currently ready operations are added to the ready set. The key is then added to the selected key set.

The way to clear the ready set of a SelectionKey is to remove the key itself from the set of selected keys. The ready set of a selection key is modified only by the Selector object during a selection operation. The idea is that only keys in the selected set are considered to have legitimate readiness information. That information persists in the key until the key is removed from the selected key set, which indicates to the selector that you have seen and dealt with it. The next time something of interest happens on the channel, the key will be set to reflect the state of the channel at that point and once again be added to the selected key set.

This scheme provides a lot of flexibility. The conventional approach is to perform a select( ) call on the selector (which updates the selected key set) then iterate over the set of keys returned by selectedKeys( ). As each key is examined in turn, the associated channel is dealt with according to the key's ready set. The key is then removed from the selected key set (by calling remove( ) on the Iterator object), and the next key is examined. When complete, the cycle repeats by calling select( ) again. The code in Example 4-1 is a typical server example.

Example 4-1. Using select( ) to service multiple channels

```
package com.ronsoft.books.nio.channels;

import java.nio.ByteBuffer;
import java.nio.channels.ServerSocketChannel;
import java.nio.channels.SocketChannel;
import java.nio.channels.Selector;
import java.nio.channels.SelectionKey;
import java.nio.channels.SelectableChannel;

import java.net.Socket;
import java.net.ServerSocket;
import java.net.InetSocketAddress;
import java.util.Iterator;

/**
 * Simple echo-back server which listens for incoming stream connections
 * and echoes back whatever it reads.  A single Selector object is used to
 * listen to the server socket (to accept new connections) and all the
 * active socket channels.
 *
 * @author Ron Hitchens (ron@ronsoft.com)
 */
public class SelectSockets
{
    public static int PORT_NUMBER = 1234;

    public static void main (String [] argv)
        throws Exception
    {
        new SelectSockets().go (argv);
    }

    public void go (String [] argv)
        throws Exception
    {
        int port = PORT_NUMBER;
```

Example 4-1. Using select() to service multiple channels (continued)

```
    if (argv.length > 0) {      // Override default listen port
        port = Integer.parseInt (argv [0]);
    }

    System.out.println ("Listening on port " + port);

    // Allocate an unbound server socket channel
    ServerSocketChannel serverChannel = ServerSocketChannel.open();
    // Get the associated ServerSocket to bind it with
    ServerSocket serverSocket = serverChannel.socket();
    // Create a new Selector for use below
    Selector selector = Selector.open();

    // Set the port the server channel will listen to
    serverSocket.bind (new InetSocketAddress (port));

    // Set nonblocking mode for the listening socket
    serverChannel.configureBlocking (false);

    // Register the ServerSocketChannel with the Selector
    serverChannel.register (selector, SelectionKey.OP_ACCEPT);

    while (true) {
        // This may block for a long time. Upon returning, the
        // selected set contains keys of the ready channels.
        int n = selector.select();

        if (n == 0) {
            continue;      // nothing to do
        }

        // Get an iterator over the set of selected keys
        Iterator it = selector.selectedKeys().iterator();

        // Look at each key in the selected set
        while (it.hasNext()) {
            SelectionKey key = (SelectionKey) it.next();

            // Is a new connection coming in?
            if (key.isAcceptable()) {
                ServerSocketChannel server =
                    (ServerSocketChannel) key.channel();
                SocketChannel channel = server.accept();

                registerChannel (selector, channel,
                    SelectionKey.OP_READ);

                sayHello (channel);
            }

            // Is there data to read on this channel?
            if (key.isReadable()) {
```

Example 4-1. Using select() to service multiple channels (continued)

```
                readDataFromSocket (key);
            }

            // Remove key from selected set; it's been handled
            it.remove( );
        }
    }
}

// -----------------------------------------------------------

/**
 * Register the given channel with the given selector for
 * the given operations of interest
 */
protected void registerChannel (Selector selector,
    SelectableChannel channel, int ops)
    throws Exception
{
    if (channel == null) {
        return;          // could happen
    }

    // Set the new channel nonblocking
    channel.configureBlocking (false);

    // Register it with the selector
    channel.register (selector, ops);
}

// -----------------------------------------------------------

// Use the same byte buffer for all channels.  A single thread is
// servicing all the channels, so no danger of concurrent acccess.
private ByteBuffer buffer = ByteBuffer.allocateDirect (1024);

/**
 * Sample data handler method for a channel with data ready to read.
 * @param key A SelectionKey object associated with a channel
 *  determined by the selector to be ready for reading.  If the
 *  channel returns an EOF condition, it is closed here, which
 *  automatically invalidates the associated key.  The selector
 *  will then de-register the channel on the next select call.
 */
protected void readDataFromSocket (SelectionKey key)
    throws Exception
{
    SocketChannel socketChannel = (SocketChannel) key.channel( );
    int count;

    buffer.clear( );            // Empty buffer
```

Example 4-1. Using select() to service multiple channels (continued)

```
        // Loop while data is available; channel is nonblocking
        while ((count = socketChannel.read (buffer)) > 0) {
            buffer.flip( );          // Make buffer readable

            // Send the data; don't assume it goes all at once
            while (buffer.hasRemaining( )) {
                socketChannel.write (buffer);
            }
            // WARNING: the above loop is evil.  Because
            // it's writing back to the same nonblocking
            // channel it read the data from, this code can
            // potentially spin in a busy loop.  In real life
            // you'd do something more useful than this.

            buffer.clear( );         // Empty buffer
        }

        if (count < 0) {
            // Close channel on EOF, invalidates the key
            socketChannel.close( );
        }
    }

    // -----------------------------------------------------------

    /**
     * Spew a greeting to the incoming client connection.
     * @param channel The newly connected SocketChannel to say hello to.
     */
    private void sayHello (SocketChannel channel)
        throws Exception
    {
        buffer.clear( );
        buffer.put ("Hi there!\r\n".getBytes( ));
        buffer.flip( );

        channel.write (buffer);
    }
}
```

Example 4-1 implements a simple server. It creates ServerSocketChannel and Selector objects and registers the channel with the selector. We don't bother saving a reference to the registration key for the server socket because it will never be deregistered. The infinite loop calls select( ) at the top, which may block indefinitely. When selection is complete, the selected key set is iterated to check for ready channels.

If a key indicates that its channel is ready to do an accept( ), we obtain the channel associated with the key and cast it to a ServerSocketChannel object. We know it's safe to do this because only ServerSocketChannel objects support the OP_ACCEPT operation. We also know our code registers only a single ServerSocketChannel object with interest in OP_ACCEPT. With a reference to the server socket channel, we invoke accept( ) on it to obtain a handle to the incoming socket. The object returned is of type SocketChannel, which is also a selectable type of channel. At this point, rather than spawning a new thread to read data from the new connection, we simply register the socket channel with the selector. We tell the selector we're interested in knowing when the new socket channel is ready for reading by passing in the OP_READ flag.

If the key did not indicate that the channel was ready for accept, we check to see if it's ready for read. Any socket channels indicating so will be one of the SocketChannel objects previously created by the ServerSocketChannel and registered for interest in reading. For each socket channel with data to read, we invoke a common routine to read and process the data socket. Note that this routine should be prepared to deal with incomplete data on the socket, which is in nonblocking mode. It should return promptly so that other channels with pending input can be serviced in a timely manner. Example 4-1 simply echoes the data back down the socket to the sender.

At the bottom of the loop, we remove the key from the selected key set by calling remove( ) on the Iterator object. Keys can be removed directly from the Set returned by selectedKeys( ), but when examining the set with an Iterator, you should use the iterator's remove( ) method to avoid corrupting the iterator's internal state.

Concurrency

Selector objects are thread-safe, but the key sets they contain are not. The key sets returned by the keys( ) and selectedKeys( ) methods are direct references to private Set objects inside the Selector object. These sets can change at any time. The registered key set is read-only. If you attempt to modify it, your reward will be a java.lang.UnsupportedOperationException, but you can still run into trouble if it's changed while you're looking at it. Iterator objects are fail-fast: they will throw java.util.ConcurrentModificationException if the underlying Set is modified, so be prepared for this if you expect to share selectors and/or key sets among threads. You're allowed to modify the selection key set directly, but be aware that you could clobber some other thread's Iterator by doing so.

If there is any question of multiple threads accessing the key sets of a selector concurrently, you must take steps to properly synchronize access. When performing a selection operation, selectors synchronize on the Selector object, the registered key set, and the selected key set objects, in that order. They also synchronize on the cancelled key set during Steps 1 and 3 of the selection process (when it deregisters channels associated with cancelled keys).

In a multithread scenario, if you need to make changes to any of the key sets, either directly or as a side effect of another operation, you should first synchronize on the same objects, in the same order. The locking order is vitally important. If competing threads do not request the same locks in the same order, there is a potential for dead-lock. If you are certain that no other threads will be accessing the selector at the same time, then synchronization is not necessary.

The close( ) method of Selector synchronizes in the same way as select( ), so there is a potential for blocking there. A thread calling close( ) will block until an in-progress selection is complete or the thread doing the selection goes to sleep. In the latter case, the selecting thread will awaken as soon as the closing thread acquires the locks and closes the selector (see the section "Stopping the Selection Process").

Asynchronous Closability

It's possible to close a channel or cancel a selection key at any time. Unless you take steps to synchronize, the states of the keys and associated channels could change unexpectedly. The presence of a key in a particular key set does not guarantee that the key is still valid or that its associated channel is still open.

Closing channels should not be a time-consuming operation. The designers of NIO specifically wanted to prevent the possibility of a thread closing a channel being blocked in an indefinite wait if the channel is involved in a select operation. When a channel is closed, its associated keys are cancelled. This does not directly affect an in-process select( ), but it does mean that a selection key that was valid when you called select( ) could be invalid upon return. You should always use the selected key set returned by the selector's selectedKeys( ) method; do not maintain your own set of keys. Understanding the selection process as outlined in the section "The Selection Process" is important to avoid running into trouble.

Refer to the section "Stopping the Selection Process" for the details of how a thread can be awakened when blocked in select( ).

If you attempt to use a key that's been invalidated, a CancelledKeyException will be thrown by most methods. You can, however, safely retrieve the channel handle from a cancelled key. If the channel has also been closed, attempting to use it will yield a ClosedChannelException in most cases.

Selection Scaling

I've mentioned several times that selectors make it easy for a single thread to multiplex large numbers of selectable channels. Using one thread to service all the channels reduces complexity and can potentially boost performance by eliminating the overhead of managing many threads. But is it a good idea to use just one thread to service all selectable channels? As always, it depends.

It could be argued that on a single CPU system it's a good idea because only one thread can be running at a time anyway. By eliminating the overhead of context switching between threads, total throughput could be higher. But what about a multi-CPU system? On a system with n CPUs, $n-1$ could be idling while the single thread trundles along servicing each channel sequentially.

Or what about the case in which different channels require different classes of service? Suppose an application logs information from a large number of distributed sensors. Any given sensor could wait several seconds while the servicing thread iterates through each ready channel. This is OK if response time is not critical. But higher-priority connections (such as operator commands) would have to wait in the queue as well if only one thread services all channels. Every application's requirements are different. The solutions you apply are affected by what you're trying to accomplish.

For the first scenario, in which you want to bring more threads into play to service channels, resist the urge to use multiple selectors. Performing readiness selection on large numbers of channels is not expensive; most of the work is done by the underlying operating system. Maintaining multiple selectors and randomly assigning channels to one of them is not a satisfactory solution to this problem. It simply makes smaller versions of the same scenario.

A better approach is to use one selector for all selectable channels and delegate the servicing of ready channels to other threads. You have a single point to monitor channel readiness and a decoupled pool of worker threads to handle the incoming data. The thread pool size can be tuned (or tune itself, dynamically) according to deployment conditions. Management of selectable channels remains simple, and simple is good.

The second scenario, in which some channels demand greater responsiveness than others, can be addressed by using two selectors: one for the command connections and another for the normal connections. But this scenario can be easily addressed in much the same way as the first. Rather than dispatching all ready channels to the same thread pool, channels can be handed off to different classes of worker threads according to function. There may be a logging thread pool, a command/control pool, a status request pool, etc.

The code in Example 4-2 is an extension of the generic selection loop code in Example 4-1. It overrides the readDataFromSocket( ) method and uses a thread pool to service channels with data to read. Rather than reading the data synchronously in the main thread, this version passes the SelectionKey object to a worker thread for servicing.

Example 4-2. Servicing channels with a thread pool

```
package com.ronsoft.books.nio.channels;

import java.nio.ByteBuffer;
import java.nio.channels.SocketChannel;
import java.nio.channels.SelectionKey;
```

Example 4-2. Servicing channels with a thread pool (continued)

```java
import java.util.List;
import java.util.LinkedList;
import java.io.IOException;

/**
 * Specialization of the SelectSockets class which uses a thread pool
 * to service channels.  The thread pool is an ad-hoc implementation
 * quicky lashed togther in a few hours for demonstration purposes.
 * It's definitely not production quality.
 *
 * @author Ron Hitchens (ron@ronsoft.com)
 */
public class SelectSocketsThreadPool extends SelectSockets
{
    private static final int MAX_THREADS = 5;

    private ThreadPool pool = new ThreadPool (MAX_THREADS);

    // -------------------------------------------------------------

    public static void main (String [] argv)
        throws Exception
    {
        new SelectSocketsThreadPool().go (argv);
    }

    // -------------------------------------------------------------

    /**
     * Sample data handler method for a channel with data ready to read.
     * This method is invoked from the go( ) method in the parent class.
     * This handler delegates to a worker thread in a thread pool to
     * service the channel, then returns immediately.
     * @param key A SelectionKey object representing a channel
     *  determined by the selector to be ready for reading.  If the
     *  channel returns an EOF condition, it is closed here, which
     *  automatically invalidates the associated key.  The selector
     *  will then de-register the channel on the next select call.
     */
    protected void readDataFromSocket (SelectionKey key)
        throws Exception
    {
        WorkerThread worker = pool.getWorker();

        if (worker == null) {
            // No threads available. Do nothing. The selection
            // loop will keep calling this method until a
            // thread becomes available.  This design could
            // be improved.
            return;
        }
```

Example 4-2. Servicing channels with a thread pool (continued)

```java
        // Invoking this wakes up the worker thread, then returns
        worker.serviceChannel (key);
    }

    // -------------------------------------------------------------------

    /**
     * A very simple thread pool class.  The pool size is set at
     * construction time and remains fixed.  Threads are cycled
     * through a FIFO idle queue.
     */
    private class ThreadPool
    {
        List idle = new LinkedList( );

        ThreadPool (int poolSize)
        {
            // Fill up the pool with worker threads
            for (int i = 0; i < poolSize; i++) {
                WorkerThread thread = new WorkerThread (this);

                // Set thread name for debugging. Start it.
                thread.setName ("Worker" + (i + 1));
                thread.start( );

                idle.add (thread);
            }
        }

        /**
         * Find an idle worker thread, if any.  Could return null.
         */
        WorkerThread getWorker( )
        {
            WorkerThread worker = null;

            synchronized (idle) {
                if (idle.size( ) > 0) {
                    worker = (WorkerThread) idle.remove (0);
                }
            }

            return (worker);
        }

        /**
         * Called by the worker thread to return itself to the
         * idle pool.
         */
        void returnWorker (WorkerThread worker)
        {
            synchronized (idle) {
```

Example 4-2. Servicing channels with a thread pool (continued)

```
            idle.add (worker);
        }
    }
}

/**
 * A worker thread class which can drain channels and echo-back
 * the input.  Each instance is constructed with a reference to
 * the owning thread pool object. When started, the thread loops
 * forever waiting to be awakened to service the channel associated
 * with a SelectionKey object.
 * The worker is tasked by calling its serviceChannel() method
 * with a SelectionKey object.  The serviceChannel() method stores
 * the key reference in the thread object then calls notify()
 * to wake it up.  When the channel has been drained, the worker
 * thread returns itself to its parent pool.
 */
private class WorkerThread extends Thread
{
    private ByteBuffer buffer = ByteBuffer.allocate (1024);
    private ThreadPool pool;
    private SelectionKey key;

    WorkerThread (ThreadPool pool)
    {
        this.pool = pool;
    }

    // Loop forever waiting for work to do
    public synchronized void run()
    {
        System.out.println (this.getName() + " is ready");

        while (true) {
            try {
                // Sleep and release object lock
                this.wait();
            } catch (InterruptedException e) {
                e.printStackTrace();
                // Clear interrupt status
                this.interrupted();
            }

            if (key == null) {
                continue;     // just in case
            }

            System.out.println (this.getName()
                + " has been awakened");

            try {
                drainChannel (key);
```

Example 4-2. Servicing channels with a thread pool (continued)

```
            } catch (Exception e) {
                System.out.println ("Caught '"
                    + e + "' closing channel");

                // Close channel and nudge selector
                try {
                    key.channel().close();
                } catch (IOException ex) {
                    ex.printStackTrace();
                }

                key.selector().wakeup();
            }

            key = null;

            // Done. Ready for more. Return to pool
            this.pool.returnWorker (this);
        }
    }

    /**
     * Called to initiate a unit of work by this worker thread
     * on the provided SelectionKey object.  This method is
     * synchronized, as is the run() method, so only one key
     * can be serviced at a given time.
     * Before waking the worker thread, and before returning
     * to the main selection loop, this key's interest set is
     * updated to remove OP_READ.  This will cause the selector
     * to ignore read-readiness for this channel while the
     * worker thread is servicing it.
     */
    synchronized void serviceChannel (SelectionKey key)
    {
        this.key = key;

        key.interestOps (key.interestOps() & (~SelectionKey.OP_READ));

        this.notify();          // Awaken the thread
    }

    /**
     * The actual code which drains the channel associated with
     * the given key.  This method assumes the key has been
     * modified prior to invocation to turn off selection
     * interest in OP_READ.  When this method completes it
     * re-enables OP_READ and calls wakeup() on the selector
     * so the selector will resume watching this channel.
     */
    void drainChannel (SelectionKey key)
        throws Exception
    {
```

Example 4-2. Servicing channels with a thread pool (continued)

```
        SocketChannel channel = (SocketChannel) key.channel( );
        int count;

        buffer.clear( );            // Empty buffer

        // Loop while data is available; channel is nonblocking
        while ((count = channel.read (buffer)) > 0) {
            buffer.flip( );         // make buffer readable

            // Send the data; may not go all at once
            while (buffer.hasRemaining( )) {
                channel.write (buffer);
            }
            // WARNING: the above loop is evil.
            // See comments in superclass.

            buffer.clear( );        // Empty buffer
        }

        if (count < 0) {
            // Close channel on EOF; invalidates the key
            channel.close( );
            return;
        }

        // Resume interest in OP_READ
        key.interestOps (key.interestOps() | SelectionKey.OP_RFAD);

        // Cycle the selector so this key is active again
        key.selector().wakeup( );
    }
  }
}
```

Because the thread doing the selection will loop back and call select( ) again almost immediately, the interest set in the key is modified to remove interest in read-readiness. This prevents the selector from repeatedly invoking readDataFromSocket( ) (because the channel will remain ready to read until the worker thread can drain the data from it). When a worker thread has finished servicing the channel, it will again update the key's interest set to reassert an interest in read-readiness. It also does an explicit wakeup( ) on the selector. If the main thread is blocked in select( ), this causes it to resume. The selection loop will then cycle (possibly doing nothing) and reenter select( ) with the updated key.

Summary

In this chapter, we covered *the* most powerful aspect of NIO. Readiness selection is essential to large-scale, high-volume server-side applications. The addition of this capability to the Java platform means that enterprise-class Java applications can now slug it out toe-to-toe with comparable applications written in any language. The key concepts covered in this chapter were:

Selector classes

> The Selector, SelectableChannel, and SelectionKey classes form the triumvirate that makes readiness selection possible on the Java platform. In the section "Selector Basics," we saw how these classes relate to each other and what they represent.

Selection keys

> In the section "Using Selection Keys," we learned more about selection keys and how they are used. The SelectionKey class encapsulates the relationship between a SelectableChannel object and a Selector with which it's registered.

Selectors

> Selection requests that the operating system determine which channels registered with a given selector are ready for I/O operation(s) of interest. We learned about the selection process in the section "Using Selectors" and how to manage the key set returned from a call to select( ). We also discussed some of the concurrency issues relating to selection.

Asynchronous closability

> Issues relating to closing selectors and channels asynchronously were touched on in the section "Selector Basics."

Multithreading

> In the section "Selection Scaling," we discussed how multiple threads can be put to work to service selectable channels without resorting to multiple Selector objects.

Selectors hold great promise for Java server applications. As this powerful new capability is integrated into commercial application servers, server-side applications will gain even greater scalability, reliability, and responsiveness.

OK, we've completed the main tour of java.nio and its subpackages. But don't put your camera away. We have a couple of bonus highlights thrown in at no extra charge. Watch your step reboarding the bus. Next stop is the enchanted land of regular expressions.

CHAPTER 5

Regular Expressions

Hey, it's a kind of magic.
—The Highlander

In this chapter, we'll discuss the API of the classes in the new `java.util.regex` package (see Figure 5-1). JSR 51, the Java Specification Request defining the new I/O capabilities, also specifies the addition of regular expression processing to the Java platform. While regular expressions, strictly speaking, are not I/O, they are most commonly used to scan text data read from files or streams.

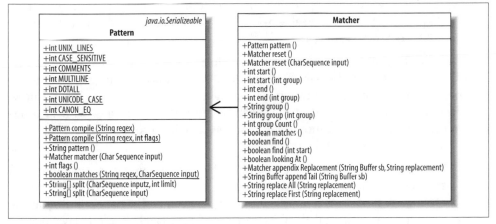

Figure 5-1. The regular expression classes

You'll learn how to use the new Java APIs to do the same powerful pattern matching that has been available to users of *perl*, egrep, and other text-processing tools. A detailed exploration of regular expression syntax is beyond the scope of this book, but a working familiarity with regular expressions is assumed. If you're new to regular expressions, want to improve your skills, or are baffled by this chapter, I recommend you pick up a good reference. O'Reilly publishes an authoritative regular expression book (it's even cited in the JDK documentation): *Mastering Regular Expressions*, by Jeffrey E. F. Friedl (*http://www.oreilly.com/catalog/regex/*).

Regular Expression Basics

A regular expression is a sequence of characters that describe, or *express*, a pattern of characters you are interested in matching within a target character sequence. Regular expressions have been widely available in the Unix world for many years by means of standard commands such as sed, grep, awk, etc. Because of its long history, the regular expression grammar used on the Unix platforms has been the basis for most regular expression processors. The Open Group, a Unix standards body, specifies regular expression syntax as a part of the Single Unix Specification (*http://www.opengroup.org/onlinepubs/7908799/xbd/re.html*).

The popular Perl[*] scripting language incorporates regular expression processing directly into its language syntax. As Perl has evolved and grown in popularity, it has added more sophisticated features and has extended the regular expression syntax. Because of its power and flexibility, Perl has become almost ubiquitous and has consequently established a de facto standard for regular expression processing.

The regular expression capabilities provided by the java.util.regex classes track those provided by Perl 5. There are minor differences confined mostly to arcane areas that typical users will rarely encounter. The specifics are detailed in the section "Java Regular Expression Syntax," in Table 5-7, and in the Javadoc API documentation for the java.util.regex.Pattern class.

In a Perl script, regular expressions are used inline to match against variable values. This tight integration of regular expression evaluation into the language has made Perl popular for scripting applications in which text files are processed. Until now, Java has been at the other end of the spectrum. Processing text files with Java has been rather cumbersome because of the shortage of built-in tools to process nontrivial patterns in text files.

While Java will never reach the level of regular expression integration that Perl enjoys, the new java.util.regex package brings the same level of expressive power to Java. The usage model is necessarily different between Perl (a procedural scripting language) and Java (a compiled, object-oriented[†] language), but the Java regular expression API is easy to use and should now allow Java to easily take on the text-processing tasks traditionally "outsourced" to Perl.

---

[*] Practical Extraction and Reporting Language (or Pathologically Eclectic Rubbish Lister, depending on how long you've been debugging).

[†] Some would argue that Perl is also object-oriented. Perl's own documentation makes it clear that Perl "objects" are little more than a syntactic illusion. If you want to argue about it, frankly, you're probably reading the wrong book.

What Is a Regular Expression?

Regular expressions derive from a mathematical notation devised by Stephen Kleene in the 1950s for describing *regular sets*. Regular expressions remained in the realm of mathematics until 1968 when Ken Thompson, a Bell Labs researcher and Unix pioneer, developed a regular expression–based search algorithm eventually integrated into the Unix ed text editor.

The g/*Regular Expression*/p (Global *Regular Expression* Print) command in ed was so useful, it spawned the standalone grep command. Other regex-based commands followed: sed, awk, lex, egrep, etc. As the uses of regular expressions proliferated and new features were added, the syntax of regular expressions used for text searches diverged from its mathematical origins.

Over time, many cooks boiled many pots, and soon there were many flavors of regular expressions. The POSIX (Portable Operating System Interface) standard was first introduced in 1986 and attempts to standardize a broad range of operating-system characteristics. POSIX defines two classes of regular expressions: basic regular expressions (BREs) and extended regular expressions (EREs).

Larry Wall released the first version of perl in 1987. Perl was useful because it brought together many powerful features in a single scripting language, not the least of which was regular expression processing woven into the fabric of the language syntax. The first version of Perl used regular expression code derived from James Gosling's version of the emacs editor. Perl is now at Version 5, which has been universally deployed for about eight years now and has become the benchmark against which most regular expression processors are measured.

Regular expression–matching engines fall into two categories: Deterministic Finite Automaton (DFA) and Nondeterministic Finite Automaton (NFA). Their differences have to do with how expressions are compiled and how they are matched against the target. DFA is usually faster because it does more work up front to build a matching tree from which unreachable branches are pruned as matching progresses. NFA can be slower because it performs a more exhaustive search and often needs to backtrack. Although DFA is faster, NFA is more full-featured. It can capture subexpressions, for example, while DFA processors cannot. The java.util.regex engine is NFA and similar in syntax to Perl 5.

—continued—

While regular expressions became an official part of the Java platform with JDK 1.4, by no means is java.util.regex the first regular expression package available for Java. The Apache organization has two open source, regular expression packages: Jakarta-ORO and Jakarta-Regexp, which have been around for quite a while. Jakarta-ORO is the successor to OROMatcher, which was donated to Apache and further enhanced. It has many features and is highly customizable. Jakarta-Regexp was also contributed to Apache but is smaller in scope. The GNU folks offer a regular expression package, gnu.regexp, with some Perl-like features. And IBM has a commercial package known as com.ibm.regex. It also provides many Perl-like features and good Unicode support.

For all the details you can stand about the history of regular expressions, types of regex processors, available implementations, and everything you ever wanted to know about regular expression syntax and usage, consult Jeffrey E.F. Friedl's book *Mastering Regular Expressions* (O'Reilly).

The Java Regular Expression API

The java.util.regex package contains only two classes for implementing Java regular expression processing. These classes are named Pattern and Matcher. This is only natural when you recall that regular expression processing consists of *pattern matching*. There is also a new interface defined in java.lang that underpins these new classes. Before looking at Pattern and Matcher, we'll take a quick look at the new CharSequence abstraction.

Additionally, as a convenience, the String class provides some new methods as shortcuts to performing regular expression matching. These are discussed in the section "Regular Expression Methods of the String Class."

The CharSequence Interface

Regular expressions do pattern matching on sequences of characters. While String objects encapsulate character sequences, they are not the only objects capable of doing so.

The JDK 1.4 release defines a new interface named CharSequence, which describes a specific, immutable sequence of characters. This new interface is an abstraction to separate the *concept* of a sequence of characters from specific implementations containing those characters. The venerable String and StringBuffer classes have been retrofitted in JDK 1.4 to implement the CharSequence interface. The new CharBuffer class (introduced in Chapter 2) also implements CharSequence. The CharSequence interface also comes into play in character set mapping (see Chapter 6).

The API defined by CharSequence is very simple. It doesn't take a lot to describe a sequence of characters, after all.

```
package java.lang;

public interface CharSequence
{
        int length( );
        char charAt (int index);

        public String toString( );
        CharSequence subSequence (int start, int end);
}
```

Every character sequence described by CharSequence has a specific length returned by the length( ) method. Individual characters of the sequence can be fetched by calling charAt( ) with the index of the desired character position. Character positions start at zero and range to one less than the length, exactly like the familiar String.charAt( ).

The toString( ) method returns a String object containing the described sequence of characters. This may be useful, for example, to print the character sequence. As noted earlier, String now implements CharSequence. Both String and CharSequence are immutable, so if CharSequence describes a complete String, the toString( ) method of CharSequence returns the underlying String object, not a copy. If the backing object is a StringBuffer or a CharBuffer, a new String will be created to hold a copy of the character sequence.

Finally, a new CharSequence describing a subrange can be created by calling the subSequence( ) method. The start and end values are specified in the same way as they are for String.substring( ): start must be a valid index of the sequence, end must be greater than start and denotes the index of the last character plus one. In other words, start is the beginning index (inclusive), and end is the ending index (exclusive).

The CharSequence interface appears to be immutable because it has no mutator methods, but the underlying implementing object may not be immutable. The CharSequence methods reflect the current state of the underlying object. If that state changes, the information returned by the CharSequence methods will also change (see Example 5-1). If you depend on a CharSequence remaining stable and are unsure of the underlying implementation, invoke the toString( ) method to make a truly immutable snapshot of the character sequence.

Example 5-1. CharSequence interface examples

```
package com.ronsoft.books.nio.regex;

import java.nio.CharBuffer;

/**
 * Demonstrate behavior of java.lang.CharSequence as implemented
 * by String, StringBuffer and CharBuffer.
 *
 * @author Ron Hitchens (ron@ronsoft.com)
```

Example 5-1. CharSequence interface examples (continued)

```java
*/
public class CharSeq
{
    public static void main (String [] argv)
    {
        StringBuffer stringBuffer = new StringBuffer ("Hello World");
        CharBuffer charBuffer = CharBuffer.allocate (20);
        CharSequence charSequence = "Hello World";

        // derived directly from a String
        printCharSequence (charSequence);

        // derived from a StringBuffer
        charSequence = stringBuffer;
        printCharSequence (charSequence);

        // Change StringBuffer
        stringBuffer.setLength (0);
        stringBuffer.append ("Goodbye cruel world");
        // same "immutable" CharSequence yields different result
        printCharSequence (charSequence);

        // Derive CharSequence from CharBuffer
        charSequence = charBuffer;
        charBuffer.put ("xxxxxxxxxxxxxxxxxxxx");
        charBuffer.clear();

        charBuffer.put ("Hello World");
        charBuffer.flip();
        printCharSequence (charSequence);

        charBuffer.mark();
        charBuffer.put ("Seeya");
        charBuffer.reset();
        printCharSequence (charSequence);

        charBuffer.clear();
        printCharSequence (charSequence);
        // Changing underlying CharBuffer is reflected in the
        // read-only CharSequnce interface
    }

    private static void printCharSequence (CharSequence cs)
    {
        System.out.println ("length=" + cs.length()
            + ", content='" + cs.toString() + "'");
    }
}
```

Here's the result of executing CharSequence:

```
length=11, content='Hello World'
length=11, content='Hello World'
```

```
length=19, content='Goodbye cruel world'
length=11, content='Hello World'
length=11, content='Seeya World'
length=20, content='Seeya Worldxxxxxxxxx'
```

The Pattern Class

The Pattern class encapsulates a regular expression, which is a pattern you want to search for in a target character sequence. Matching regular expressions can be expensive because of the huge number of possible permutations, especially if the pattern will be applied repeatedly. Most regular expression processors (including Perl, under the covers) compile expressions first, then use this compiled representation to perform pattern detection in the input.

The Java regular expression package is no different. Instances of the Pattern class encapsulate a single, compiled regular expression. Let's take a look at the complete API of Pattern to see how it's used. Remember, this is not a syntactically complete class file, just the method signatures with the class bodies left out.

```
package java.util.regex;

public final class Pattern implements java.io.Serializable
{
        public static final int UNIX_LINES
        public static final int CASE_INSENSITIVE
        public static final int COMMENTS
        public static final int MULTILINE
        public static final int DOTALL
        public static final int UNICODE_CASE
        public static final int CANON_EQ

        public static boolean matches (String regex, CharSequence input)

        public static Pattern compile (String regex)
        public static Pattern compile (String regex, int flags)

        public String pattern( )
        public int flags( )

        public String[] split (CharSequence input, int limit)
        public String[] split (CharSequence input)

        public Matcher matcher (CharSequence input)
}
```

The first method listed above, matches( ), is a convenience method that does a complete matching operation and returns a boolean indication of whether the regular expression matches the *entire* input sequence. This is handy because you don't need to keep track of any objects; just call a simple static method and test the result.

```
public boolean goodAnswer (String answer)
{
```

```
            return (Pattern.matches ("[Yy]es|[Yy]|[Tt]rue", answer));
    }
```

This is appropriate for cases in which default settings are acceptable and the test need to be done only once. If you will be checking for the same pattern repeatedly, if you want to find patterns that are subsequences of the input, or if you need to set nondefault options, you should create a Pattern object and make use of its API methods.

Note that there are no public constructors for the Pattern class. New instances can be created only by invoking one of the static factory methods. Both forms of compile() take a regular expression String argument. The returned Pattern object contains that regular expression translated to a compiled internal form. The compile() factory methods may throw the java.util.regex.PatternSyntaxException if the regular expression you provide is malformed. This is an unchecked exception, so if you're not confident that the expression you're using will work (because it's a variable passed to you, for example), wrap the call to compile() in a try/catch block.

The second form of compile() accepts a bit mask of flags that affect the default compilation of the regular expression. These flags enable optional behaviors of the compiled pattern, such as how line boundaries are handled or case insensitivity. Each of these flags (except CANON_EQ) can also be enabled by an embedded sub-expression within the expression itself. Flags can be combined in a boolean OR expression, like this:

```
    Pattern pattern = Pattern.compile ("[A-Z][a-zA-Z]*",
            Pattern.CASE_INSENSITIVE | Pattern.UNIX_LINES);
```

All flags are off by default. The meaning of each compile-time option is summarized in Table 5-1.

Table 5-1. Flag values affecting regular expression compilation

Flag name	Embedded expression	Description
UNIX_LINES	(?d)	Enables Unix lines mode.
		In this mode, only the newline character (\n) is recognized as the line terminator. This affects the behavior of ., ^, and $. If this flag is not set (the default), then all of the following are considered to be line terminators: \n, \r, \r\n, \u0085 (next line), \u2028 (line separator), and \u2029 (paragraph separator).
		Unix line mode can also be specified by the embedded expression (?d).
CASE_INSENSITIVE	(?i)	Enables case-insensitive pattern matching and may incur a small performance penalty.
		Use of this flag presupposes that only characters from the US-ASCII character set are being matched. If you're working with character sets of other languages, specify the UNICODE_CASE flag as well to enable Unicode-aware case folding.

Table 5-1. Flag values affecting regular expression compilation (continued)

Flag name	Embedded expression	Description
UNICODE_CASE	(?iu)	Unicode-aware, case-folding mode.
		When used in conjunction with the CASE_INSENSITIVE flag, case-insensitive character matching is done in accordance with the Unicode standard. This ensures that upper- and lowercase characters are treated equally in all the languages encoded by the Unicode charset.
		This option may incur a performance penalty.
COMMENTS	(?x)	Permits whitespace and comments in the pattern.
		When this mode is in effect, any whitespace in the pattern is ignored, and comments beginning with the # character are ignored to end-of-line.
MULTILINE	(?m)	Turns on multiline mode.
		In multiline mode, the ^ and $ expressions match just after or just before (respectively) a line separator or the beginning or end of the character sequence. In normal mode, these expressions match only the beginning or end of the entire character sequence.
DOTALL	(?s)	Dot (.) character matches any character, even line separators.
		By default, the dot expression does not match line separators. This option is equivalent to Perl's single-line mode, hence the (?s) embedded flag name.
CANON_EQ	None	Enables canonical equivalence.
		When this flag is specified, characters will be considered a match if and only if their canonical decompositions match.
		For example, the two-character sequence a\u030A (Unicode symbol "LATIN SMALL LETTER A" followed by symbol "COMBINING RING ABOVE") will match the single character \u00E5 ("LATIN SMALL LETTER A WITH RING") when this flag is given.
		Canonical equivalence is not evaluated by default. See the character map definitions at *http://www.unicode.org* for canonical-equivalence details.
		This flag may incur a significant performance penalty. There is no embedded flag expression to enable canonical equivalence.

Instances of the Pattern class are immutable; each is tied to a specific regular expression and cannot be modified. Pattern objects are also thread-safe and can be used concurrently by multiple threads.

So, once you have a Pattern, what can you do with it?

```
package java.util.regex;

public final class Pattern implements java.io.Serializable
{
        // This is a partial API listing

        public String pattern()
        public int flags()
```

```
        public String[] split (CharSequence input, int limit)
        public String[] split (CharSequence input)

        public Matcher matcher (CharSequence input)
    }
```

The next two methods of the `Pattern` class API return information about the encapsulated expression. The `pattern()` method returns the `String` used to initially create the `Pattern` instance (the string passed to `compile()` when the object was created). The next, `flags()`, returns the flag bit mask provided when the pattern was compiled. If the `Pattern` object was created by the no-argument version of `compile()`, `flags()` will return 0. The returned value reflects only the explicit flag values provided to `compile()`; it does not include the equivalent of any flags set by embedded expressions within the regular expression pattern, as listed in the second column of Table 5-1.

The instance method `split()` is a convenience that tokenizes a character sequence using the pattern as delimiter. This is reminiscent of the `StringTokenizer` class but is more powerful because the delimiter can be a multicharacter sequence matched by the regular expression. Also, the `split()` method is stateless, returning an array of string tokens rather than requiring multiple invocations to iterate through them:

```
    Pattern spacePat = Pattern.compile ("\\s+");
    String [] tokens = spacePat.split (input);
```

Invoking `split()` with only one argument is equivalent to invoking the two-argument version with zero as the second argument. The second argument for `split()` denotes a limit on the number of times the input sequence will be split by the regular expression. The meaning of the limit argument is overloaded. Nonpositive values have special meanings.

If the limit value provided for `split()` is negative (any negative number), the character sequence will be split indefinitely until the input is exhausted. The returned array could have any length. If the limit is given as zero, the input will be split indefinitely, but trailing empty strings will not be included in the result array. If the limit is positive, it sets the maximum size of the returned `String` array. For a limit value of n, the regular expression will be applied at most $n-1$ times. These combinations are summarized in Table 5-2, and the code that generated the table is listed in Example 5-2.

Table 5-2. Matrix of split() behavior

Input: poodle zoo	Regex = " "	Regex = "d"	Regex="o"
Limit = 1	"poodle zoo"	"poodle zoo"	"poodle zoo"
Limit = 2	"poodle","zoo"	"poo","le zoo"	"p","odle zoo"
Limit = 5	"poodle","zoo"	"poo","le ","oo"	"p",,"dle z",,
Limit = -2	"poodle","zoo"	"poo","le ","oo"	"p",,"dle z",,
Limit = 0	"poodle","zoo"	"poo","le ","oo"	"p",,"dle z"

Finally, matcher( ) is a factory method that creates a Matcher object for the compiled pattern. A matcher is a stateful matching engine that knows how to match a pattern (the Pattern object it was created from) against a target character sequence. You must provide an initial input target when creating a Matcher, but different input can be provided later (discussed in the section "The Matcher Class").

Splitting strings with the Pattern class

Example 5-2 generates a matrix of the result of splitting the same input string with several different regular expression patterns and limit values.

Example 5-2. Splitting strings with Pattern

```
package com.ronsoft.books.nio.regex;

import java.util.regex.Pattern;
import java.util.List;
import java.util.LinkedList;

/**
 * Demonstrate behavior of splitting strings.  The XML output created
 * here can be styled into HTML or some other useful form.
 * See poodle.xsl.
 *
 * @author Ron Hitchens (ron@ronsoft.com)
 */
public class Poodle
{
    /**
     * Generate a matrix table of how Pattern.split() behaves with
     * various regex patterns and limit values.
     */
    public static void main (String [] argv)
        throws Exception
    {
        String input = "poodle zoo";
        Pattern space = Pattern.compile (" ");
        Pattern d = Pattern.compile ("d");
        Pattern o = Pattern.compile ("o");
        Pattern [] patterns = { space, d, o };
        int limits [] = { 1, 2, 5, -2, 0 };

        // Use supplied args, if any.  Assume that args are good.
        // Usage: input pattern [pattern ...]
        // Don't forget to quote the args.
        if (argv.length != 0) {
            input = argv [0];
            patterns = collectPatterns (argv);
        }

        generateTable (input, patterns, limits);
    }
```

Example 5-2. Splitting strings with Pattern (continued)

```java
/**
 * Output a simple XML document with the results of applying
 * the list of regex patterns to the input with each of the
 * limit values provided.  I should probably use the JAX APIs
 * to do this, but I want to keep the code simple.
 */
private static void generateTable (String input,
    Pattern [] patterns, int [] limits)
{
    System.out.println ("<?xml version='1.0'?>");
    System.out.println ("<table>");
    System.out.println ("\t<row>");
    System.out.println ("\t\t<head>Input: "
        + input + "</head>");

    for (int i = 0; i < patterns.length; i++) {
        Pattern pattern = patterns [i];

        System.out.println ("\t\t<head>Regex: <value>"
            + pattern.pattern() + "</value></head>");
    }

    System.out.println ("\t</row>");

    for (int i = 0; i < limits.length; i++) {
        int limit = limits [i];

        System.out.println ("\t<row>");
        System.out.println ("\t\t<entry>Limit: "
            + limit + "</entry>");

        for (int j = 0; j < patterns.length; j++) {
            Pattern pattern = patterns [j];
            String [] tokens = pattern.split (input, limit);

            System.out.print ("\t\t<entry>");

            for (int k = 0; k < tokens.length; k++) {
                System.out.print ("<value>"
                    + tokens [k] + "</value>");
            }

            System.out.println ("</entry>");
        }

        System.out.println ("\t</row>");
    }

    System.out.println ("</table>");
}

/**
 * If command line args were given, compile all args after the
```

Example 5-2. Splitting strings with Pattern (continued)

```
     * first as a Pattern.  Return an array of Pattern objects.
     */
    private static Pattern [] collectPatterns (String [] argv)
    {
        List list = new LinkedList();

        for (int i = 1; i < argv.length; i++) {
            list.add (Pattern.compile (argv [i]));
        }

        Pattern [] patterns = new Pattern [list.size()];

        list.toArray (patterns);

        return (patterns);
    }
}
```

Example 5-2 outputs an XML document describing the result matrix. The XSL stylesheet in Example 5-3 converts the XML to HTML for display in a web browser.

Example 5-3. Split matrix styelsheet

```
<?xml version="1.0"?>
<xsl:stylesheet xmlns:xsl="http://www.w3.org/1999/XSL/Transform" version="1.0">

<!--
    XSL stylesheet to transform the simple XML output of Poodle.java
    to HTML for display in a browser.  Use an XSL processor such as
    xalan with this stylesheet to convert the XML to HTML.

    @author Ron Hitchens (ron@ronsoft.com)
  -->

<xsl:output method="html"/>

<xsl:template match="/">
    <html><head><title>Poodle Zoo</title></head><body>
    <xsl:apply-templates/>
    </body></html>
</xsl:template>

<xsl:template match="table">
    <table align="center" border="1" cellpadding="5">
    <xsl:apply-templates/>
    </table>
</xsl:template>

<xsl:template match="row">
    <tr>
    <xsl:apply-templates/>
    </tr>
</xsl:template>
```

Example 5-3. Split matrix styelsheet (continued)

```
<xsl:template match="entry">
    <td>
    <xsl:apply-templates/>
    </td>
</xsl:template>

<xsl:template match="head">
    <th>
    <xsl:apply-templates/>
    </th>
</xsl:template>

<xsl:template match="entry/value">
    <xsl:if test="position() != 1">
        <xsl:text>, </xsl:text>
    </xsl:if>
    <xsl:call-template name="simplequote"/>
</xsl:template>

<xsl:template name="simplequote" match="value">
    <code>
    <xsl:text>&quot;</xsl:text>
    <xsl:apply-templates/>
    <xsl:text>&quot;</xsl:text>
    </code>
</xsl:template>

</xsl:stylesheet>
```

The Matcher Class

The Matcher class provides a rich API for matching regular expression patterns against character sequences. A Matcher instance is always created by invoking the matcher( ) method of a Pattern object, and it always applies the regular expression pattern encapsulated by that Pattern:

```
package java.util.regex;

public final class Matcher
{
        public Pattern pattern( )

        public Matcher reset( )
        public Matcher reset (CharSequence input)

        public boolean matches( )
        public boolean lookingAt( )
        public boolean find( )
        public boolean find (int start)

        public int start( )
```

```
            public int start (int group)
            public int end( )
            public int end (int group)

            public int groupCount( )
            public String group( )
            public String group (int group)

            public String replaceFirst (String replacement)
            public String replaceAll (String replacement)
            public StringBuffer appendTail (StringBuffer sb)
            public Matcher appendReplacement (StringBuffer sb, String replacement)
    }
```

Instances of the Matcher class are stateful objects that encapsulate the matching of a specific regular expression against a specific input character sequence. Matcher objects are not thread-safe because they hold internal state between method invocations.

Every Matcher instance is derived from a Pattern instance, and the pattern( ) method of Matcher returns a back reference to the Pattern object that created it.

Matcher objects can be used repeatedly, but because of their stateful nature, they must be placed in a known state to begin a new series of matching operations. This is done by calling the reset( ) method, which prepares the object for pattern matching at the beginning of the CharSequence associated with the matcher. The no-argument version of reset( ) will reuse the last CharSequence given to the Matcher. If you want to perform matching against a new sequence of characters, pass a new CharSequence to reset( ), and subsequent matching will be done against that target. For example, as you read each line of a file, you could pass it to reset( ). See Example 5-4.

Example 5-4. Simple file grep

```
package com.ronsoft.books.nio.regex;

import java.util.regex.Pattern;
import java.util.regex.Matcher;
import java.io.FileReader;
import java.io.BufferedReader;
import java.io.IOException;

/**
 * Simple implementation of the ubiquitous grep command.
 * First argument is the regular expression to search for (remember to
 * quote and/or escape as appropriate).  All following arguments are
 * filenames to read and search for the regular expression.
 *
 * @author Ron Hitchens (ron@ronsoft.com)
 */
public class SimpleGrep
{
    public static void main (String [] argv)
        throws Exception
```

Example 5-4. Simple file grep (continued)

```
{
    if (argv.length < 2) {
        System.out.println ("Usage: regex file [ ... ]");
        return;
    }

    Pattern pattern = Pattern.compile (argv [0]);
    Matcher matcher = pattern.matcher ("");

    for (int i = 1; i < argv.length; i++) {
        String file = argv [i];
        BufferedReader br = null;
        String line;

        try {
            br = new BufferedReader (new FileReader (file));
        } catch (IOException e) {
            System.err.println ("Cannot read '" + file
                + "': " + e.getMessage());
            continue;
        }

        while ((line = br.readLine()) != null) {
            matcher.reset (line);

            if (matcher.find()) {
                System.out.println (file + ": " + line);
            }
        }

        br.close();
    }
}
}
```

Example 5-5 demonstrates a more sophisticated use of the reset( ) method to allow a Matcher to work on several different character sequences.

Example 5-5. Extracting matched expressions

```
package com.ronsoft.books.nio.regex;

import java.util.regex.Pattern;
import java.util.regex.Matcher;

/**
 * Validates email addresses.
 *
 * Regular expression found in the Regular Expression Library
 * at regxlib.com.  Quoting from the site,
 * "Email validator that adheres directly to the specification
```

Example 5-5. Extracting matched expressions (continued)

```
 * for email address naming.  It allows for everything from
 * ipaddress and country-code domains, to very rare characters
 * in the username."
 *
 * @author Michael Daudel (mgd@ronsoft.com) (original)
 * @author Ron Hitchens (ron@ronsoft.com) (hacked)
 */
public class EmailAddressFinder
{
    public static void main (String[] argv)
    {
        if (argv.length < 1) {
            System.out.println ("usage: emailaddress ...");
        }

        // Compile the email address detector pattern
        Pattern pattern = Pattern.compile (
            "([a-zA-Z0-9_\\-\\.]+)@((\\[[0-9]{1,3}\\.[0-9]"
            + "{1,3}\\.[0-9]{1,3}\\.)|(([a-zA-Z0-9\\-]+\\.)+))"
            + "([a-zA-Z]{2,4}|[0-9]{1,3})(\\]?)",
            Pattern.MULTILINE);

        // Make a Matcher object for the pattern
        Matcher matcher = pattern.matcher ("");

        // Loop through the args and find the addrs in each one
        for (int i = 0; i < argv.length; i++) {
            boolean matched = false;

            System.out.println ("");
            System.out.println ("Looking at " + argv [i] + " ...");

            // Reset the Matcher to look at the current arg string
            matcher.reset (argv [i]);

            // Loop while matches are encountered
            while (matcher.find())
            {
                // found one
                System.out.println ("\t" + matcher.group());

                matched = true;
            }

            if ( ! matched) {
                System.out.println ("\tNo email addresses found");
            }
        }
    }
}
```

Here's the output from `EmailAddressFinder` when run on some typical addresses:

```
Looking at Ron Hitchens ,ron@ronsoft.com., fred@bedrock.com, barney@rubble.org, Wilma
<wflintstone@rockvegas.com> ...
ron@ronsoft.com
fred@bedrock.com
barney@rubble.org
wflintstone@rockvegas.com
```

The next group of methods return boolean indications of how the regular expression applies to the target character sequence. The first, `matches( )`, returns `true` if the *entire* character sequence is matched by the regular expression pattern. If the pattern matches only a subsequence, `false` is returned. This can be useful to select lines in a file that fit a certain pattern exactly. This behavior is identical to the convenience method `matches( )` on the `Pattern` class.

The `lookingAt( )` method is similar to `matches( )` but does not require that the entire sequence be matched by the pattern. If the regular expression pattern matches the *beginning* of the character sequence, then `lookingAt( )` returns `true`. The `lookingAt( )` method always begins scanning at the beginning of the sequence. The name of this method is intended to indicate if the matcher is currently "looking at" a target that starts with the pattern. If it returns `true`, then the `start( )`, `end( )`, and `group( )` methods can be called to determine the extent of the matched subsequence (more about those methods shortly).

The `find( )` method performs the same sort of matching operation as `lookingAt( )`, but remembers the position of the previous match and resumes scanning after it. This allows successive calls to `find( )` to step through the input and find embedded matches. On the first call following a reset, scanning begins at the first character of the input sequence. On subsequent calls, it resumes scanning at the first character following the previously matched subsequence. For each invocation, `true` is returned if the pattern was found; otherwise, `false` is returned. Typically, you'll use `find( )` to iterate over some text to find all the matching patterns within it.

The version of `find( )` that takes a positional argument does an implicit reset and begins scanning the input at the provided index position. Afterwards, no-argument `find( )` calls can be made to scan the remainder of the input sequence if needed.

Once a match has been detected, you can determine where in the character sequence the match is located by calling `start( )` and `end( )`. The `start( )` method returns the index of the first character of the matched sequence; `end( )` returns the index of the last character of the match plus one. These values are consistent with `CharSequence.subsequence( )` and can be used directly to extract the matched subsequence.

```
CharSequence subseq;

if (matcher.find( )) {
        subseq = input.subSequence (matcher.start(), matcher.end( ));
}
```

Some regular expressions can match the empty string, in which case start( ) and end( ) will return the same value. The start( ) and end( ) methods return only meaningful values only if a match has previously been detected by matches( ), lookingAt( ), or find( ). If no match has been made, or the last matching attempt returned false, then invoking start( ) or end( ) will result in a java.lang.IllegalStateException.

To understand the forms of start( ) and end( ) that take a group argument, we first need to understand *expression capture groups*. (See Figure 5-2.)

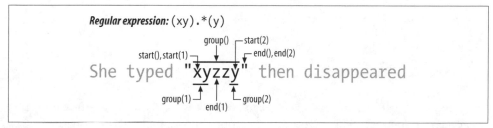

Figure 5-2. start( ), end( ), and group( ) values

Regular expressions may contain subexpressions, known as capture groups, enclosed in parentheses. During the evaluation of the regular expression, the subsequences of the input matching these capture group expressions are saved and can be referenced later in the expression. Once the full matching operation is complete, these saved snippets can be retrieved from the Matcher object by specifying a corresponding group number.

Capture groups can be nested and are numbered by counting their opening parens from left to right. The entire expression, whether or not it has any subgroups, is always counted as capture group zero. For example, the regular expression A((B)(C(D))) would have capture groups numbered as in Table 5-3.

Table 5-3. Regular expression capture groups of A((B)(C(D)))

Group number	Expression group
0	A((B)(C(D)))
1	((B)(C(D)))
2	(B)
3	(C(D))
4	(D)

There are exceptions to this grouping syntax. A group beginning with (? is a pure, or noncapturing, group. Its value is not saved, and it's not counted for purposes of numbering capture groups. (See Table 5-7 for syntax details.)

Let's look in more detail at the methods for working with capture groups:

```java
package java.util.regex;

public final class Matcher
{
        // This is a partial API listing

        public int start( )
        public int start (int group)
        public int end( )
        public int end (int group)

        public int groupCount( )
        public String group( )
        public String group (int group)
}
```

The number of capture groups in the regular expression pattern is returned by the groupCount( ) method. This value derives from the original Pattern object and is immutable. Group numbers must be positive and less than the value returned by groupCount( ). Passing a group number out of range will result in a java.lang. IndexOutOfBoundsException.

A capture group number can be passed to start( ) and end( ) to determine the subsequence matching the given capture group subexpression. It's possible for the overall expression to successfully match but one or more capture groups not to have matched. The start( ) and end( ) methods will return a value of -1 if the requested capture group is not currently set. As mentioned earlier, the entire regular expression is considered to be group zero. Invoking start( ) or end( ) with no argument is equivalent to passing an argument of zero. Invoking start( ) or end( ) for group zero will never return -1.

You can extract a matching subsequence from the input CharSequence using the values returned by start( ) and end( ) (as shown previously), but the group( ) methods provide an easier way to do this. Invoking group( ) with a numeric argument returns a String that is the matching subsequence for that particular capture group. If you call the version of group( ) that takes no argument, the subsequence matched by the entire regular expression (group zero) is returned. This code:

```java
String match0 = input.subSequence (matcher.start(), matcher.end()).toString( );
String match2 = input.subSequence (matcher.start (2), matcher.end (2)).toString( );
```

is equivalent to this:

```java
String match0 = matcher.group( );
String match2 = matcher.group(2);
```

Finally, let's look at the methods of the Matcher object that deal with modifying a character sequence. One of the most common applications of regular expressions is to do a search-and-replace. The replaceFirst( ) and replaceAll( ) methods make this very easy to do. They behave identically except that replaceFirst( ) stops after the first match it finds, while replaceAll( ) iterates until all matches have been replaced. Both take a String argument that is the replacement value to substitute for the matched pattern in the input character sequence.

```
package java.util.regex;

public final class Matcher
{
        // This is a partial API listing

        public String replaceFirst (String replacement)
        public String replaceAll (String replacement)
}
```

As mentioned earlier, capture groups can be back-referenced within the regular expression. They can also be referenced from the replacement string you provide to replaceFirst( ) or replaceAll( ). Capture group numbers can be embedded in the replacement string by preceding them with a dollar sign character. When the replacement string is substituted into the result string, each occurrence of $g is replaced by the value that would be returned by group(g). If you want to use a literal dollar sign in the replacement string, you must precede it with a backslash character (\$). To pass through a backslash, you must double it (\\). If you want to concatenate literal numeric digits following a capture group reference, separate them from the group number with a backslash, like this: 123$2\456. See Table 5-4 for some examples. See also Example 5-6 for sample code.

Table 5-4. Replacement of matched patterns

Regex pattern	Input	Replacement	replaceFirst( )	replaceAll( )
a*b	aabfooaabfooab foob	-	-fooaabfooabfoob	-foo-foo-foo-
\p{Blank}	fee fie foe fum	_	fee_fie foe fum	fee_fie_foe_fum
([bB])yte	Byte for byte	$1ite	Bite for byte	Bite for bite
\d\d\d\d([-])	card #1234-5678-1234	xxxx$1	card #xxxx-5678-1234	card #xxxx-xxxx-1234
(up|left)(*)(right|down)	left right, up down	$3$2$1	right left, up down	right left, down up
([CcPp][hl]e[ea]se)	I want cheese. Please.	\<b\> $1 \</b\>	I want \<b\> cheese \</b\>. Please.	I want \<b\> cheese \</b\>. \<b\> Please \</b\>.

Example 5-6. Regular expression replacement

```
package com.ronsoft.books.nio.regex;

import java.util.regex.Pattern;
import java.util.regex.Matcher;

/**
 * Exercise the replacement capabilities of the java.util.regex.Matcher class.
 * Run this code from the command line with three or more arguments.
 * 1) First argument is a regular expression
 * 2) Second argument is a replacement string, optionally with capture group
 *    references ($1, $2, etc)
 * 3) Any remaining arguments are treated as input strings to which the
 *    regular expression and replacement strings will be applied.
 * The effect of calling replaceFirst() and replaceAll() for each input string
 * will be listed.
 *
 * Be careful to quote the commandline arguments if they contain spaces or
 * special characters.
 *
 * @author Ron Hitchens (ron@ronsoft.com)
 */
public class RegexReplace
{
    public static void main (String [] argv)
    {
        // sanity check, need at least three args
        if (argv.length < 3) {
            System.out.println ("usage: regex replacement input ...");
            return;
        }

        // Save the regex and replacment strings with mnemonic names
        String regex = argv [0];
        String replace = argv [1];

        // Compile the expression; needs to be done only once
        Pattern pattern = Pattern.compile (regex);
        // Get a Matcher instance and use a dummy input string for now
        Matcher matcher = pattern.matcher ("");

        // print out for reference
        System.out.println ("        regex: '" + regex + "'");
        System.out.println ("  replacement: '" + replace + "'");

        // For each remaining arg string, apply the regex/replacment
        for (int i = 2; i < argv.length; i++) {
            System.out.println ("------------------------");

            matcher.reset (argv [i]);

            System.out.println ("        input: '"
                + argv [i] + "'");
```

Example 5-6. Regular expression replacement (continued)

```
            System.out.println ("replaceFirst(): '"
                + matcher.replaceFirst (replace) + "'");
            System.out.println ("  replaceAll(): '"
                + matcher.replaceAll (replace) + "'");
        }



    }
}
```

And here's the output from running `RegexReplace`:

```
            regex: '([bB])yte'
      replacement: '$1ite'
-----------------------
            input: 'Bytes is bytes'
   replaceFirst(): 'Bites is bytes'
     replaceAll(): 'Bites is bites'
```

Remember that regular expressions interpret backslashes in the strings you provide. Also remember that the Java compiler expects two backslashes for each one in a literal `String`. This means that if you want to escape a backslash in the regex, you'll need two backslashes in the compiled `String`. To get two backslashes in a row in the compiled regex string, you'll need four backslashes in a row in the Java source code.

To generate a replacement sequence of a\b, the `String` literal argument to `replaceAll()` must be a\\\\b (see Example 5-7). Be careful when counting those backslashes!

Example 5-7. Backslashes in regular expressions

```
package com.ronsoft.books.nio.regex;

import java.util.regex.Pattern;
import java.util.regex.Matcher;

/**
 * Demonstrate behavior of backslashes in regex patterns.
 *
 * @author Ron Hitchens (ron@ronsoft.com)
 */
public class BackSlashes
{
    public static void main (String [] argv)
    {
        // Substitute "a\b" for XYZ or ABC in input
        String rep = "a\\\\b";
        String input = "> XYZ <=> ABC <";
        Pattern pattern = Pattern.compile ("ABC|XYZ");
        Matcher matcher = pattern.matcher (input);
```

Example 5-7. Backslashes in regular expressions (continued)

```
        System.out.println (matcher.replaceFirst (rep));
        System.out.println (matcher.replaceAll (rep));

        // Change all newlines in input to escaped, DOS-like CR/LF
        rep = "\\\\r\\\\n";
        input = "line 1\nline 2\nline 3\n";
        pattern = Pattern.compile ("\\n");
        matcher = pattern.matcher (input);

        System.out.println ("");
        System.out.println ("Before:");
        System.out.println (input);

        System.out.println ("After (dos-ified, escaped):");
        System.out.println (matcher.replaceAll (rep));
    }
}
```

Here's the output from running BackSlashes:

```
> a\b <=> ABC <
> a\b <=> a\b <

Before:
line 1
line 2
line 3

After (dos-ified, escaped):
line 1\r\nline 2\r\nline 3\r\n
```

The two append methods listed in the Matcher API are useful when iterating though an input character sequence, repeatedly invoking find( ):

```
package java.util.regex;

public final class Matcher
{
        // This is a partial API listing

        public StringBuffer appendTail (StringBuffer sb)
        public Matcher appendReplacement (StringBuffer sb, String replacement)
}
```

Rather than returning a new String with the replacement already performed, the append methods append to a StringBuffer object you provide. This allows you to make decisions about the replacement at each point a match is found or to accumulate the result of matching against multiple input strings. Using appendReplacement( ) and appendTail( ) gives you total control of the search-and-replace process.

One of the bits of state information remembered by Matcher objects is an *append position*. The append position is used to remember the amount of the input character sequence that has already been copied out by previous invocations of appendReplacement(). When appendReplacement() is invoked, the following process takes place:

1. Characters are read from the input starting at the current append position and appended to the provided StringBuffer. The last character copied is the one just before the first character of the matched pattern. This is the character at the index returned by start() minus one.

2. The replacement string is appended to the StringBuffer and substitutes any embedded capture group references as described earlier.

3. The append position is updated to be the index of the character following the matched pattern, which is the value returned by end().

The appendReplacement() method works properly only if a previous match operation was successful (usually a call to find()). You will be rewarded with a delightful java.lang.IllegalStateException if the last match returned false or if the method is called immediately following a reset.

But don't forget that there may be remaining characters in the input beyond the last match of the pattern. You probably don't want to lose those, but appendReplacement() will not have copied them otherwise, and end() won't return a useful value after find() fails to find any more matches. The appendTail() method is there to copy the remainder of your input in this situation. It simply copies any characters from the current append position to the end of the input and appends them to the given StringBuffer. The following code is a typical usage scenario for appendReplacement() and appendTail():

```
Pattern pattern = Pattern.compile ("([Tt])hanks");
Matcher matcher = pattern.matcher ("Thanks, thanks very much");
StringBuffer sb = new StringBuffer();

while (matcher.find()) {
        if (matcher.group(1).equals ("T")) {
                matcher.appendReplacement (sb, "Thank you");
        } else {
                matcher.appendReplacement (sb, "thank you");
        }
}

matcher.appendTail (sb);
```

Table 5-5 shows the sequence of changes applied to the StringBuffer by the above code.

Table 5-5. Using appendReplacement( ) and appendTail( )

Append position	Execute	Resulting StringBuffer
0	appendReplacement (sb, "Thank you")	Thank you
6	appendReplacement (sb, "thank you")	Thank you, thank you
14	appendTail (sb)	Thank you, thank you very much

This sequence of append operations results in the StringBuffer object sb containing the string "Thank you, thank you very much". Example 5-8 is a complete code example showing this type of replacement, as well as alternate ways of performing the same substitution. In this simple case, the value of a capture group can be used because the first letter of the matched pattern is the same as that of the replacement. In a more complex case, there may not be an overlap between the input and the replacement values. Using Matcher.find( ) and Matcher.appendReplacement( ) allows you to programmatically mediate each replacement, possibly injecting different replacement values at each point along the way.

Example 5-8. Regular expression append/replace

```
package com.ronsoft.books.nio.regex;

import java.util.regex.Pattern;
import java.util.regex.Matcher;

/**
 * Test the appendReplacement() and appendTail() methods of the
 * java.util.regex.Matcher class.
 *
 * @author Ron Hitchens (ron@ronsoft.com)
 */
public class RegexAppend
{
    public static void main (String [] argv)
    {
        String input = "Thanks, thanks very much";
        String regex = "([Tt])hanks";
        Pattern pattern = Pattern.compile (regex);
        Matcher matcher = pattern.matcher (input);
        StringBuffer sb = new StringBuffer();

        // Loop while matches are encountered
        while (matcher.find()) {
            if (matcher.group(1).equals ("T")) {
                matcher.appendReplacement (sb, "Thank you");
            } else {
                matcher.appendReplacement (sb, "thank you");
            }
        }

        // Complete the transfer to the StringBuffer
        matcher.appendTail (sb);
```

Example 5-8. Regular expression append/replace (continued)

```
        // Print the result
        System.out.println (sb.toString());

        // Let's try that again using the $n escape in the replacement
        sb.setLength (0);
        matcher.reset();

        String replacement = "$1hank you";

        // Loop while matches are encountered
        while (matcher.find()) {
            matcher.appendReplacement (sb, replacement);
        }

        // Complete the transfer to the StringBuffer
        matcher.appendTail (sb);

        // Print the result
        System.out.println (sb.toString());

        // and once more, the easy way (because this example is simple)
        System.out.println (matcher.replaceAll (replacement));

        // one last time, using only the String
        System.out.println (input.replaceAll (regex, replacement));

    }
}
```

Regular Expression Methods of the String Class

It should be pretty obvious from the preceding sections that strings and regular expressions go hand in hand. It's only natural then that our old friend the String class has added some convenience methods to do common regular expression operations:

```
package java.lang;

public final class String
        implements java.io.Serializable, Comparable, CharSequence
{
        // This is a partial API listing

        public boolean matches (String regex)
        public String [] split (String regex)
        public String [] split (String regex, int limit)
        public String replaceFirst (String regex, String replacement)
        public String replaceAll (String regex, String replacement)
}
```

All the new `String` methods are pass-through calls to methods of the `Pattern` or `Matcher` classes. Now that you know how `Pattern` and `Matcher` are used and interoperate, using these `String` convenience methods should be a no brainer. Instead of describing each method, they are summarized in Table 5-6.

Table 5-6. Regular expression methods of the String class

String method signature	java.util.regex equivalent
input.matches (String regex)	Pattern.matches (String regex, CharSequence input)
input.split (String regex)	pat.split (CharSequence input)
input.split (String regex, int limit)	pat.split (CharSequence input, int limit)
input.replaceFirst (String regex, String replacement)	match.replaceFirst (String replacement)
input.replaceAll (String regex, String replacement)	match.replaceAll (String replacement)

In Table 5-6, assume that there is a `String` named input, a `Pattern` object named pat, and a `Matcher` named match:

```
String input = "Mary had a little lamb";
String [] tokens = input.split ("\\s+");   // split on whitespace
```

As of JDK 1.4, none of these regular expression convenience methods cache any expressions or do any other optimizations. Some JVM implementations may choose to cache and reuse pattern objects, but you should not rely on them. If you expect to apply the same pattern-matching operations repeatedly, it will be more efficient to use the classes in `java.util.regex`.

Java Regular Expression Syntax

Following is a summary of the regular expression syntax supported by the `java.util.regex` package, as released in JDK 1.4. Things change quickly in the Java world, so you should always check the current documentation provided with the Java implementation you're using. The information provided here is a quick reference to get you started.

The `java.util.regex` classes are fully Unicode-aware and follow the guidelines in *Unicode Technical Report #18: Unicode Regular Expression Guidelines*, found at *http://www.unicode.org/unicode/reports/tr18*.

As mentioned previously, the syntax is similar to Perl, but not exactly the same. The main feature missing in `java.util.regex` is the ability to embed Perl code in an expression (which would require dragging in a full Perl interpreter). The primary addition to the Java syntax is *possessive quantifiers*, which are greedier than regular greedy quantifiers. Possessive quantifiers match as much of the target as possible even if it means that the remainder of the expression would fail to match. Java regular expressions also support some Unicode escape sequences not supported by Perl. Consult the Javadoc page for `java.util.regex.Pattern` for complete details.

Table 5-7 is a regular expression quick reference. It is reproduced from *Java In A Nutshell, Fourth Edition* (O'Reilly).

Table 5-7. Java regular expression syntax quick reference

Syntax	Matches
Single characters	
x	The character *x*, as long as *x* is not a punctuation character with special meaning in the regular expression syntax.
p	The punctuation character *p*.
\\\\	The backslash character.
\n	The newline character \u000A.
\t	The tab character \u0009.
\r	The carriage return character \u000D.
\f	The form feed character \u000C.
\e	The escape character \u001B.
\a	The bell (alert) character \u0007.
\u*hhhh*	The Unicode character with hexadecimal code *hhhh*.
\x*hh*	The character with hexadecimal code *hh*.
\0*n*	The character with octal code *n*.
\0*nn*	The character with octal code *nn*.
\0*nnn*	Character with octal code *nnn*, in which *nnn* <= 377.
\c*x*	The control character ^*x*.
Character classes	
[...]	One of the characters between the brackets. Characters may be specified literally, and the syntax also allows the specification of character ranges, with intersection, union and subtraction operators. See specific examples that follow.
[^...]	Any one character not between the brackets.
[a-z0-9]	The character range: a character between (inclusive) a and z or 0 and 9.
[0-9[a-fA-F]]	The union of classes: same as [0-9a-fA-F].
[a-z&&[aeiou]]	The intersection of classes: same as [aeiou].
[a-z&&[^aeiou]]	Subtraction: the characters a through z, except for the vowels.
.	Any character, except a line terminator. If the DOTALL flag is set, it matches any character, including line terminators.
\d	An ASCII digit: [0-9].
\D	Anything but an ASCII digit: [^\d].
\s	ASCII whitespace: [\t\n\f\r\x0B].
\S	Anything but ASCII whitespace: [^\s].

Table 5-7. Java regular expression syntax quick reference (continued)

Syntax	Matches
\w	An ASCII word character: [a-zA-Z0-9_].
\W	Anything but an ASCII word character: [^\w].
\p{*group*}	Any character in the named group. See the following group names. Many of the group names are from POSIX, which is why p is used for this character class.
\P{*group*}	Any character not in the named group.
\p{Lower}	An ASCII lowercase letter: [a-z].
\p{Upper}	An ASCII uppercase letter: [A-Z].
\p{ASCII}	Any ASCII character: [\x00-\x7f].
\p{Alpha}	An ASCII letter: [a-zA-Z].
\p{Digit}	An ASCII digit: [0-9]
\p{XDigit}	A hexadecimal digit: [0-9a-fA-F].
\p{Alnum}	ASCII letter or digit: [\p{Alpha}\p{Digit}].
\p{Punct}	ASCII punctuation: one of ! "#$%&'( )*+,-./:;<=>?@[\]^_`{|}~].
\p{Graph}	A visible ASCII character: [\p{Alnum}\p{Punct}].
\p{Print}	A visible ASCII character: same as \p{Graph}.
\p{Blank}	An ASCII space or tab: [\t].
\p{Space}	ASCII whitespace: [\t\n\f\r\x0b].
\p{Cntrl}	An ASCII control character: [\x00-\x1f\x7f].
\p{*category*}	Any character in the named Unicode category. Category names are one- or two-letter codes defined by the Unicode standard. One-letter codes include L for letter, N for number, S for symbol, Z for separator, and P for punctuation. Two-letter codes represent subcategories, such as Lu for uppercase letter, Nd for decimal digit, Sc for currency symbol, Sm for math symbol, and Zs for space separator. See java.lang.Character for a set of constants that correspond to these subcategories, and note that the full set of one- and two-letter codes is not documented in this book.
\p{*block*}	Any character in the named Unicode block. In Java regular expressions, block names begin with "In", followed by mixed-case capitalization of the Unicode block name, without spaces or underscores. For example: \p{InOgham} or \p{InMathematicalOperators}. See java.lang.Character.UnicodeBlock for a list of Unicode block names.

Sequences, alternatives, groups, and references

xy	Match *x* followed by *y*.
x|y	Match *x* or *y*.
(...)	Grouping. Group subexpression within parentheses into a single unit that can be used with *, +, ?, |, and so on. Also "capture" the characters that match this group for later use.
(?:...)	Grouping only. Group subexpression as with ( ), but do not capture the text that matched.
n	Match the same characters that were matched when capturing group number *n* was first matched. Be careful when *n* is followed by another digit: the largest number that is a valid group number will be used.

Table 5-7. Java regular expression syntax quick reference (continued)

Syntax	Matches
Repetition[a]	
x?	Zero or one occurrence of *x*; i.e., *x* is optional.
*x**	Zero or more occurrences of *x*.
x+	One or more occurrences of *x*.
x{*n*}	Exactly *n* occurrences of *x*.
x{*n*,}	*n* or more occurrences of *x*.
x{*n,m*}	At least *n*, and at most *m* occurrences of *x*.
Anchors[b]	
^	The beginning of the input string or, if the `MULTILINE` flag is specified, the beginning of the string or of any new line.
$	The end of the input string or, if the `MULTILINE` flag is specified, the end of the string or of line within the string.
\b	A word boundary: a position in the string between a word and a non-word character.
\B	A position in the string that is not a word boundary.
\A	The beginning of the input string. Like ^, but never matches the beginning of a new line, regardless of what flags are set.
\Z	The end of the input string, ignoring any trailing line terminator.
\z	The end of the input string, including any line terminator.
\G	The end of the previous match.
(?=*x*)	A positive look-ahead assertion. Require that the following characters match *x*, but do not include those characters in the match.
(?!*x*)	A negative look-ahead assertion. Require that the following characters do not match the pattern *x*.
(?<=*x*)	A positive look-behind assertion. Require that the characters immediately before the position match *x*, but do not include those characters in the match. *x* must be a pattern with a fixed number of characters.
(?<!*x*)	A negative look-behind assertion. Require that the characters immediately before the position do not match *x*. *x* must be a pattern with a fixed number of characters.
Miscellaneous	
(?>*x*)	Match *x* independently of the rest of the expression, without considering whether the match causes the rest of the expression to fail to match. Useful to optimize certain complex regular expressions. A group of this form does not capture the matched text.
(?*onflags-offflags*)	Don't match anything, but turn on the flags specified by *onflags*, and turn off the flags specified by *offflags*. These two strings are combinations in any order of the following letters and correspond to the following `Pattern` constants: i (CASE_INSENSITIVE), d (UNIX_LINES), m (MULTILINE), s (DOTALL), u (UNICODE_CASE), and x (COMMENTS). Flag settings specified in this way take effect at the point that they appear in the expression and persist until the end of the expression, or until the end of the parenthesized group of which they are a part, or until overridden by another flag setting expression.
(?*onflags-offflags*:*x*)	Match *x*, applying the specified flags to this subexpression only. This is a noncapturing group, such as (?:...), with the addition of flags.

Table 5-7. Java regular expression syntax quick reference (continued)

Syntax	Matches
\Q	Don't match anything, but quote all subsequent pattern text until \E. All characters within such a quoted section are interpreted as literal characters to match, and none (except \E) have special meanings.
\E	Don't match anything; terminate a quote started with \Q.
#comment	If the COMMENT flag is set, pattern text between a # and the end of the line is considered a comment and is ignored.

[a] These repetition characters are known as *greedy quantifiers* because they match as many occurrences of *x* as possible while still allowing the rest of the regular expression to match. If you want a "reluctant quantifier," which matches as few occurrences as possible while still allowing the rest of the regular expression to match, follow the previous quantifiers with a question mark. For example, use *? instead of *, and {2,}? instead of {2,}. Or, if you follow a quantifier with a plus sign instead of a question mark, then you specify a "possessive quantifier," which matches as many occurrences as possible, even if it means that the rest of the regular expression will not match. Possessive quantifiers can be useful when you are sure that they will not adversely affect the rest of the match, because they can be implemented more efficiently than regular greedy quantifiers.

[b] Anchors do not match characters but instead match the zero-width positions between characters, "anchoring" the match to a position at which a specific condition holds.

An Object-Oriented File Grep

Example 5-9 implements an object oriented form of the familiar grep command. Instances of the Grep class are constructed with a regular expression and can be used to scan different files for the same pattern. The result of the Grep.grep( ) method is a type-safe array of Grep.MatchedLine objects. The MatchedLine class is a contained class within Grep. You must refer to it as Grep.MatchedLine or import it separately.

Example 5-9. Object-oriented grep

```
package com.ronsoft.books.nio.regex;

import java.io.File;
import java.io.FileReader;
import java.io.LineNumberReader;
import java.io.IOException;
import java.util.List;
import java.util.LinkedList;
import java.util.Iterator;
import java.util.regex.Matcher;
import java.util.regex.Pattern;

/**
 * A file searching class, similar to grep, which returns information about
 * lines matched in the specified files.  Instances of this class are tied
 * to a specific regular expression pattern and may be applied repeatedly
 * to multiple files.  Instances of Grep are thread safe, they may be shared.
 *
 * @author Michael Daudel (mgd@ronsoft.com) (original)
 * @author Ron Hitchens (ron@ronsoft.com) (hacked)
 */
```

Example 5-9. Object-oriented grep (continued)

```java
public class Grep
{
    // the pattern to use for this instance
    private Pattern pattern;

    /**
     * Instantiate a Grep object for the given pre-compiled Pattern object.
     * @param pattern A java.util.regex.Pattern object specifying the
     *  pattern to search for.
     */
    public Grep (Pattern pattern)
    {
        this.pattern = pattern;
    }

    /**
     * Instantiate a Grep object and compile the given regular expression
     * string.
     * @param regex The regular expression string to compile into a
     *  Pattern for internal use.
     * @param ignoreCase If true, pass Pattern.CASE_INSENSITIVE to the
     *  Pattern constuctor so that seaches will be done without regard
     *  to alphabetic case.  Note, this only applies to the ASCII
     *  character set.  Use embedded expressions to set other options.
     */
    public Grep (String regex, boolean ignoreCase)
    {
        this.pattern = Pattern.compile (regex,
            (ignoreCase) ? Pattern.CASE_INSENSITIVE : 0);

    }

    /**
     * Instantiate a Grep object with the given regular expression string,
     * with default options.
     */
    public Grep (String regex)
    {
        this (regex, false);
    }

    // ---------------------------------------------------------------

    /**
     * Perform a grep on the given file.
     * @param file A File object denoting the file to scan for the
     *  regex given when this Grep instance was constructed.
     * @return A type-safe array of Grep.MatchedLine objects describing
     *  the lines of the file matched by the pattern.
     * @exception IOException If there is a problem reading the file.
     */
    public MatchedLine [] grep (File file)
```

Example 5-9. Object-oriented grep (continued)

```
    throws IOException
{
    List list = grepList (file);
    MatchedLine matches [] = new MatchedLine [list.size()];

    list.toArray (matches);

    return (matches);
}

/**
 * Perform a grep on the given file.
 * @param file A String filename denoting the file to scan for the
 *   regex given when this Grep instance was constructed.
 * @return A type-safe array of Grep.MatchedLine objects describing
 *   the lines of the file matched by the pattern.
 * @exception IOException If there is a problem reading the file.
 */
public MatchedLine [] grep (String fileName)
    throws IOException
{
    return (grep (new File (fileName)));
}

/**
 * Perform a grep on the given list of files.  If a given file cannot
 * be read, it will be ignored as if empty.
 * @param files An array of File objects to scan.
 * @return A type-safe array of Grep.MatchedLine objects describing
 *   the lines of the file matched by the pattern.
 */
public MatchedLine [] grep (File [] files)
{
    List aggregate = new LinkedList();

    for (int i = 0; i < files.length; i++) {
        try {
            List temp = grepList (files [i]);

            aggregate.addAll (temp);
        } catch (IOException e) {
            // ignore I/O exceptions
        }
    }

    MatchedLine matches [] = new MatchedLine [aggregate.size()];

    aggregate.toArray (matches);

    return (matches);
}

// ------------------------------------------------------------
```

Example 5-9. Object-oriented grep (continued)

```
/**
 * Encapsulation of a matched line from a file.  This immutable
 * object has five read-only properties:<ul>
 * <li>getFile(): The File this match pertains to.</li>
 * <li>getLineNumber(): The line number (1-relative) within the
 *   file where the match was found.</li>
 * <li>getLineText(): The text of the matching line</li>
 * <li>start(): The index within the line where the matching
 *   pattern begins.</li>
 * <li>end(): The index, plus one, of the end of the matched
 *   character sequence.</li>
 * </ul>
 */
public static class MatchedLine
{
    private File file;
    private int lineNumber;
    private String lineText;
    private int start;
    private int end;

    MatchedLine (File file, int lineNumber, String lineText,
        int start, int end)
    {
        this.file - file;
        this.lineNumber = lineNumber;
        this.lineText = lineText;
        this.start = start;
        this.end = end;
    }

    public File getFile()
    {
        return (this.file);
    }

    public int getLineNumber()
    {
        return (this.lineNumber);
    }

    public String getLineText()
    {
        return (this.lineText);
    }

    public int start()
    {
        return (this.start);
    }

    public int end()
```

Example 5-9. Object-oriented grep (continued)

```java
    {
        return (this.end);
    }
}

// -------------------------------------------------------------

/**
 * Run the grepper on the given File.
 * @return A (non-type-safe) List of MatchedLine objects.
 */
private List grepList (File file)
    throws IOException
{
    if ( ! file.exists()) {
        throw new IOException ("Does not exist: " + file);
    }

    if ( ! file.isFile()) {
        throw new IOException ("Not a regular file: " + file);
    }

    if ( ! file.canRead()) {
        throw new IOException ("Unreadable file: " + file);
    }

    LinkedList list = new LinkedList();
    FileReader fr = new FileReader (file);
    LineNumberReader lnr = new LineNumberReader (fr);
    Matcher matcher = this.pattern.matcher ("");
    String line;

    while ((line = lnr.readLine()) != null) {
        matcher.reset (line);

        if (matcher.find()) {
            list.add (new MatchedLine (file,
                lnr.getLineNumber(), line,
                matcher.start(), matcher.end()));
        }
    }

    lnr.close();

    return (list);
}

// -------------------------------------------------------------

/**
 * Test code to run grep operations.  Accepts two command-line
 * options: -i or --ignore-case, compile the given pattern so
```

Example 5-9. Object-oriented grep (continued)

```
 * that case of alpha characters is ignored.  Or -1, which runs
 * the grep operation on each individual file, rather that passing
 * them all to one invocation.  This is just to test the different
 * methods.  The printed ouptut is slightly different when -1 is
 * specified.
 */
public static void main (String [] argv)
{
    // Set defaults
    boolean ignoreCase = false;
    boolean onebyone = false;
    List argList = new LinkedList( );    // to gather args

    // Loop through the args, looking for switches and saving
    // the patterns and filenames
    for (int i = 0; i < argv.length; i++) {
        if (argv [i].startsWith ("-")) {
            if (argv [i].equals ("-i")
                || argv [i].equals ("--ignore-case"))
            {
                ignoreCase = true;
            }

            if (argv [i].equals ("-1")) {
                onebyone = true;
            }

            continue;
        }

        // not a switch, add it to the list
        argList.add (argv [i]);
    }

    // Enough args to run?
    if (argList.size( ) < 2) {
        System.err.println ("usage: [options] pattern filename ...");
        return;
    }

    // First arg on the list will be taken as the regex pattern.
    // Pass the pattern to the new Grep object, along with the
    // current value of the ignore case flag.
    Grep grepper = new Grep ((String) argList.remove (0),
        ignoreCase);

    // somewhat arbitrarily split into two ways of calling the
    // grepper and printing out the results
    if (onebyone) {
        Iterator it = argList.iterator( );
```

Example 5-9. Object-oriented grep (continued)

```
            // Loop through the filenames and grep them
            while (it.hasNext( )) {
                String fileName = (String) it.next( );

                // Print the filename once before each grep
                System.out.println (fileName + ":");

                MatchedLine [] matches = null;

                // Catch exceptions
                try {
                    matches = grepper.grep (fileName);
                } catch (IOException e) {
                    System.err.println ("\t*** " + e);
                    continue;
                }

                // Print out info about the matched lines
                for (int i = 0; i < matches.length; i++) {
                    MatchedLine match = matches [i];

                    System.out.println ("   "
                        + match.getLineNumber( )
                        + " [" + match.start( )
                        + "-" + (match.end( ) - 1)
                        + "]: "
                        + match.getLineText( ));
                }
            }
        } else {
            // Convert the filename list to an array of File
            File [] files = new File [argList.size( )];

            for (int i = 0; i < files.length; i++) {
                files [i] = new File ((String) argList.get (i));
            }

            // Run the grepper; unreadable files are ignored
            MatchedLine [] matches = grepper.grep (files);

            // Print out info about the matched lines
            for (int i = 0; i < matches.length; i++) {
                MatchedLine match = matches [i];

                System.out.println (match.getFile().getName( )
                    + ", " + match.getLineNumber( ) + ": "
                    + match.getLineText( ));
            }
        }
    }
}
```

Summary

In this chapter, we discussed the long-awaited regular expression classes added to the J2SE platform in the 1.4 release:

CharSequence

> We were introduced to the new CharSequence interface in the section "The CharSequence Interface" and learned that it is implemented by several classes to describe sequences of characters in an abstract way.

Pattern

> The Pattern class encapsulates a regular expression in an immutable object instance. In the section "The Pattern Class," we saw the API of Pattern and learned how to create instances by compiling expression strings. We also saw some static utility methods for doing one-time matches.

Matcher

> The Matcher class is a state machine object that applies a Pattern object to an input character sequence to find matching patterns in that input. The section "The Matcher Class" described the Matcher API, including how to create new Matcher instances from a Pattern object and how to perform various types of matching operations.

String

> The String class has had new regular expression convenience methods added in 1.4. These were summarized in the section "Regular Expression Methods of the String Class."

The syntax of the regular expressions supported by java.util.regex.Pattern is listed in Table 5-7. The syntax closely matches that of Perl 5.

Now we add a little international flavor to the tour. In the next chapter, you'll be introduced to the exotic and sometimes mysterious world of character sets.

CHAPTER 6

Character Sets

Here, put this fish in your ear.
—Ford Prefect

We live in a diverse and ever-changing universe. Even on this rather mundane M-class planet we call Earth, we speak hundreds of different languages. In *The Hitchhikers Guide to the Galaxy*, Arthur Dent solved his language problem by placing a Babelfish in his ear. He could then understand the languages spoken by the diverse (to say the least) characters he encountered along his involuntary journey through the galaxy.[*]

On the Java platform, we don't have the luxury of Babelfish technology (at least not yet).[†] We must still deal with multiple languages and the many characters that comprise those languages. Luckily, Java was the first widely used programming language to use Unicode internally to represent characters. Compared to byte-oriented programming languages such as C or C++, native support of Unicode greatly simplifies character data handling, but it by no means makes character handling automatic. You still need to understand how character mapping works and how to handle multiple character sets.

Character Set Basics

Before discussing the details of the new classes in `java.nio.charsets`, let's define some terms related to character sets and character transcoding. The new character set classes present a more standardized approach to this realm, so it's important to be clear on the terminology used.

---

[*] He didn't manage to prevent Earth being blown up, but that's beside the point.

[†] Though *http://babelfish.altavista.com* is getting there.

Character set

> A set of characters, i.e., symbols with specific semantic meanings. The letter "A" is a character. So is "%". Neither has any intrinsic numeric value, nor any direct relationship to ASCII, Unicode, or even computers. Both symbols existed long before the first computer was invented.

Coded character set

> A assignment of numeric values to a set of characters. Assigning codes to characters so they can be represented digitally results in a specific set of character codings. Other coded character sets might assign a different numeric value to the same character. Character set mappings are usually determined by standards bodies, such as US-ASCII, ISO 8859-1, Unicode (ISO 10646-1), and JIS X0201.

Character-encoding scheme

> A mapping of the members of a coded character set to a sequence of octets (eight bit bytes). The encoding scheme defines how a sequence of character encodings will be represented as a sequence of bytes. The numeric values of the character encodings do not need to be the same as the encoded bytes, nor even a one-to-one or one-to-many relationship. Think of character set encoding and decoding as similar in principle to object serialization and deserialization.
>
> Character data is usually encoded for transmission over a network or for storage in a file. An encoding scheme is not a character set, it's a mapping; but because of the close relationship between them, most encodings are associated with a single character set. UTF-8, for example, is used only to encode the Unicode character set. However, it's possible for one encoding scheme to handle more than one character set. For example, EUC can encode characters from several Asian languages.
>
> Figure 6-1 is a graphical representation of encoding a Unicode character sequence to a sequence of bytes using the UTF-8 encoding scheme. UTF-8 encodes character code values less than 0x80 as a single-byte value (standard ASCII). All other Unicode characters are encoded as multibyte sequences of two to six bytes (*http://www.ietf.org/rfc/rfc2279.txt*).

Charset

> The term *charset* is defined in RFC2278 (*http://ietf.org/rfc/rfc2278.txt*). It's the combination of a coded character set and a character-encoding scheme. The anchor class of the `java.nio.charset` package is `Charset`, which encapsulates the charset abstraction.

Unicode is a 16-bit character encoding.[*] It attempts to unify the character sets of all the languages around the world into a single, comprehensive mapping. It's gaining ground, but there are still many other character encodings in wide use today. Most

---

[*] Or so it seems. Unicode now defines character codings larger than 16 bits. These new, expanded codings are not expected to be supported by Java until at least the 1.5 release.

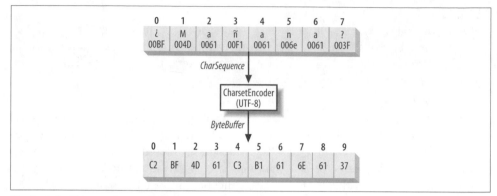

Figure 6-1. Characters encoded as UTF-8

operating systems are still byte-oriented in terms of I/O and file storage, so whatever encoding is used, be it Unicode or something else, there is still a need to translate between byte sequences and character set encodings.

The classes comprising the `java.nio.charset` package address this need. This is not the first time the Java platform has addressed character set encoding, but it's the most systematic, comprehensive, and flexible solution. The `java.nio.charset.spi` package provides a Server Provider Interface (SPI), which allows new encoders and decoders to be plugged in as needed.

Charsets

As of JDK 1.4, every JVM implementation is required to support a standard set of charsets, listed in Table 6-1. JVM implementations are free to support additional charsets but must provide this minimum set. (Consult your JVM's release documentation for information on whether additional charsets are available.) Note that although all JVMs must support at least this list of charsets, the default charset is not specified and is not required to be one of these standard charsets. The default is determined at JVM startup and depends on the underlying operating-system environment, locale setting, and/or the JVM configuration. If you need a specific charset, it's safest to name it explicitly. Don't assume that the deployment default is the same as it is for your development environment.

Table 6-1. Required charsets

Charset name	Description
US-ASCII	Seven-bit ASCII, ISO 646-US. The basic Latin block of the Unicode character set. This is the familiar American-English character set.
ISO-8859-1	ISO-LATIN-1. The character set used for most European languages. This is a superset of US-ASCII and includes most non-English European characters. (See *http://www.unicode.org/charts/*.) The characters of ISO-LATIN-1 are encoded within eight bits.

Table 6-1. Required charsets (continued)

Charset name	Description
UTF-8	Eight-bit UCS Transformation Format. Specified by RFC 2279 and by the Unicode Standard 3.0 (amended). This is a byte-oriented character encoding. The ASCII characters, those less than 0x80, are encoded as single bytes. Other characters are encoded as two or more bytes. For multiple sequences, if the high-order bits of the first byte encode the number of following bytes. (See *http://www.ietf.org/rfc/rfc2279.txt*.) UTF-8 interoperates well with ASCII because a simple ASCII file is a well-formed UTF-8 encoding, and a UTF-8 encoding of characters less than 0x80 is an ASCII file.
UTF-16BE	16-bit UCS Transformation Format, big-endian byte order. Every Unicode character is encoded as a two-byte sequence, with the high-order eight bits written first.
UTF-16LE	16-bit UCS Transformation Format, little-endian byte order. Every Unicode character is encoded as a two-byte sequence, with the low-order eight bits written first.
UTF-16	16-bit UCS Transformation Format. Byte order is determined by an optional byte-order mark. The UTF-16 charsets are specified in RFC 2781. The UTF-16BE and UTF-16BE formats encode into 16-bit quantities and are thus byte order–dependent. UTF-16 is a portability encoding that uses a leading byte mark to indicate whether the remainder of the encoded byte stream is UTF-16BE or UTF-16LE. See Table 6-2.

Charset names are case-insensitive, i.e., upper- and lowercase letters are considered to be equivalent when comparing charset names.

The Internet Assigned Names Authority (IANA) maintains the official registry of charset names, and all the names listed in Table 6-1 are standardized names registered with the IANA.

UTF-16BE and UTF-16LE encode each character as a two-byte numeric value. The decoder of such an encoding must therefore have prior knowledge of how the data was encoded or a means of determining the byte order from the encoded data stream itself. The UTF-16 encoding recognizes a byte-order mark: the Unicode character \uFEFF. The byte-order mark has special meaning only when it occurs at the beginning of an encoded stream. If this value is encountered later, it is mapped according to its defined Unicode value (zero width, nonbreaking space). Foreign, little-endian systems might prepend \uFFFE and encode the stream as UTF-16LE. Using the UTF-16 encoding to prepend and recognize the byte-order mark allows systems with different internal byte orders to exchange Unicode data.

Table 6-2 illustrates the actions taken by the Java platform for the various combinations.

Table 6-2. UTF-16 charset encode/decode

	UTF-16	UTF-16BE	UTF-16LE
Encode	Prepend byte mark \uFEFF, encode as UTF-16BE.	No byte mark, encode big-endian byte order.	No byte mark, encode little-endian byte order.
Decode: no byte mark	Decode as UTF-16BE (Java's native byte order).	Decode, assuming big-endian byte order.	Decode, assuming little-endian byte order.

Table 6-2. UTF-16 charset encode/decode (continued)

	UTF-16	UTF-16BE	UTF-16LE
Decode: mark = \uFEFF	Discard mark. Decode as UTF-16BE.	Discard mark. Decode as big-endian byte order.	Discard mark. Decode as little-endian byte order. Note that decoding will be byte-swapped, which may result in a runtime exception.
Decode: mark = \uFFFE	Discard mark. Decode as UTF-16LE.	Discard mark. Decode as big-endian byte order. Note that decoding will be byte-swapped, which may result in runtime exception.	Discard mark. Decode as little-endian byte order.

Example 6-1 demonstrates how characters are translated to byte sequences by various Charset implementations.

Example 6-1. Encoding with the standard charsets

```
package com.ronsoft.books.nio.charset;

import java.nio.charset.Charset;
import java.nio.ByteBuffer;

/**
 * Charset encoding test.  Run the same input string, which contains
 * some non-ascii characters, through several Charset encoders and dump out
 * the hex values of the resulting byte sequences.
 *
 * @author Ron Hitchens (ron@ronsoft.com)
 */
public class EncodeTest
{
    public static void main (String [] argv)
        throws Exception
    {
        // This is the character sequence to encode
        String input = "\u00bfMa\u00f1ana?";

        // the list of charsets to encode with
        String [] charsetNames = {
            "US-ASCII", "ISO-8859-1", "UTF-8", "UTF-16BE",
            "UTF-16LE", "UTF-16" // , "X-ROT13"
        };

        for (int i = 0; i < charsetNames.length; i++) {
            doEncode (Charset.forName (charsetNames [i]), input);
        }
    }

    /**
     * For a given Charset and input string, encode the chars
     * and print out the resulting byte encoding in a readable form.
```

Example 6-1. Encoding with the standard charsets (continued)

```
    */
   private static void doEncode (Charset cs, String input)
   {
       ByteBuffer bb = cs.encode (input);

       System.out.println ("Charset: " + cs.name());
       System.out.println ("  Input: " + input);
       System.out.println ("Encoded: ");

       for (int i = 0; bb.hasRemaining(); i++) {
           int b = bb.get();
           int ival = ((int) b) & 0xff;
           char c = (char) ival;

           // Keep tabular alignment pretty
           if (i < 10) System.out.print (" ");

           // Print index number
           System.out.print ("   " + i + ": ");

           // Better formatted output is coming someday...
           if (ival < 16) System.out.print ("0");

           // Print the hex value of the byte
           System.out.print (Integer.toHexString (ival));

           // If the byte seems to be the value of a
           // printable character, print it.  No guarantee
           // it will be.
           if (Character.isWhitespace (c) ||
               Character.isISOControl (c))
           {
               System.out.println ("");
           } else {
               System.out.println (" (" + c + ")");
           }
       }

       System.out.println ("");
   }
}
```

Here is the output from running EncodeTest:

```
Charset: US-ASCII
  Input: ¿Mañana?
Encoded:
    0: 3f (?)
    1: 4d (M)
    2: 61 (a)
    3: 3f (?)
    4: 61 (a)
    5: 6e (n)
```

```
  6: 61 (a)
  7: 3f (?)

Charset: ISO-8859-1
  Input: ¿Mañana?
Encoded:
  0: bf (¿)
  1: 4d (M)
  2: 61 (a)
  3: f1 (ñ)
  4: 61 (a)
  5: 6e (n)
  6: 61 (a)
  7: 3f (?)

Charset: UTF-8
  Input: ¿Mañana?
Encoded:
  0: c2 (Â)
  1: bf (¿)
  2: 4d (M)
  3: 61 (a)
  4: c3 (Ã)
  5: b1 (±)
  6: 61 (a)
  7: 6e (n)
  8: 61 (a)
  9: 3f (?)

Charset: UTF-16BE
  Input: ¿Mañana?
Encoded:
   0: 00
   1: bf (¿)
   2: 00
   3: 4d (M)
   4: 00
   5: 61 (a)
   6: 00
   7: f1 (ñ)
   8: 00
   9: 61 (a)
  10: 00
  11: 6e (n)
  12: 00
  13: 61 (a)
  14: 00
  15: 3f (?)

Charset: UTF-16LE
  Input: ¿Mañana?
Encoded:
  0: bf (¿)
```

```
    1: 00
    2: 4d (M)
    3: 00
    4: 61 (a)
    5: 00
    6: f1 (ñ)
    7: 00
    8: 61 (a)
    9: 00
   10: 6e (n)
   11: 00
   12: 61 (a)
   13: 00
   14: 3f (?)
   15: 00

Charset: UTF-16
  Input: ¿Mañana?
Encoded:
    0: fe ( æ)
    1: ff (ÿ)
    2: 00
    3: bf (¿)
    4: 00
    5: 4d (M)
    6: 00
    7: 61 (a)
    8: 00
    9: f1 (ñ)
   10: 00
   11: 61 (a)
   12: 00
   13: 6e (n)
   14: 00
   15: 61 (a)
   16: 00
 17: 3f (?)
```

The Charset Class

Let's dig into the Charset class API (summarized in Figure 6-2):

```
package java.nio.charset;

public abstract class Charset implements Comparable
{
        public static boolean isSupported (String charsetName)
        public static Charset forName (String charsetName)
        public static SortedMap availableCharsets()

        public final String name()
        public final Set aliases()
        public String displayName()
```

```
    public String displayName (Locale locale)

    public final boolean isRegistered( )

    public boolean canEncode( )
    public abstract CharsetEncoder newEncoder( );
    public final ByteBuffer encode (CharBuffer cb)
    public final ByteBuffer encode (String str)

    public abstract CharsetDecoder newDecoder( );
    public final CharBuffer decode (ByteBuffer bb)

    public abstract boolean contains (Charset cs);
    public final boolean equals (Object ob)
    public final int compareTo (Object ob)

    public final int hashCode( )
    public final String toString( )
}
```

The Charset class encapsulates immutable information about a specific charset. Charset is abstract. Concrete instances are obtained by invoking the static factory method forName( ), passing in the name of the desired charset. All the Charset methods are thread-safe; a single instance can be shared among multiple threads.

The boolean class method isSupported( ) can be called to determine if a particular charset is currently available in the running JVM. New charsets can be installed dynamically through the Charset SPI mechanism, so the answer for a given charset name can change over time. The Charset SPI is discussed in the section "The Charset Service Provider Interface."

A charset can have multiple names. It always has a *canonical* name but can also have zero or more aliases. The canonical name or any of the aliases can be used with forName( ) and isSupported( ).

Some charsets also have historical names, which are used in previous Java platform releases and are retained for backward compatibility. Historical charset names are returned by the getEncoding( ) method of the InputStreamReader and OutputStreamWriter classes. If a charset has an historical name, it will be the canonical name or one of the aliases of the Charset. The Charset class does not provide an indication of which names are historical.

The last of the static class methods, availableCharsets( ), will return a java.util. SortedMap of all the charsets currently active in the JVM. As with isSupported( ), the values returned could change over time if new charsets are installed. The members of the returned map will be Charset objects with their canonical names as keys. When iterated, the map will be traversed in alphanumeric order by canonical name.

The availableCharsets( ) method is potentially slow. Although many charsets can be supported, they are typically not created until explicitly requested. Invoking

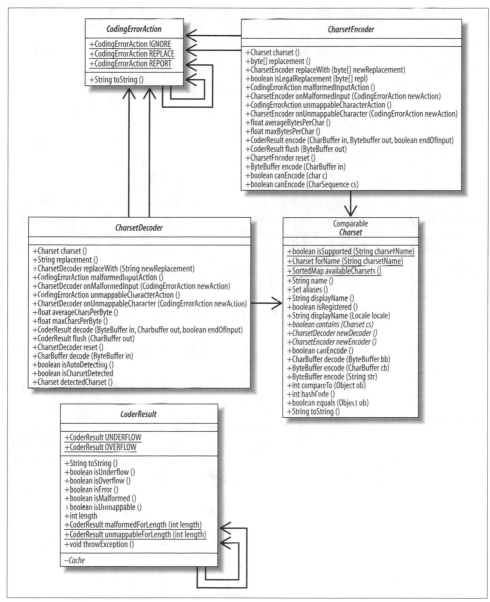

Figure 6-2. The charset classes

availableCharsets() requires that all known Charset objects be instantiated. Instantiating a Charset may require that libraries be loaded, network resources accessed, translation tables computed, etc. If you know the name of the charset you want to use, use the forName() method. Use availableCharsets() when you need to enumerate all available charsets—for example, to present a selection to an interactive user. Assuming that no new charsets are installed in the interim, the Map returned by availableCharsets( ) contains exactly the same charsets that are returnable by forName( ).

Once a reference to a Charset instance has been obtained, the name( ) method will return the canonical name of the charset, and aliases( ) will give you a Set containing the aliases. The Set returned by aliases( ) will never be null, but may be empty.

Each Charset object has two displayName( ) methods as well. The default implementations of these methods simply return the canonical charset name. These methods can provide a localized display name to use in a menu or selection box, for example. The displayName( ) method can take a Locale argument to specify a locale for localization. The no-argument version uses the default locale setting.

As mentioned at the beginning of this section, the IANA maintains the definitive registry of charset names. If a given Charset object represents a charset registered with the IANA, then the isRegistered( ) method will return true. If this is the case, then the Charset object is expected to comply with several requirements:

- Its canonical name should match the name in the IANA registry for the charset.
- If the IANA registry has multiple names for the charset, the canonical name returned by the object should match the MIME-preferred name denoted in the IANA registry.
- If the charset name is removed from the registry, the current canonical name should be retained as an alias.
- If the charset is not registered with the IANA, its canonical name must begin with either "X-" or "x-".

For the most part, only JVM vendors are concerned with these rules. However, if you plan to supply your own charsets as part of an application, it's good to know what you shouldn't do. You should return false for isRegistered( ) and name your charset with a leading "X-". See the section "The Charset Service Provider Interface."

Comparing Charsets

The following contains the API methods of Charset that we'll discuss in this section:

```
public abstract class Charset implements Comparable
{
        // This is a partial API listing

        public abstract boolean contains (Charset cs);
        public final boolean equals (Object ob)
        public final int compareTo (Object ob)

        public final int hashCode( )
        public final String toString( )
}
```

Recall that a charset is the combination of a coded set of characters and the encoding scheme for that character set. Like any set, it's possible for one charset to be a subset of another charset. One charset (C1) is said to *contain* another (C2), if every character that can be represented in C2 can also be represented identically in C1. Every charset is considered to contain itself. If this containment relationship holds, then any string you can encode in C2 (the contained subcharset) is guaranteed to be encodable in C1 without the need for any substitutions.

The contains( ) instance method indicates whether the Charset object passed as an argument is known to be contained by the charset encapsulated by that Charset object. This method does not do a runtime comparison of the charsets; it returns true only if the concrete Charset class knows that the given charset is contained. If contains( ) returns false, it indicates either that a containment relationship is known not to exist or that nothing is known about the containment relationship.

If a charset is contained by another, this does not imply that the encoded byte sequences generated will be identical for a given input character sequence.

The Charset class explicitly overrides the Object.equals( ) method. Instances of Charset are considered to be equal if they have the same canonical name (as returned by name( )). In the JDK 1.4.0 release, the comparison performed by equals( ) is a simple comparison of the canonical name strings, which means that the test is case-sensitive. This is a bug that should be corrected in future releases. Since the Charset.equals( ) method overrides the default method in the Object class, it must declare a parameter of type Object rather than Charset. A Charset object is never equal to any other class of object.

 The implementation of Charset in JDK 1.4 returns the same object handle for all invocations of forName( ) that map to the same charset. This means that comparing Charset object references with the == operator appears to work as well as using the equals( ) method. Always use the equals( ) method to test equality. The implementation could change in the future, and if it does, your code will break.

You probably noticed in the previous listing that Charset implements the Comparable interface, which implies that it provides a compareTo( ) method. Like equals( ), compareTo( ) returns a result based on a the canonical name of the Charset object. The compareTo( ) method of Charset ignores case when doing comparisons. If a set of Charset objects are sorted, they will be ordered by their canonical names, ignoring case. Again, because the compareTo( ) method defined in Comparable takes an Object as the argument type, the one defined here does too. If you pass a non-Charset object to the compareTo( ) method you will generate a ClassCastException. compareTo( ) cannot compare dissimilar object instances.

Continuing the theme of identifying Charset objects by their canonical names, the hashCode( ) method returns the hash code of the String returned by the name( )

method (which means that the hash code is case-sensitive). The toString( ) method of Charset returns the canonical name. Most of the time, the implementation of the hashCode( ) and toString( ) methods are not of much interest. They are mentioned here because the Charset class overrides them, which could affect how they behave if used in hash maps or how they appear in a debugger.

Now that we've covered the simple API methods, let's take a look at character set coders. This is where the conversion between characters and byte streams is actually done.

Charset Encoders

Charsets are composed of a coded character set and a related encoding scheme. The CharsetEncoder and CharsetDecoder classes implement the transcoding scheme. (See Figure 6-1.)

```
public abstract class Charset implements Comparable
{
        // This is a partial API listing

        public boolean canEncode( )
        public abstract CharsetEncoder newEncoder();
        public final ByteBuffer encode (CharBuffer cb)
        public final ByteBuffer encode (String str)
}
```

The first API method of interest here is canEncode( ). This method indicates whether encoding is allowed by this charset. Nearly all charsets support encoding. The main exceptions are charsets with decoders that are capable of autodetecting how a byte sequence was encoded and then selecting an appropriate decoding scheme. These charsets typically only support decoding and do not create encodings of their own.

The canEncode( ) method returns true if this Charset object is capable of encoding a sequence of characters. If false, the other three methods listed above should not be called on that object. Doing so results in an UnsupportedOperationException.

Calling newEncoder( ) returns a CharsetEncoder object capable of converting character sequences to byte sequences using the encoding scheme associated with the charset. We'll look at the API of the CharsetEncoder class later in this section, but we'll first take a quick look at the two remaining methods of Charset.

The two encode( ) methods of Charset are conveniences that perform encodings using default values for the encoder associated with the charset. Both return new ByteBuffer objects containing an encoded byte sequence corresponding to the characters of the given String or CharBuffer. Encoders always operate on CharBuffer objects. The form of encode( ) that takes a String argument creates a temporary CharBuffer for you automatically that is equivalent to this:

```
charset.encode (CharBuffer.wrap (string));
```

Invoking encode( ) on a Charset object uses default settings for the encoder and is equivalent to the following code:

```
charset.newEncoder( )
        .onMalformedInput (CodingErrorAction.REPLACE)
        .onUnmappableCharacter (CodingErrorAction.REPLACE)
        .encode (charBuffer);
```

As we'll learn in a later discussion, this runs an encoder that replaces any unrecognized or invalid input characters with a default byte sequence.

Let's look at the API for CharsetEncoder to more fully understand the process of character encoding:

```
package java.nio.charset;

public abstract class CharsetEncoder
{
        public final Charset charset( )
        public final float averageBytesPerChar( )
        public final float maxBytesPerChar( )

        public final CharsetEncoder reset( )
        public final ByteBuffer encode (CharBuffer in) throws
                CharacterCodingException
        public final CoderResult encode (CharBuffer in, ByteBuffer out,
                boolean endOfInput)
        public final CoderResult flush (ByteBuffer out)

        public boolean canEncode (char c)
        public boolean canEncode (CharSequence cs)

        public CodingErrorAction malformedInputAction( )
        public final CharsetEncoder onMalformedInput (CodingErrorAction newAction)
        public CodingErrorAction unmappableCharacterAction( )
        public final CharsetEncoder onUnmappableCharacter (
                CodingErrorAction newAction)

        public final byte [] replacement( )
        public boolean isLegalReplacement (byte[] repl)
        public final CharsetEncoder replaceWith (byte[] newReplacement)
}
```

A CharsetEncoder object is a stateful transformation engine: characters go in and bytes come out. Several calls to the encoder may be required to complete a transformation. The encoder remembers the state of the transformation between calls.

The first group of methods listed here provide immutable information about the CharsetEncoder object. Every encoder is associated with a Charset object, and the charset( ) method returns a back reference.

The averageBytesPerChar( ) method returns a floating-point value representing the average number of bytes needed to encode a character of the set. Note that this can be a fractional value. An encoding algorithm may choose to span byte boundaries when encoding characters, or some characters may encode into more bytes than others (UTF-8 works in this way). This method is useful as a heuristic to determine the approximate size of the ByteBuffer needed to contain the encoded bytes of a given sequence of characters.

Finally, the maxBytesPerChar( ) method indicates the largest number of bytes needed to encode a single character in the set. This is also a float value. Like averageBytesPerChar( ), this method can be used to size a ByteBuffer. Multiplying the value returned from maxBytesPerChar( ) by the number of characters to be encoded will yield a worst-case output buffer size.

Before we get into the nitty gritty of encoding, a note about the CharsetEncoder API: the first, simpler form of encode( ) is a convenience form that does an all-in-one encoding of the CharBuffer you provide in a newly allocated ByteBuffer. This is the method ultimately invoked when you call encode( ) directly on the Charset class.

When using the CharsetEncoder object, you have the option of setting error-handling preferences before or during encoding. (We'll discuss handling encoding errors later in this section.) Invoking the single-argument form of encode( ) performs a complete encoding cycle (reset, encode, and flush), so any prior internal state of the encoder will be lost.

Let's look closer at how the encoding process works. The CharsetEncoder class is a stateful encoding engine. The fact that encoders are stateful implies that they are not thread-safe; CharsetEncoder objects should not be shared among threads. Encoding can be done in a single step, as in the first form of encode( ) described above, or by calling the second form of encode( ) repeatedly. The process of encoding occurs as follows:

1. Reset the state of the encoder by calling the reset( ) method. This prepares the encoding engine to begin generating an encoded byte stream. A newly created CharsetEncoder object does not need to be reset, but it doesn't hurt to do so.

2. Invoke encode( ) zero or more times to supply characters to the encoder, with the endOfInput argument false to indicate that more characters may follow. Characters will be consumed from the given CharBuffer, and the encoded byte sequence will be appended to the provided ByteBuffer.

   Upon return, the input CharBuffer may not be fully empty. The output ByteBuffer may have filled up, or the encoder may require more input to complete a multicharacter translation. The encoder itself may also be holding state that could affect how subsequent translations are performed. Compact the input buffer before refilling it.

3. Call encode( ) a final time, passing true for the endOfInput argument. The provided CharBuffer may contain additional characters to be encoded or may be

empty. The important thing is that endOfInput is true on the last invocation. This lets the encoding engine know that no more input is coming, which allows it to detect malformed input.

4. Invoke the flush( ) method to complete any unfinished encoding and output all remaining bytes. If there is insufficient room in the output ByteBuffer, it may be necessary to call this method multiple times.

The encode( ) method returns when it has consumed all the input, when the output ByteBuffer is full, or when a coding error has been detected. In any case, a CoderResult object will be returned to indicate what happened. The result object can indicate one of the following result conditions:

Underflow

This is normal and indicates that more input is required. Either the input CharBuffer content has been exhausted or, if it's not empty, the remaining characters cannot be processed without additional input. The position of the CharBuffer is updated to account for any characters consumed by the encoder.

Fill the CharBuffer with more characters to be encoded (calling compact( ) on the buffer first, if nonempty) and call encode( ) again to continue. If you're finished, call encode( ) with the empty CharBuffer and true for endOfInput, then call flush( ) to make sure that all bytes have been sent to the ByteBuffer.

An underflow condition always returns the same object instance: a static class variable named CharsetEncoder.UNDERFLOW. This allows you to use the equality operator (==) on the returned object handle to test for underflow.

Overflow

This indicates that the encoder has filled the output ByteBuffer and needs to generate more encoded output. The input CharBuffer object may or may not be exhausted. This is a normal condition and does not indicate an error. You should drain the ByteBuffer but not disturb the CharBuffer, which will have had its position updated, then invoke encode( ) again. Repeat until you get an underflow result.

Like underflow, overflow returns a unity instance, CharsetEncoder.OVERFLOW, which can be used directly in equality comparisons.

Malformed input

When encoding, this usually means that a character contains a 16-bit numeric value that is not a valid Unicode character. For decode, this means that the decoder encountered a sequence of bytes it doesn't recognize.

The returned CoderResult instance will not be a singleton reference as it is for underflow and overflow. See the API of CoderResult in the section "The Coder-Result class."

Unmappable character

This indicates that the encoder is unable to map a character or sequence of characters to bytes—for example, if you're using the ISO-8859-1 encoding but your input CharBuffer contains non-Latin Unicode characters. For decode, the decoder understands the input byte sequence but does not know how to create corresponding characters.

While encoding, the encoder returns result objects if it encounters malformed or unmappable input. You can also test individual characters, or sequences of characters, to determine if they can be encoded. Here are the methods for testing whether encoding is possible:

```
package java.nio.charset;

public abstract class CharsetEncoder
{
        // This is a partial API listing

        public boolean canEncode (char c)
        public boolean canEncode (CharSequence cs)
}
```

The two forms of canEncode( ) return a boolean result indicating whether the encoder is capable of encoding the given input. Both methods perform an encoding of the input into a temporary buffer. This will cause changes to the encoder's internal state, so these methods should not be called while the encoding process is underway. Use these methods to check your input prior to starting the encoding process.

The second form of canEncode( ) takes an argument of type CharSequence, which was introduced in Chapter 5. Any object that implements CharSequence (currently CharBuffer, String, or StringBuffer) can be passed to canEncode( ).

The remaining methods of CharsetEncoder are involved with handling encoding errors:

```
public abstract class CharsetEncoder
{
        // This is a partial API listing

        public CodingErrorAction malformedInputAction( )
        public final CharsetEncoder onMalformedInput (CodingErrorAction newAction)

        public CodingErrorAction unmappableCharacterAction( )
        public final CharsetEncoder onUnmappableCharacter (
                CodingErrorAction newAction)

        public final byte [] replacement( )
        public boolean isLegalReplacement (byte[] repl)
        public final CharsetEncoder replaceWith (byte[] newReplacement)
}
```

As mentioned earlier, a CoderResult object can be returned from encode( ) indicating problems with encoding a character sequence. There are two defined coding-error conditions: *malformed* and *unmappable*. An encoder instance can be configured to take different actions on each of these error conditions. The CodingErrorAction class encapsulates the possible actions to take when one of these conditions occurs. CodingErrorAction is a trivial class with no useful methods. It's a simple, type-safe enumeration that contains static, named instances of itself. The CodingErrorAction class defines three public fields:

REPORT
> The default action when a CharsetEncoder is created. This action indicates that coding errors should be reported by returning a CoderResult object, as described earlier.

IGNORE
> Indicates that coding errors should be ignored and any erroneous input dropped as if it wasn't there.

REPLACE
> Handles coding errors by dropping the erroneous input and outputting the replacement byte sequence currently defined for this CharsetEncoder.

Now that we know the possible error actions, how to use the first four methods in the previous API listing should be fairly obvious. The malformedInputAction() method returns the action in effect for malformed input. Calling onMalformedInput() sets the CodingErrorAction value to be used from then on. A similar pair of methods for unmappable characters sets error actions and returns the CharsetEncoder object handle. By returning the CharsetEncoder, these methods allow invocation chaining. For example:

```
CharsetEncoder encoder = charset.newEncoder()
        .onMalformedInput (CodingErrorAction.REPLACE)
        .onUnmappableCharacter (CodingErrorAction.IGNORE);
```

The final group of methods on CharsetEncoder deal with managing the replacement sequence to be used when the action is CodingErrorAction.REPLACE.

The current replacement byte sequence can be retrieved by calling the replacement() method. If you haven't set your own replacement sequence, this will return the default.

You can test the legality of a replacement sequence by calling the isLegalReplacement() method with the byte array you'd like to use. The replacement byte sequence must be a valid encoding for the charset. Remember, character set encoding transforms characters into byte sequences for later decoding. If the replacement sequence cannot be decoded into a valid character sequence, the encoded byte sequence becomes invalid.

Finally, you can set a new replacement sequence by calling replaceWith() and passing in a byte array. The given byte sequence will be output when a coding error occurs and the corresponding error action is set to CodingErrorAction.REPLACE. The byte sequence in the array must be a legal replacement value; java.lang.IllegalArgumentException will be thrown if it is not. The return value is the CharsetEncoder object itself.

The CoderResult class

Let's take a look at the CoderResult class mentioned earlier. CoderResult objects are returned by CharsetEncoder and CharsetDecoder objects:

```
package java.nio.charset;

public class CoderResult {
        public static final CoderResult OVERFLOW
        public static final CoderResult UNDERFLOW

        public boolean isUnderflow( )
        public boolean isOverflow( )
        public boolean isError( )
        public boolean isMalformed( )
        public boolean isUnmappable( )

        public int length( )

        public static CoderResult malformedForLength (int length)
        public static CoderResult unmappableForLength (int length)
        public void throwException( ) throws CharacterCodingException
}
```

As mentioned earlier, unity instances of CoderResult are returned for every underflow and overflow condition. You can see these defined above as public static fields in the CoderResult class. These instances can make it easier to test for the common cases. You can directly compare a CoderResult object against these public fields using the == operator (see Example 6-2). Regardless of which CoderResult object you have, you can always use the API to determine the meaning of the returned result.

The first two methods, isUnderflow( ) and isOverflow( ), are not considered errors. If either of these methods return true, then no further information can be obtained from the CoderResult object. The CoderResult.UNDERFLOW instance always returns true for isUnderflow( ), and CoderResult.OVERFLOW always returns true for isOverflow( ).

The other two boolean functions, isMalformed( ) and isUnmappable( ), are error conditions. The isError( ) method is a convenience method that returns true if either of these methods would return true.

If the CoderResult instance represents an error condition, the length( ) method tells you the length of the erroneous input sequence. For normal underflow/overflow conditions, there is no associated length (which is why a single instance can be shared). If you invoke length( ) on an instance of CoderResult that doesn't represent an error (isError( ) returns false), it throws the unchecked java.lang.UnsupportedOperation-Exception, so be careful. For instances with a length, the input CharBuffer would have been positioned to the first erroneous character.

The CoderResult class also includes three convenience methods to make life easier for developers of custom encoders and decoders (which you'll see how to do in the section

---

"The Charset Service Provider Interface"). The CoderResult constructor is private: you can't instantiate it directly or subclass it to make your own. We've already seen that CoderResult instances representing overflow and underflow are singletons. For instances representing errors, the only unique bit of information they contain is the value returned by length( ). The two factory methods malformedForLength( ) and unmappableForLength( ) return an instance of CoderResult returns true from isMalformed( ) or isUnmappable( ), respectively, and whose length( ) method returns the value you provide. These factory methods always return the same CoderResult instance for a given length.

In some contexts, it's more appropriate to throw an exception than to pass along a CoderResult object. For example, the all-in-one encode( ) method of the CharsetEncoder class throws an exception if it encounters a coding error. The throwException( ) method is a convenience that throws an appropriate subclass of CharacterCodingException, as summarized in Table 6-3.

Table 6-3. Exceptions thrown by CoderResult.throwException( )

Result type	Exception
isUnderflow( )	BufferUnderflowException
isOverflow( )	BufferOverflowException
isMalformed( )	MalformedInputException
isUnmappable( )	UnmappableCharacterException

Charset Decoders

A charset decoder is the inverse of an encoder. It transforms a sequence of bytes encoded by a particular encoding scheme into a sequence of 16-bit Unicode characters. Like CharsetEncoder, CharsetDecoder is a stateful transformation engine. Neither is thread-safe because state is remembered across calls to their methods.

```
package java.nio.charset;

public abstract class CharsetDecoder
{
        public final Charset charset( )
        public final float averageCharsPerByte( )
        public final float maxCharsPerByte( )

        public boolean isAutoDetecting( )
        public boolean isCharsetDetected( )
        public Charset detectedCharset( )

        public final CharsetDecoder reset( )
        public final CharBuffer decode (ByteBuffer in)
                throws CharacterCodingException
```

```
public final CoderResult decode (ByteBuffer in, CharBuffer out,
        boolean endOfInput)
public final CoderResult flush (CharBuffer out)

public CodingErrorAction malformedInputAction()
public final CharsetDecoder onMalformedInput (CodingErrorAction newAction)
public CodingErrorAction unmappableCharacterAction()
public final CharsetDecoder onUnmappableCharacter (
        CodingErrorAction newAction)

public final String replacement()
public final CharsetDecoder replaceWith (String newReplacement)
}
```

As you can see, the API of CharsetDecoder is nearly a mirror image of CharsetEncoder. In this section, we'll concentrate on the differences, proceeding with the assumption that you've already read the section "Charset Encoders."

The first group of methods in the previous listing is self-evident. The associated Charset object can be obtained by calling charset(). The average and maximum number of characters decoded from each byte in this encoding are returned by averageCharsPerByte() and maxCharsPerByte(), respectively. These values can be used to size a CharBuffer object to receive decoded characters.

The CharsetDecoder class has its own set of methods that are unique to it. In the previous listing, these methods have to do with charset autodetection. The first method, isAutoDetecting(), returns a boolean value indicating whether this decoder is capable of autodetecting the encoding scheme used by an encoded byte sequence.

If isAutoDetecting() returns true, then the two methods following it in the previous listing are meaningful. The isCharsetDetected() method will return true if the decoder has read enough bytes from the input byte sequence to determine the type of encoding used. This method is useful only when the decoding process has begun (because it must read some of the bytes and examine them). Following a call to reset(), it will always return false. This method is optional and meaningful only for autodetecting charsets. The default implementation always throws a java.lang.UnsupportedOperationException.

If a charset has been detected (indicated by isCharsetDetected() returning true), then a Charset object representing that charset can be obtained by calling detectedCharset(). You shouldn't call this method unless you know that a charset has actually been detected. If the decoder has not yet read enough input to determine the charset represented by the encoding, a java.lang.IllegalStateException will be thrown. The detectedCharset() method is also optional and will throw the same java.lang.UnsupportedOperationException if the charset is not autodetecting. Use isAutoDetecting() and isCharsetDetected() sensibly, and you shouldn't have any problem.

Now, let's turn to the methods that actually do the decoding:

```
package java.nio.charset;

public abstract class CharsetDecoder
{
        // This is a partial API listing

        public final CharsetDecoder reset()
        public final CharBuffer decode (ByteBuffer in)
            throws CharacterCodingException
        public final CoderResult decode (ByteBuffer in, CharBuffer out,
            boolean endOfInput)
        public final CoderResult flush (CharBuffer out)
}
```

The decoding process is similar to encoding. It includes the same basic steps:

1. Reset the decoder, by invoking reset( ), to place the decoder in a known state ready to accept input.

2. Invoke decode( ) zero or more times with endOfInput set to false to feed bytes into the decoding engine. Characters will be added to the given CharBuffer as decoding progresses.

3. Invoke decode( ) one time with endOfInput set to true to let the decoder know that all input has been provided.

4. Call flush( ) to ensure that all decoded characters have been sent to the output.

This is essentially the same process as for encoding (refer to the section "Charset Encoders" for more details). The decode( ) method also returns CoderResult objects to indicate what happened. The meaning of these result objects is identical to those returned by CharsetEncoder.encode( ). Input and output buffers should be managed in the same way as for encoding when underflow or overflow indications are returned.

And now, the methods for handling errors:

```
package java.nio.charset;

public abstract class CharsetDecoder
{
        // This is a partial API listing

        public CodingErrorAction malformedInputAction()
        public final CharsetDecoder onMalformedInput (CodingErrorAction newAction)
        public CodingErrorAction unmappableCharacterAction()
        public final CharsetDecoder onUnmappableCharacter (
            CodingErrorAction newAction)

        public final String replacement()
        public final CharsetDecoder replaceWith (String newReplacement)
}
```

The API methods dealing with replacement sequences operate on Strings rather than on byte arrays. When decoding, byte sequences are converted to character sequences, so the replacement sequence for a decode operation is specified as a String containing characters to be inserted in the output CharBuffer on an error condition. Note that there is no isLegalReplacement( ) method to test the replacement sequence. Any string you can construct is a legal replacement sequence, unless it's longer than the value returned by maxCharsPerByte( ). Invoking replaceWith( ) with a string that's too long will result in a java.lang.IllegalArgumentException.

This section is intentionally terse. For more detailed information, flip back a few pages to the section "Charset Encoders."

Example 6-2 illustrates how to decode a stream of bytes representing a character set encoding.

Example 6-2. Charset decoding

```java
package com.ronsoft.books.nio.charset;

import java.nio.*;
import java.nio.charset.*;
import java.nio.channels.*;
import java.io.*;

/**
 * Test charset decoding.
 * @author Ron Hitchens (ron@ronsoft.com)
 */
public class CharsetDecode
{
    /**
     * Test charset decoding in the general case, detecting and handling
     * buffer under/overflow and flushing the decoder state at end of
     * input.
     * This code reads from stdin and decodes the ASCII-encoded byte
     * stream to chars.  The decoded chars are written to stdout.  This
     * is effectively a 'cat' for input ascii files, but another charset
     * encoding could be used by simply specifying it on the command line.
     */
    public static void main (String [] argv)
        throws IOException
    {
        // Default charset is standard ASCII
        String charsetName = "ISO-8859-1";

        // Charset name can be specified on the command line
        if (argv.length > 0) {
            charsetName = argv [0];
        }

        // Wrap a Channel around stdin, wrap a channel around stdout,
        // find the named Charset and pass them to the decode method.
```

Example 6-2. Charset decoding (continued)

```
        // If the named charset is not valid, an exception of type
        // UnsupportedCharsetException will be thrown.
        decodeChannel (Channels.newChannel (System.in),
            new OutputStreamWriter (System.out),
            Charset.forName (charsetName));
    }

    /**
     * General purpose static method which reads bytes from a Channel,
     * decodes them according
     * @param source A ReadableByteChannel object which will be read to
     *   EOF as a source of encoded bytes.
     * @param writer A Writer object to which decoded chars will be written.
     * @param charset A Charset object, whose CharsetDecoder will be used
     *   to do the character set decoding.
     */
    public static void decodeChannel (ReadableByteChannel source,
        Writer writer, Charset charset)
        throws UnsupportedCharsetException, IOException
    {
        // Get a decoder instance from the Charset
        CharsetDecoder decoder = charset.newDecoder();

        // Tell decoder to replace bad chars with default mark
        decoder.onMalformedInput (CodingErrorAction.REPLACE);
        decoder.onUnmappableCharacter (CodingErrorAction.REPLACE);

        // Allocate radically different input and output buffer sizes
        // for testing purposes
        ByteBuffer bb = ByteBuffer.allocateDirect (16 * 1024);
        CharBuffer cb = CharBuffer.allocate (57);

        // Buffer starts empty; indicate input is needed
        CoderResult result = CoderResult.UNDERFLOW;
        boolean eof = false;

        while ( ! eof) {
            // Input buffer underflow; decoder wants more input
            if (result == CoderResult.UNDERFLOW) {
                // decoder consumed all input, prepare to refill
                bb.clear();

                // Fill the input buffer; watch for EOF
                eof = (source.read (bb) == -1);

                // Prepare the buffer for reading by decoder
                bb.flip();
            }

            // Decode input bytes to output chars; pass EOF flag
            result = decoder.decode (bb, cb, eof);
```

Example 6-2. Charset decoding (continued)

```
            // If output buffer is full, drain output
            if (result == CoderResult.OVERFLOW) {
                drainCharBuf (cb, writer);
            }
        }

        // Flush any remaining state from the decoder, being careful
        // to detect output buffer overflow(s)
        while (decoder.flush (cb) == CoderResult.OVERFLOW) {
            drainCharBuf (cb, writer);
        }

        // Drain any chars remaining in the output buffer
        drainCharBuf (cb, writer);

        // Close the channel; push out any buffered data to stdout
        source.close( );
        writer.flush( );
    }

    /**
     * Helper method to drain the char buffer and write its content to
     * the given Writer object.  Upon return, the buffer is empty and
     * ready to be refilled.
     * @param cb A CharBuffer containing chars to be written.
     * @param writer A Writer object to consume the chars in cb.
     */
    static void drainCharBuf (CharBuffer cb, Writer writer)
        throws IOException
    {
        cb.flip( );          // Prepare buffer for draining

        // This writes the chars contained in the CharBuffer but
        // doesn't actually modify the state of the buffer.
        // If the char buffer was being drained by calls to get( ),
        // a loop might be needed here.
        if (cb.hasRemaining( )) {
            writer.write (cb.toString( ));
        }

        cb.clear( );          // Prepare buffer to be filled again
    }
}
```

That pretty much wraps up charsets and their related encoders and decoders. The next section will cover the Charset SPI.

The Charset Service Provider Interface

The Charset SPI provides a mechanism for developers to add new Charset implementations to the running JVM environment. If you have a need to create your own charsets, or port a charset not provided on the JVM platform you're using, the charset SPI is what you'll use.

The pluggable SPI architecture is used throughout the Java environment in many different contexts. There are eight packages in the 1.4 JDK named spi and several others that go by other names. Pluggability is a powerful design technique, one of the cornerstones upon which Java's portability and adaptability are built.

Charsets are formally defined by the IANA, and standardized charsets are registered there. Charset handling in Java as of 1.4 is based solidly upon the conventions and standards promulgated by the IANA. The IANA not only registers names, but also has rules about the structure and content of those names (RFC 2278). If you create new Charset implementations, you should follow the conventions for charset names. The Charset class enforces the same rules. For example, the name of a charset must be composed from the set of characters listed in Table 6-4, and the first character must be a letter or a digit.

Table 6-4. Legal characters for charset names

Character(s)	Unicode value(s)	RFC 2278 name
A–Z	\u0041–\u005a	
a–z	\u0061–\u007a	
0–9	\u0030–\u0039	
- (dash)	\u002d	HYPHEN-MINUS
. (period)	\u002e	FULLSTOP
: (colon)	\u003a	COLON
_ (underscore)	\u005f	LOWLINE

Before looking at the API, a little explanation of how the Charset SPI works is needed. The java.nio.charset.spi package contains only one abstract class, CharsetProvider. Concrete implementations of this class supply information about Charset objects they provide. To define a custom charset, you must first create concrete implementations of Charset, CharsetEncoder, and CharsetDecoder from the java.nio.charset package. You then create a custom subclass of CharsetProvider, which will provide those classes to the JVM.

A complete sample implementation of a custom charset and provider is listed in the section "Custom Charset Example."

Creating Custom Charsets

Before looking at the one and only class in the java.nio.charset.spi package, let's linger a bit longer in java.nio.charset and discuss what's needed to implement a custom charset. You need to create a Charset object before you can make it available in a running JVM. Let's take another look at the Charset API, adding the constructor and noting the abstract methods:

```
package java.nio.charset;

public abstract class Charset implements Comparable
{
        protected Charset (String canonicalName, String [] aliases)

        public static SortedMap availableCharsets( )
        public static boolean isSupported (String charsetName)
        public static Charset forName (String charsetName)

        public final String name( )
        public final Set aliases( )
        public String displayName( )
        public String displayName (Locale locale)

        public final boolean isRegistered( )

        public boolean canEncode( )
        public abstract CharsetEncoder newEncoder( );
        public final ByteBuffer encode (CharBuffer cb)
        public final ByteBuffer encode (String str)

        public abstract CharsetDecoder newDecoder( );
        public final CharBuffer decode (ByteBuffer bb)

        public abstract boolean contains (Charset cs);
        public final boolean equals (Object ob)
        public final int compareTo (Object ob)

        public final int hashCode( )
        public final String toString( )
}
```

The minimum you'll need to do is create a subclass of java.nio.charset.Charset and provide concrete implementations of the three abstract methods and a constructor. The Charset class does not have a default, no-argument constructor. This means that your custom charset class must have a constructor, even if it doesn't take arguments. This is because you must invoke Charset's constructor at instantiation time (by calling super( ) at the beginning of your constructor) to provide it with your charset's canonical name and aliases. Doing this lets methods in the Charset class handle the name-related stuff for you, so it's a good thing.

Two of the three abstract methods are simple factories by which your custom encoder and decoder classes will be obtained. You'll also need to implement the boolean method contains( ), but you can punt this by always returning false, which indicates that you don't know if your charset contains the given charset. All the other Charset methods have default implementations that will work in most cases. If your charset has special needs, override the default methods as appropriate.

You'll also need to provide concrete implementations of CharsetEncoder and Charset-Decoder. Recall that a charset is a set of coded characters and an encode/decode scheme. As we've seen in previous sections, encoding and decoding are nearly symmetrical at the API level. A brief discussion of what's needed to implement an encoder is given here; the same applies to building a decoder. This is the listing for the CharsetEncoder class, with its constructors and protected and abstract methods added:

```
package java.nio.charset;

public abstract class CharsetEncoder
{
        protected CharsetEncoder (Charset cs,
                float averageBytesPerChar, float maxBytesPerChar)

        protected CharsetEncoder (Charset cs,
                float averageBytesPerChar, float maxBytesPerChar,
                byte [] replacement)

        public final Charset charset( )
        public final float averageBytesPerChar( )
        public final float maxBytesPerChar( )

        public final CharsetEncoder reset( )
        protected void implReset( )
        public final ByteBuffer encode (CharBuffer in)
                throws CharacterCodingException
        public final CoderResult encode (CharBuffer in, ByteBuffer out,
                boolean endOfInput)
        public final CoderResult flush (ByteBuffer out)
        protected CoderResult implFlush(ByteBuffer out)

        public boolean canEncode (char c)
        public boolean canEncode (CharSequence cs)

        public CodingErrorAction malformedInputAction( )
        public final CharsetEncoder onMalformedInput (CodingErrorAction newAction)
        protected void implOnMalformedInput (CodingErrorAction newAction)
        public CodingErrorAction unmappableCharacterAction( )
        public final CharsetEncoder onUnmappableCharacter (
                CodingErrorAction newAction)
        protected void implOnUnmappableCharacter (CodingErrorAction newAction)

        public final byte [] replacement( )
        public boolean isLegalReplacement (byte[] repl)
```

```
        public final CharsetEncoder replaceWith (byte[] newReplacement)
        protected void implReplaceWith (byte[] newReplacement)

        protected abstract CoderResult encodeLoop (CharBuffer in,
                ByteBuffer out);
    }
```

Like Charset, CharsetEncoder does not have a default constructor, so you'll need to call super( ) in your concrete class constructor to provide the needed parameters.

Take a look at the last method first. To provide your own CharsetEncoder implementation, the minimum you need to do is provide a concrete encodeLoop( ) method. For a simple encoding algorithm, the default implementations of the other methods should work fine. Note that encodeLoop( ) takes arguments similar to encode( )'s, excluding the boolean flag. The encode( ) method delegates the actual encoding to encodeLoop( ), which only needs to be concerned about consuming characters from the CharBuffer argument and outputting the encoded bytes to the provided ByteBuffer.

The main encode( ) method takes care of remembering state across invocations and handling coding errors. Like encode( ), the encodeLoop( ) method returns CoderResult objects to indicate what happened while processing the buffers. If your encodeLoop( ) fills the output ByteBuffer, it should return CoderResult.OVERFLOW. If the input CharBuffer is exhausted, CoderResult.UNDERFLOW should be returned. If your encoder requires more input than what is in the input buffer to make a coding decision, you can perform a look-ahead by returning UNDERFLOW until sufficient input is present in the CharBuffer to continue.

The remaining protected methods listed above—those beginning with impl—are status change callback hooks that notify the implementation (your code) when changes are made to the state of the encoder. The default implementations of all these methods are stubs that do nothing. For example, if you maintain additional state in your encoder, you may need to know when the encoder is being reset. You can't override the reset( ) method itself becase it's declared as final. The implReset( ) method is provided to call you when reset( ) is invoked on CharsetEncoder to let you know what happened in a cleanly decoupled way. The other impl classes play the same role for the other events of interest.

For reference, this is the equivalent API listing for CharsetDecoder:

```
    package java.nio.charset;

    public abstract class CharsetDecoder
    {
        protected CharsetDecoder (Charset cs, float averageCharsPerByte,
                float maxCharsPerByte)

        public final Charset charset( )
        public final float averageCharsPerByte( )
        public final float maxCharsPerByte( )
```

```
        public boolean isAutoDetecting( )
        public boolean isCharsetDetected( )
        public Charset detectedCharset( )

        public final CharsetDecoder reset( )
        protected void implReset( )
        public final CharBuffer decode (ByteBuffer in)
                throws CharacterCodingException
        public final CoderResult decode (ByteBuffer in, CharBuffer out,
                boolean endOfInput)
        public final CoderResult flush (CharBuffer out)
        protected CoderResult implFlush (CharBuffer out)

        public CodingErrorAction malformedInputAction( )
        public final CharsetDecoder onMalformedInput (CodingErrorAction newAction)
        protected void implOnMalformedInput (CodingErrorAction newAction)
        public CodingErrorAction unmappableCharacterAction( )
        public final CharsetDecoder onUnmappableCharacter (
                CodingErrorAction newAction)
        protected void implOnUnmappableCharacter (CodingErrorAction newAction)

        public final String replacement( )
        public final CharsetDecoder replaceWith (String newReplacement)
        protected void implReplaceWith (String newReplacement)

        protected abstract CoderResult decodeLoop (ByteBuffer in, CharBuffer out);
    }
```

Now that we've seen how to implement custom charsets, including the associated encoders and decoders, let's see how to hook them into the JVM so that running code can make use of them.

Providing Your Custom Charsets

To provide your own Charset implementation to the JVM runtime environment, you must create a concrete subclass of the CharsetProvider class in java.nio. charsets.spi, one with a no-argument constructor. The no-argument constructor is important because your CharsetProvider class will be located by reading its fully qualified name from a configuration file. This class name string will then be passed to Class.newInstance( ) to instantiate your provider, which works only for objects with no-argument constructors.

The configuration file read by the JVM to locate charset providers is named *java.nio. charset.spi.CharsetProvider*. It is located in a resource directory (*META-INF/services*) in the JVM classpath. Every Java Archive (JAR) file has a *META-INF* directory that can contain information about the classes and resources in that JAR. A directory named *META-INF* can be placed at the top of a regular directory hierarchy in the JVM classpath as well.

Each file in the *META-INF/services* directory has the name of a fully qualified service provider class. The content of each file is a list of fully qualified class names that are concrete implementations of that class (so each of the classes named within a file must be an instanceof the class represented by the name of the file). See the JAR specification at *http://java.sun.com/j2se/1.4/docs/guide/jar/jar.html* for full details.

If a *META-INF/services* directory exists when a classpath component (either a JAR or a directory) is first examined by the class loader, then each of the files that it contains will be processed. Each is read and all the classes listed are instantiated and registered as service providers for the class identified by the name of the file. By placing the fully qualified name of your CharsetProvider class in a file named *java.nio.charset.spi.CharsetProvider*, you are registering it as a provider of charsets.

The format of the configuration file is a simple list of fully qualified class names, one per line. The comment character is the hash sign (#, \u0023). The file must be encoded in UTF-8 (standard text file). The classes named in this services list do not need to reside in the same JAR, but the classes must be visible to the same context class loader (i.e., be in the same classpath). If the same CharsetProvider class is named in more than one services file, or more than once in the same file, it will be added only once as a service provider.

This mechanism makes it easy to install a new CharsetProvider and the Charset implementation(s) it provides. The JAR containing your charset implementation, and the services file naming it, only needs to be in the classpath of the JVM. You can also install it as an extension to your JVM by placing a JAR in the defined extension directory for your operating system (*jre/lib/ext* in most cases). Your custom charset would then be available every time the JVM runs.

There is no specified API mechanism to add new charsets to the JVM programmatically. Individual JVM implementations can provide an API, but JDK 1.4 does not provide a means to do so.

Now that we know how the CharsetProvider class is used to add charsets, let's look at the code. The API of CharsetProvider is almost trivial. The real work of providing custom charsets is in creating your custom Charset, CharsetEncoder, and CharsetDecoder classes. CharsetProvider is merely a facilitator that connects your charset to the runtime environment.

```
package java.nio.charset.spi;

public abstract class CharsetProvider
{
        protected CharsetProvider( ) throws SecurityException

        public abstract Iterator charsets( );
        public abstract Charset charsetForName (String charsetName);
}
```

Note the protected constructor. CharsetProvider should not be instantiated directly by your code. CharsetProvider objects will be instantiated by the low-level service provider facility. Define a default constructor in your CharsetProvider class if you need to set up the charsets your provider will make available. This could involve loading charset mapping information from an external resource, algorithmically generating translation maps, etc. Also note that the constructor for CharsetProvider can throw a java.lang.SecurityException.

Instantiation of CharsetProvider objects is checked by the SecurityManager (if one is installed). The security manager must allow java.lang.RuntimePermission("charset-Provider"), or no new charset providers can be installed. Charsets can be involved in security-sensitive operations, such as encoding URLs and other data content. The potential for mischief is significant. You may want to install a security manager that disallows new charsets if there is a potential for untrusted code running within your application. You may also want to examine untrusted JARs to see if they contain service configuration files under *META-INF/service* to install custom charset providers (or custom service providers of any sort).

The two methods defined on CharsetProvider are called by consumers of the Charset implementations you're providing. In most cases, your provider will be called by the static methods of the Charset class to discover information about available charsets, but other classes can call these methods as well.

The charsets( ) method is called to obtain a list of the Charset classes your provider class makes available. It should return a java.util.Iterator, enumerating references to the provided Charset instances. The map returned by the Charset.availableCharsets( ) method is an aggregate of invoking the charsets( ) method on each currently installed CharsetProvider instance.

The other method, charsetForName( ), is called to map a charset name, either canonical or an alias, to a Charset object. This method should return null if your provider does not provide a charset by the requested name.

That's all there is to it. You now have all the necessary tools to create your own custom charsets and their associated encoders and decoders, and to plug them into a live, running JVM. Implementation of a custom Charset and CharsetProvider is presented in Example 6-3, which contains sample code illustrating the use of character sets, encoding and decoding, and the Charset SPI. Example 6-3 implements a custom Charset.

Example 6-3. The custom Rot13 charset

```
package com.ronsoft.books.nio.charset;

import java.nio.CharBuffer;
import java.nio.ByteBuffer;
import java.nio.charset.Charset;
import java.nio.charset.CharsetEncoder;
```

Example 6-3. The custom Rot13 charset (continued)

```java
import java.nio.charset.CharsetDecoder;
import java.nio.charset.CoderResult;
import java.util.Map;
import java.util.Iterator;
import java.io.Writer;
import java.io.PrintStream;
import java.io.PrintWriter;
import java.io.OutputStreamWriter;
import java.io.BufferedReader;
import java.io.InputStreamReader;
import java.io.FileReader;

/**
 * A Charset implementation which performs Rot13 encoding.  Rot-13 encoding
 * is a simple text obfuscation algorithm which shifts alphabetical characters
 * by 13 so that 'a' becomes 'n', 'o' becomes 'b', etc.  This algorithm
 * was popularized by the Usenet discussion forums many years ago to mask
 * naughty words, hide answers to questions, and so on.  The Rot13 algorithm
 * is symmetrical, applying it to text that has been scrambled by Rot13 will
 * give you the original unscrambled text.
 *
 * Applying this Charset encoding to an output stream will cause everything
 * you write to that stream to be Rot13 scrambled as it's written out.  And
 * appying it to an input stream causes data read to be Rot13 descrambled
 * as it's read.
 *
 * @author Ron Hitchens (ron@ronsoft.com)
 */
public class Rot13Charset extends Charset
{
    // the name of the base charset encoding we delegate to
    private static final String BASE_CHARSET_NAME = "UTF-8";

    // Handle to the real charset we'll use for transcoding between
    // characters and bytes.  Doing this allows us to apply the Rot13
    // algorithm to multibyte charset encodings. But only the
    // ASCII alpha chars will be rotated, regardless of the base encoding.
    Charset baseCharset;

    /**
     * Constructor for the Rot13 charset.  Call the superclass
     * constructor to pass along the name(s) we'll be known by.
     * Then save a reference to the delegate Charset.
     */
    protected Rot13Charset (String canonical, String [] aliases)
    {
        super (canonical, aliases);

        // Save the base charset we're delegating to
        baseCharset = Charset.forName (BASE_CHARSET_NAME);
    }

    // ----------------------------------------------------------
```

Example 6-3. The custom Rot13 charset (continued)

```
    /**
     * Called by users of this Charset to obtain an encoder.
     * This implementation instantiates an instance of a private class
     * (defined below) and passes it an encoder from the base Charset.
     */
    public CharsetEncoder newEncoder()
    {
        return new Rot13Encoder (this, baseCharset.newEncoder());
    }


    /**
     * Called by users of this Charset to obtain a decoder.
     * This implementation instantiates an instance of a private class
     * (defined below) and passes it a decoder from the base Charset.
     */
    public CharsetDecoder newDecoder()
    {
        return new Rot13Decoder (this, baseCharset.newDecoder());
    }


    /**
     * This method must be implemented by concrete Charsets.  We always
     * say no, which is safe.
     */
    public boolean contains (Charset cs)
    {
        return (false);
    }


    /**
     * Common routine to rotate all the ASCII alpha chars in the given
     * CharBuffer by 13.  Note that this code explicitly compares for
     * upper and lower case ASCII chars rather than using the methods
     * Character.isLowerCase and Character.isUpperCase.  This is because
     * the rotate-by-13 scheme only works properly for the alphabetic
     * characters of the ASCII charset and those methods can return
     * true for non-ASCII Unicode chars.
     */
    private void rot13 (CharBuffer cb)
    {
        for (int pos = cb.position(); pos < cb.limit(); pos++) {
            char c = cb.get (pos);
            char a = '\u0000';

            // Is it lowercase alpha?
            if ((c >= 'a') && (c <= 'z')) {
                a = 'a';
            }

            // Is it uppercase alpha?
            if ((c >= 'A') && (c <= 'Z')) {
                a = 'A';
            }
```

Example 6-3. The custom Rot13 charset (continued)

```
        // If either, roll it by 13
        if (a != '\u0000') {
            c = (char)((((c - a) + 13) % 26) + a);
            cb.put (pos, c);
        }
    }
}


// --------------------------------------------------------

/**
 * The encoder implementation for the Rot13 Charset.
 * This class, and the matching decoder class below, should also
 * override the "impl" methods, such as implOnMalformedInput() and
 * make passthrough calls to the baseEncoder object.  That is left
 * as an exercise for the hacker.
 */
private class Rot13Encoder extends CharsetEncoder
{
    private CharsetEncoder baseEncoder;

    /**
     * Constructor, call the superclass constructor with the
     * Charset object and the encodings sizes from the
     * delegate encoder.
     */
    Rot13Encoder (Charset cs, CharsetEncoder baseEncoder)
    {
        super (cs, baseEncoder.averageBytesPerChar( ),
            baseEncoder.maxBytesPerChar( ));

        this.baseEncoder = baseEncoder;
    }

    /**
     * Implementation of the encoding loop.  First, we apply
     * the Rot13 scrambling algorithm to the CharBuffer, then
     * reset the encoder for the base Charset and call it's
     * encode() method to do the actual encoding.  This may not
     * work properly for non-Latin charsets.  The CharBuffer
     * passed in may be read-only or re-used by the caller for
     * other purposes so we duplicate it and apply the Rot13
     * encoding to the copy.  We DO want to advance the position
     * of the input buffer to reflect the chars consumed.
     */
    protected CoderResult encodeLoop (CharBuffer cb, ByteBuffer bb)
    {
        CharBuffer tmpcb = CharBuffer.allocate (cb.remaining( ));
```

Example 6-3. The custom Rot13 charset (continued)

```
            while (cb.hasRemaining()) {
                tmpcb.put (cb.get());
            }

            tmpcb.rewind();

            rot13 (tmpcb);

            baseEncoder.reset();

            CoderResult cr = baseEncoder.encode (tmpcb, bb, true);

            // If error or output overflow, we need to adjust
            // the position of the input buffer to match what
            // was really consumed from the temp buffer.  If
            // underflow (all input consumed), this is a no-op.
            cb.position (cb.position() - tmpcb.remaining());

            return (cr);
        }
    }

    // ----------------------------------------------------------

    /**
     * The decoder implementation for the Rot13 Charset.
     */
    private class Rot13Decoder extends CharsetDecoder
    {
        private CharsetDecoder baseDecoder;

        /**
         * Constructor, call the superclass constructor with the
         * Charset object and pass alon the chars/byte values
         * from the delegate decoder.
         */
        Rot13Decoder (Charset cs, CharsetDecoder baseDecoder)
        {
            super (cs, baseDecoder.averageCharsPerByte(),
                baseDecoder.maxCharsPerByte());

            this.baseDecoder = baseDecoder;
        }

        /**
         * Implementation of the decoding loop.  First, we reset
         * the decoder for the base charset, then call it to decode
         * the bytes into characters, saving the result code.  The
         * CharBuffer is then de-scrambled with the Rot13 algorithm
         * and the result code is returned.  This may not
         * work properly for non-Latin charsets.
         */
```

Example 6-3. The custom Rot13 charset (continued)

```
    protected CoderResult decodeLoop (ByteBuffer bb, CharBuffer cb)
    {
        baseDecoder.reset( );

        CoderResult result = baseDecoder.decode (bb, cb, true);

        rot13 (cb);

        return (result);
    }
}

// --------------------------------------------------------

/**
 * Unit test for the Rot13 Charset.  This main( ) will open and read
 * an input file if named on the command line, or stdin if no args
 * are provided, and write the contents to stdout via the X-ROT13
 * charset encoding.
 * The "encryption" implemented by the Rot13 algorithm is symmetrical.
 * Feeding in a plain-text file, such as Java source code for example,
 * will output a scrambled version.  Feeding the scrambled version
 * back in will yield the original plain-text document.
 */
public static void main (String [] argv)
    throws Exception
{
    BufferedReader in;

    if (argv.length > 0) {
        // Open the named file
        in = new BufferedReader (new FileReader (argv [0]));
    } else {
        // Wrap a BufferedReader around stdin
        in = new BufferedReader (new InputStreamReader (System.in));
    }

    // Create a PrintStream that uses the Rot13 encoding
    PrintStream out = new PrintStream (System.out, false, "X-ROT13");

    String s = null;

    // Read all input and write it to the output.
    // As the data passes through the PrintStream,
    // it will be Rot13-encoded.
    while ((s = in.readLine( )) != null) {
        out.println (s);
    }

    out.flush( );
    }
}
```

To use this Charset and its encoder and decoder, it must be made available to the Java runtime environment. This is done with the CharsetProvider class (Example 6-4).

Example 6-4. Custom charset provider

```java
package com.ronsoft.books.nio.charset;

import java.nio.charset.Charset;
import java.nio.charset.spi.CharsetProvider;
import java.util.Set;
import java.util.HashSet;
import java.util.Iterator;

/**
 * A CharsetProvider class which makes available the charsets
 * provided by Ronsoft.  Currently there is only one, namely the X-ROT13
 * charset.  This is not a registered IANA charset, so it's
 * name begins with "X-" to avoid name clashes with offical charsets.
 *
 * To activate this CharsetProvider, it's necessary to add a file to
 * the classpath of the JVM runtime at the following location:
 *   META-INF/services/java.nio.charsets.spi.CharsetProvider
 *
 * That file must contain a line with the fully qualified name of
 * this class on a line by itself:
 *   com.ronsoft.books.nio.charset.RonsoftCharsetProvider
 *
 * See the javadoc page for java.nio.charsets.spi.CharsetProvider
 * for full details.
 *
 * @author Ron Hitchens (ron@ronsoft.com)
 */
public class RonsoftCharsetProvider extends CharsetProvider
{
    // the name of the charset we provide
    private static final String CHARSET_NAME = "X-ROT13";

    // a handle to the Charset object
    private Charset rot13 = null;

    /**
     * Constructor, instantiate a Charset object and save the reference.
     */
    public RonsoftCharsetProvider( )
    {
        this.rot13 = new Rot13Charset (CHARSET_NAME, new String [0]);
    }

    /**
     * Called by Charset static methods to find a particular named
     * Charset.  If it's the name of this charset (we don't have
     * any aliases) then return the Rot13 Charset, else return null.
     */
```

Example 6-4. Custom charset provider (continued)

```java
    public Charset charsetForName (String charsetName)
    {
        if (charsetName.equalsIgnoreCase (CHARSET_NAME)) {
            return (rot13);
        }

        return (null);
    }

    /**
     * Return an Iterator over the set of Charset objects we provide.
     * @return An Iterator object containing references to all the
     *    Charset objects provided by this class.
     */
    public Iterator charsets( )
    {
        HashSet set = new HashSet (1);

        set.add (rot13);

        return (set.iterator( ));
    }
}
```

For this charset provider to be seen by the JVM runtime environment, a file named *META_INF/services/java.nio.charset.spi.CharsetProvider* must exist in one of the JARs or directories of the classpath. The content of that file must be:

```
    com.ronsoft.books.nio.charset.RonsoftCharsetProvider
```

Adding X-ROT13 to the list of charsets in Example 6-1 produces this additional output:

```
Charset: X-ROT13
  Input: ¿Mañana?
Encoded:
    0: c2 (Â)
    1: bf (¿)
    2: 5a (Z)
    3: 6e (n)
    4: c3 (Ã)
    5: b1 (±)
    6: 6e (n)
    7: 61 (a)
    8: 6e (n)
    9: 3f (?)
```

The letters a and n are coincidentally 13 letters apart, so they appear to switch places in this particular word. Note how the non-ASCII and nonalphabetic characters remain unchanged from UTF-8 encoding.

Summary

Many Java programmers will never need to deal with character set transcoding issues, and most will never need to create custom charsets. But for those who do, the suite of classes in java.nio.charset and java.nio.charset.spi provide powerful and flexible machinery for character handling.

In this chapter, we learned about the new character-coding features of JDK 1.4. The important points covered were:

The Charset *class*
> Encapsulates a coded character set and the encoding scheme used to represent a sequence of characters from that character set as a byte sequence.

The CharsetEncoder *class*
> An encoding engine that converts a sequence of characters into a sequence of bytes. The byte sequence can later be decoded to reconstitute the original character sequence.

The CharsetDecoder *class*
> A decoding engine that converts an encoded byte sequence into a sequence of characters.

The CharsetProvider *SPI*
> Used by the service provider mechanism to locate and make Charset implementations available to use within the runtime environment.

And that pretty much wraps up our magical mystery tour of NIO. Check around your seat and in the overhead compartments for any personal belongings you may have left behind. Thank you very much for your kind attention. Be sure to visit us on the Web at *http://www.javanio.info/*. Bye now, bubye, bye, bye now.

NIO and the JNI

The Street finds its own uses for technology.
—William Gibson

As discussed in Chapter 2, direct buffers provide a means by which a Java buffer object can encapsulate system, or "raw," memory and use that memory as its backing store. In the Java realm, you do this by invoking ByteBuffer.allocateDirect( ), which allocates the system memory and wraps a Java object around it.

This approach—allocating system memory and constructing a Java object to encapsulate it—is new in JDK 1.4. In previous releases, it was not possible for the Java side to use memory allocated by native code. It's possible for native code invoked through the Java Native Interface (JNI) to call back to the JVM and request that memory be allocated from the JVM heap, but not the other way around. Memory allocated in this way can be used by Java code, but there are severe restrictions on how the memory can be accessed by native code. This made it awkward for Java and native code to share memory spaces.

In JDK 1.2, things got a little better with the introduction of GetPrimitiveArrayCritical( ) and ReleasePrimitiveArrayCritical( ). These new JNI functions gave native code better control of the memory area. For example, you could be confident that the garbage collector would leave it alone during a critical section. However, these methods also have serious restrictions, and the allocated memory still comes from the JVM heap.

Enhancements in JDK 1.4 brought three new JNI functions that invert this memory-allocation model. The JNI function NewDirectByteBuffer( ) takes a system memory address and size as arguments and constructs and returns a ByteBuffer object that uses the memory area as its backing store. This is a powerful capability that makes the following possible:

- Memory can be allocated by native code, then wrapped in a buffer object to be used by pure Java code.

- Full Java semantics apply to the wrapping buffer object (e.g., bounds checking, scoping, garbage collection, etc.).

- The wrapping object is a `ByteBuffer`. Views of it can be created, it can be sliced, its byte order can be set, and it can participate in I/O operations on channels (providing the underlying memory space is eligible for I/O).

- The natively allocated memory does not need to lie within the JVM heap or even within the JVM process space. This makes it possible to wrap a `ByteBuffer` around specialized memory spaces, such as video memory or a device controller.

The other two new JNI functions make it easy for JNI code to interact with direct buffers created on the Java side. `GetDirectBufferAddress( )` and `GetDirectBufferCapacity( )` let native code discover the location and size of the backing memory of a direct byte buffer. Direct `ByteBuffer` objects created by `ByteBuffer.allocateDirect( )` allocates system memory and wrap it in an object (as described above), but these objects also take steps to deallocate the system memory when the Java object is garbage collected.

This means that you can instantiate a byte buffer object with `ByteBuffer.allocateDirect( )`, then pass that object to a native method that can use the system memory space without worrying that it might be disturbed by the garbage collector. Upon return, Java code can examine the buffer to get the result and ultimately allow the buffer to be garbage collected when finished (which will automatically release the associated system memory). This reduces complexity, eliminates buffer copying, maintains object semantics (including garbage collection), prevents memory leaks, and requires less coding on your part. For situations in which native code must do the memory allocation, such as gaining access to video memory, you'll need to make sure that the native code releases memory properly when you're finished with the buffer object.

If you plan to share direct byte buffers with native code, you should explicitly set the byte order of the buffer to the native byte order. The byte order of the underlying system may not be the same as Java's. This is a good idea even if you won't be viewing the buffer content as other data types. It may enable more efficient access to the underlying memory.

```
buffer.order (ByteOrder.nativeOrder( ));
```

For details of the JNI API, consult the JNI spec on Sun's web site at *http://java.sun.com/j2se/1.4/docs/guide/jni/*.

Probably the best known, and most dramatic, example of the NIO/JNI interface's power is OpenGL For Java (a.k.a. GL4Java) from Jausoft (*www.jausoft.com/*). This OpenGL binding uses native OpenGL libraries, without modification, and provides a pure Java API to OpenGL. It consists mostly of (script-generated) glue code that passes buffer references to the OpenGL library with little or no buffer copying involved.

This allows for sophisticated, real-time 3D applications to be written entirely in Java without a single line of native code. Sun created an application using OpenGL For Java called JCanyon, which they demonstrated at JavaOne 2001 and JavaOne 2002. It's a real-time, interactive F16 flight simulator that uses satellite imagery of the Grand Canyon for the terrain. It even models fog. JCanyon also takes full advantage of NIO channels and memory mapping to prefetch the terrain data. The entire application—F16 simulation, terrain management, fog, everything—is 100% Java. The OpenGL library is accessed through the GL4Java API—no system-specific native code is needed at all—and it runs on a typical laptop.

In the nine months between JavaOne 2001 and 2002, as NIO matured from work-in-progress to final release, the frame-rate of JCanyon roughly doubled.

The JCanyon code is open source and can be downloaded from Sun's web site at *http://java.sun.com/products/jfc/tsc/articles/jcanyon/*. The Jausoft OpenGL binding, also open source, is bundled with the JCanyon code, or you can get it directly from *www.jausoft.com/*. The Jausoft site also has many smaller-scale OpenGL demos.

APPENDIX B
Selectable Channels SPI

If you build it, he will come.
—An Iowa Cornfield

The selectable-channel architecture, like several other components of the Java platform, is pluggable by means of a Service Provider Interface (SPI). Chapter 6 showed how to use the pluggable Charset SPI, and the Channel SPI works essentially the same way. Channel, Selector, and even SelectionKey implementations can be quite complex and are necessarily operating system–dependent. A sample channel implementation is beyond the scope of this book. This appendix only summarizes the SPI at a high level. If you are setting out to create your own custom channel implementation, you will require more detailed information than can be presented here.

As we saw in "The Charset Service Provider Interface" in Chapter 6, services are facilitated by a provider class instantiated by the low-level services mechanism. For channels, the base provider class is java.nio.channels.spi.SelectorProvider. Note that this isn't named ChannelProvider. This SPI applies only to selectable channels, not all channel types. There's a tight dependency between selectable channels and related selectors (and selection keys, which associate one with the other). Channels and selectors from different providers will not work together.

```
package java.nio.channels.spi;

public abstract class SelectorProvider
{
        public static SelectorProvider provider()

        // The following methods all throw IOException

        public abstract AbstractSelector openSelector()
        public abstract ServerSocketChannel openServerSocketChannel()
        public abstract SocketChannel openSocketChannel()
        public abstract DatagramChannel openDatagramChannel()
        public abstract Pipe openPipe()
}
```

A SelectorProvider instance exposes factory methods to create concrete Selector objects, the three types of socket channel objects, and Pipe objects. The Selector objects produced must interoperate with socket channel objects from the same provider (and the channels produced by a Pipe object from that provider). Channels, selectors, and selection keys from a given provider can have access to each other's internal implementation details.

The API of SelectorProvider is pretty obvious, with the possible exception of the first method listed above. The provider( ) method is a class method on SelectorProvider that returns a reference to the default system provider. The default provider is determined at JVM startup in the same manner as CharsetProvider objects (see the javadoc for SelectorProvider for details). You can obtain a SelectorProvider by other means if you choose (such as by instantiating it directly, if that's allowed), then invoke the instance factory methods directly on the provider object. The default factory methods of the channel classes, such as SocketChannel.open( ), pass through to the corresponding factory methods on the default SelectorProvider object.

There are four other classes in the java.nio.channels.spi package: AbstractInterruptibleChannel, AbstractSelectableChannel, AbstractSelectionKey, and AbstractSelector. You may remember from Figure 3-2 that AbstractSelectableChannel extends AbstractInterruptibleChannel by way of java.nio.channels.SelectableChannel. AbstractInterruptibleChannel provides a common framework for managing channels that can be interrupted, and AbstractSelectableChannel provides similar support for selectable channels. Because AbstractInterruptibleChannel is the ancestor of AbstractSelectableChannel, all selectable channels are interruptible.

```
package java.nio.channels.spi;

public abstract class AbstractInterruptibleChannel
        implements Channel, InterruptibleChannel
{
        protected AbstractInterruptibleChannel( )

        public final void close( ) throws IOException
        public final boolean isOpen( )

        protected final void begin( )
        protected final void end (boolean completed)
        protected abstract void implCloseChannel( ) throws IOException;
}

public abstract class AbstractSelectableChannel
        extends java.nio.channels.SelectableChannel
{
        protected AbstractSelectableChannel (SelectorProvider provider)

        public final SelectorProvider provider( )
        public final boolean isRegistered( )
        public final SelectionKey keyFor (Selector sel)
```

```
        public final SelectionKey register (Selector sel,
                int ops, Object att)
        public final boolean isBlocking( )
        public final Object blockingLock( )
        public final SelectableChannel configureBlocking (boolean block)
                throws IOException

        protected final void implCloseChannel( )
                throws IOException
        protected abstract void implCloseSelectableChannel( )
                throws IOException;
        protected abstract void implConfigureBlocking (boolean block)
                throws IOException;
    }
```

Any channel implementation that wants to support selection must extend
AbstractSelectableChannel. Most of the methods provided by the two classes listed
above are default implementations that you've already seen in the APIs of the channel classes in Chapter 3. Each has a small number of protected methods that subclasses can (or must) implement to create a new selectable channel class.

The other two classes, AbstractSelector and AbstractSelectionKey, provide similar
templates from which concrete implementation classes must extend:

```
package java.nio.channels.spi;

public abstract class AbstractSelector
        extends Selector
{
        protected AbstractSelector(SelectorProvider provider)
        public final void close( ) throws IOException
        public final boolean isOpen( )
        public final SelectorProvider provider( )

        protected abstract SelectionKey register (
                AbstractSelectableChannel ch, int ops, Object att);
        protected final void deregister (AbstractSelectionKey key)
        protected final Set cancelledKeys( )
        protected final void begin( )
        protected final void end( )
        protected abstract void implCloseSelector( ) throws IOException;
}

public abstract class AbstractSelectionKey
        extends SelectionKey
{
        protected AbstractSelectionKey( )

        public final boolean isValid( )
        public final void cancel( )
}
```

Again, you can see the default implementations of public methods and protected methods used only by subclasses. In AbstractSelector, you can see the internal hooks for the cancelled key set and explicit channel deregistration.

Few "civilian" Java programmers will ever need to concern themselves with the channels SPI. This is a realm primarily inhabited by JVM vendors and/or vendors of high-end products such as application servers. Creating a new selectable-channel implementation is a nontrivial undertaking that requires specialized skills and significant resources.

NIO Quick Reference

I still haven't found what I'm looking for.
—U2

This appendix is a quick reference to the NIO classes and interfaces. Packages, classes, and methods are sorted alphabetically to make things easier to find. The API listings were created programmatically using the Java Reflection API to extract information directly from the compiled class files of the JDK. Regular expressions (auto-generated from the class information) were used to retrieve parameter names from the source. Descriptive text (such as this) was composed in XML then processed by an XSL stylesheet to merge with the API information (by invoking the Java code as an extension function) for each class.

The same convention is used here as in the main text. A missing semicolon at the end of a method signature implies that the method body follows in the source. Abstract methods end with a semicolon because they have no concrete body. The values to which constants are initialized are not listed.

This reference was generated against the J2SE 1.4.0 release.

Package java.nio

The java.nio package contains Buffer classes used by classes in the java.nio.channels and java.nio.charset subpackages.

Buffer

Buffer is the base class from which all other buffer classes extend. It contains generic methods common to all buffer types.

```
public abstract class Buffer
{
    public final int capacity()
    public final Buffer clear()
```

```
    public final Buffer flip()
    public final boolean hasRemaining()
    public abstract boolean isReadOnly();
    public final int limit()
    public final Buffer limit (int newLimit)
    public final Buffer mark()
    public final int position()
    public final Buffer position (int newPosition)
    public final int remaining()
    public final Buffer reset()
    public final Buffer rewind()
}
```

See also: ByteBuffer

BufferOverflowException

BufferOverflowException (unchecked) is thrown when a simple relative put() is attempted with a buffer's position equal to its limit, or when a bulk put() would cause the position to exceed the limit.

```
public class BufferOverflowException
    extends RuntimeException
{
    public BufferOverflowException()
}
```

See also: Buffer

BufferUnderflowException

BufferUnderflowException (unchecked) is thrown when a simple relative get() is attempted with a buffer's position equal to its limit, or when a bulk get() would cause the position to exceed the limit.

```
public class BufferUnderflowException
    extends RuntimeException
{
    public BufferUnderflowException()
}
```

See also: Buffer

ByteBuffer

ByteBuffer is the most complex and versatile of all the buffer classes. Only byte buffers can participate in I/O operations on channels to send and receive data.

```
public abstract class ByteBuffer
    extends Buffer
    implements Comparable
{
```

```
public static ByteBuffer allocate (int capacity)
public static ByteBuffer allocateDirect (int capacity)
public final byte [] array()
public final int arrayOffset()
public abstract CharBuffer asCharBuffer();
public abstract DoubleBuffer asDoubleBuffer();
public abstract FloatBuffer asFloatBuffer();
public abstract IntBuffer asIntBuffer();
public abstract LongBuffer asLongBuffer();
public abstract ByteBuffer asReadOnlyBuffer();
public abstract ShortBuffer asShortBuffer();
public abstract ByteBuffer compact();
public int compareTo (Object ob)
public abstract ByteBuffer duplicate();
public boolean equals (Object ob)
public abstract byte get();
public ByteBuffer get (byte [] dst)
public abstract byte get (int index);
public ByteBuffer get (byte [] dst, int offset, int length)
public abstract char getChar();
public abstract char getChar (int index);
public abstract double getDouble();
public abstract double getDouble (int index);
public abstract float getFloat();
public abstract float getFloat (int index);
public abstract int getInt();
public abstract int getInt (int index);
public abstract long getLong();
public abstract long getLong (int index);
public abstract short getShort();
public abstract short getShort (int index);
public final boolean hasArray()
public int hashCode()
public abstract boolean isDirect();
public final ByteOrder order()
public final ByteBuffer order (ByteOrder bo)
public abstract ByteBuffer put (byte b);
public final ByteBuffer put (byte [] src)
public ByteBuffer put (ByteBuffer src)
public abstract ByteBuffer put (int index, byte b);
public ByteBuffer put (byte [] src, int offset, int length)
public abstract ByteBuffer putChar (char value);
public abstract ByteBuffer putChar (int index, char value);
public abstract ByteBuffer putDouble (double value);
public abstract ByteBuffer putDouble (int index, double value);
public abstract ByteBuffer putFloat (float value);
public abstract ByteBuffer putFloat (int index, float value);
public abstract ByteBuffer putInt (int value);
public abstract ByteBuffer putInt (int index, int value);
public abstract ByteBuffer putLong (long value);
public abstract ByteBuffer putLong (int index, long value);
public abstract ByteBuffer putShort (short value);
public abstract ByteBuffer putShort (int index, short value);
```

```
        public abstract ByteBuffer slice();
        public String toString()
        public static ByteBuffer wrap (byte [] array)
        public static ByteBuffer wrap (byte [] array, int offset, int length)
    }
```

See also: Buffer, ByteOrder

ByteOrder

ByteOrder is a type-safe enumeration that cannot be instantiated directly. Two publicly accessible instances of ByteOrder are visible as static class fields. A class method is provided to determine the native byte order of the underlying operating system, which may not be the same as the Java platform default.

```
    public final class ByteOrder
    {
        public static final ByteOrder BIG_ENDIAN
        public static final ByteOrder LITTLE_ENDIAN

        public static ByteOrder nativeOrder()
        public String toString()
    }
```

See also: ByteBuffer

CharBuffer

CharBuffer manages data elements of type char and implements the CharSequence interface that allows it to participate in character-oriented operations such as regular expression matching. CharBuffer is also used by classes in the java.nio.charset package.

```
    public abstract class CharBuffer
        extends Buffer
        implements Comparable, CharSequence
    {
        public static CharBuffer allocate (int capacity)
        public final char [] array()
        public final int arrayOffset()
        public abstract CharBuffer asReadOnlyBuffer();
        public final char charAt (int index)
        public abstract CharBuffer compact();
        public int compareTo (Object ob)
        public abstract CharBuffer duplicate();
        public boolean equals (Object ob)
        public abstract char get();
        public CharBuffer get (char [] dst)
        public abstract char get (int index);
        public CharBuffer get (char [] dst, int offset, int length)
        public final boolean hasArray()
```

```
public int hashCode()
public abstract boolean isDirect();
public final int length()
public abstract ByteOrder order();
public abstract CharBuffer put (char c);
public final CharBuffer put (char [] src)
public final CharBuffer put (String src)
public CharBuffer put (CharBuffer src)
public abstract CharBuffer put (int index, char c);
public CharBuffer put (char [] src, int offset, int length)
public CharBuffer put (String src, int start, int end)
public abstract CharBuffer slice();
public abstract CharSequence subSequence (int start, int end);
public String toString()
public static CharBuffer wrap (char [] array)
public static CharBuffer wrap (CharSequence csq)
public static CharBuffer wrap (char [] array, int offset, int length)
public static CharBuffer wrap (CharSequence csq, int start, int end)
}
```

See also: Buffer, java.lang.CharSequence, java.util.regex.Matcher

DoubleBuffer

DoubleBuffer manages data elements of type double.

```
public abstract class DoubleBuffer
    extends Buffer
    implements Comparable
{
    public static DoubleBuffer allocate (int capacity)
    public final double [] array()
    public final int arrayOffset()
    public abstract DoubleBuffer asReadOnlyBuffer();
    public abstract DoubleBuffer compact();
    public int compareTo (Object ob)
    public abstract DoubleBuffer duplicate();
    public boolean equals (Object ob)
    public abstract double get();
    public DoubleBuffer get (double [] dst)
    public abstract double get (int index);
    public DoubleBuffer get (double [] dst, int offset, int length)
    public final boolean hasArray()
    public int hashCode()
    public abstract boolean isDirect();
    public abstract ByteOrder order();
    public abstract DoubleBuffer put (double d);
    public final DoubleBuffer put (double [] src)
    public DoubleBuffer put (DoubleBuffer src)
    public abstract DoubleBuffer put (int index, double d);
    public DoubleBuffer put (double [] src, int offset, int length)
    public abstract DoubleBuffer slice();
    public String toString()
```

```
        public static DoubleBuffer wrap (double [] array)
        public static DoubleBuffer wrap (double [] array, int offset, int length)
    }
```

See also: Buffer

FloatBuffer

FloatBuffer manages data elements of type float.

```
    public abstract class FloatBuffer
        extends Buffer
        implements Comparable
    {
        public static FloatBuffer allocate (int capacity)
        public final float [] array()
        public final int arrayOffset()
        public abstract FloatBuffer asReadOnlyBuffer();
        public abstract FloatBuffer compact();
        public int compareTo (Object ob)
        public abstract FloatBuffer duplicate();
        public boolean equals (Object ob)
        public abstract float get();
        public FloatBuffer get (float [] dst)
        public abstract float get (int index);
        public FloatBuffer get (float [] dst, int offset, int length)
        public final boolean hasArray()
        public int hashCode()
        public abstract boolean isDirect();
        public abstract ByteOrder order();
        public abstract FloatBuffer put (float f);
        public final FloatBuffer put (float [] src)
        public FloatBuffer put (FloatBuffer src)
        public abstract FloatBuffer put (int index, float f);
        public FloatBuffer put (float [] src, int offset, int length)
        public abstract FloatBuffer slice();
        public String toString()
        public static FloatBuffer wrap (float [] array)
        public static FloatBuffer wrap (float [] array, int offset, int length)
    }
```

See also: Buffer

IntBuffer

IntBuffer manages data elements of type int.

```
    public abstract class IntBuffer
        extends Buffer
        implements Comparable
    {
        public static IntBuffer allocate (int capacity)
        public final int [] array()
        public final int arrayOffset()
```

```
        public abstract IntBuffer asReadOnlyBuffer();
        public abstract IntBuffer compact();
        public int compareTo (Object ob)
        public abstract IntBuffer duplicate();
        public boolean equals (Object ob)
        public abstract int get();
        public abstract int get (int index);
        public IntBuffer get (int [] dst)
        public IntBuffer get (int [] dst, int offset, int length)
        public final boolean hasArray()
        public int hashCode()
        public abstract boolean isDirect();
        public abstract ByteOrder order();
        public abstract IntBuffer put (int i);
        public final IntBuffer put (int [] src)
        public IntBuffer put (IntBuffer src)
        public abstract IntBuffer put (int index, int i);
        public IntBuffer put (int [] src, int offset, int length)
        public abstract IntBuffer slice();
        public String toString()
        public static IntBuffer wrap (int [] array)
        public static IntBuffer wrap (int [] array, int offset, int length)
    }
```

See also: Buffer

InvalidMarkException

InvalidMarkException (unchecked) is thrown when reset() is invoked on a buffer that does not have a mark set.

```
    public class InvalidMarkException
        extends IllegalStateException
    {
        public InvalidMarkException()
    }
```

See also: Buffer

LongBuffer

LongBuffer manages data elements of type long.

```
    public abstract class LongBuffer
        extends Buffer
        implements Comparable
    {
        public static LongBuffer allocate (int capacity)
        public final long [] array()
        public final int arrayOffset()
        public abstract LongBuffer asReadOnlyBuffer();
        public abstract LongBuffer compact();
        public int compareTo (Object ob)
```

```
    public abstract LongBuffer duplicate();
    public boolean equals (Object ob)
    public abstract long get();
    public abstract long get (int index);
    public LongBuffer get (long [] dst)
    public LongBuffer get (long [] dst, int offset, int length)
    public final boolean hasArray()
    public int hashCode()
    public abstract boolean isDirect();
    public abstract ByteOrder order();
    public LongBuffer put (LongBuffer src)
    public abstract LongBuffer put (long l);
    public final LongBuffer put (long [] src)
    public abstract LongBuffer put (int index, long l);
    public LongBuffer put (long [] src, int offset, int length)
    public abstract LongBuffer slice();
    public String toString()
    public static LongBuffer wrap (long [] array)
    public static LongBuffer wrap (long [] array, int offset, int length)
}
```

See also: Buffer

MappedByteBuffer

MappedByteBuffer is a special type of ByteBuffer whose data elements are the content of a disk file. MappedByteBuffer objects can be created only by invoking the map() method of a FileChannel object.

```
public abstract class MappedByteBuffer
    extends ByteBuffer
{
    public final MappedByteBuffer force()
    public final boolean isLoaded()
    public final MappedByteBuffer load()
}
```

See also: Buffer, java.nio.channels.FileChannel

ReadOnlyBufferException

ReadOnlyBufferException (unchecked) is thrown when a method that would modify the buffer content, such as put() or compact(), is invoked on a read-only buffer.

```
public class ReadOnlyBufferException
    extends UnsupportedOperationException
{
    public ReadOnlyBufferException()
}
```

See also: Buffer

ShortBuffer

ShortBuffer manages data elements of type short.

```
public abstract class ShortBuffer
    extends Buffer
    implements Comparable
{
    public static ShortBuffer allocate (int capacity)
    public final short [] array()
    public final int arrayOffset()
    public abstract ShortBuffer asReadOnlyBuffer();
    public abstract ShortBuffer compact();
    public int compareTo (Object ob)
    public abstract ShortBuffer duplicate();
    public boolean equals (Object ob)
    public abstract short get();
    public abstract short get (int index);
    public ShortBuffer get (short [] dst)
    public ShortBuffer get (short [] dst, int offset, int length)
    public final boolean hasArray()
    public int hashCode()
    public abstract boolean isDirect();
    public abstract ByteOrder order();
    public ShortBuffer put (ShortBuffer src)
    public abstract ShortBuffer put (short s);
    public final ShortBuffer put (short [] src)
    public abstract ShortBuffer put (int index, short s);
    public ShortBuffer put (short [] src, int offset, int length)
    public abstract ShortBuffer slice();
    public String toString()
    public static ShortBuffer wrap (short [] array)
    public static ShortBuffer wrap (short [] array, int offset, int length)
}
```

See also: Buffer

Package java.nio.channels

The java.nio.channels package contains the classes and interfaces related to channels and selectors.

AlreadyConnectedException

AlreadyConnectedException (unchecked) is thrown when connect() is invoked on a SocketChannel object that is already connected.

```
public class AlreadyConnectedException
    extends IllegalStateException
{
```

```
    public AlreadyConnectedException()
}
```
See also: java.net.Socket, SocketChannel

AsynchronousCloseException

AsynchronousCloseException (subclass of IOException) is thrown when a thread is blocked on a channel operation, such as read() or write(), and the channel is closed by another thread.

```
public class AsynchronousCloseException
    extends ClosedChannelException
{
    public AsynchronousCloseException()
}
```
See also: ClosedByInterruptException

ByteChannel

ByteChannel is an empty aggregation interface. It combines ReadableByteChannel and WritableByteChannel into a single interface but doesn't define any new methods.

```
public interface ByteChannel
    extends ReadableByteChannel, WritableByteChannel
{
}
```
See also: Channel, ReadableByteChannel, WritableByteChannel

CancelledKeyException

CancelledKeyException (unchecked) is thrown when something attempts to use a SelectionKey object that has been invalidated.

```
public class CancelledKeyException
    extends IllegalStateException
{
    public CancelledKeyException()
}
```
See also: SelectionKey, Selector

Channel

Channel is the superinterface of all other channel interfaces. It defines the methods common to all concrete channel classes.

```
public interface Channel
{
    public void close()
```

```
        throws java.io.IOException;
    public boolean isOpen();
}
```

See also: ByteChannel, GatheringByteChannel, ReadableByteChannel, ScatteringByte-Channel, WritableByteChannel

Channels

Channels is a utility class that makes it possible for channels to interoperate with traditional byte and character streams. The factory methods return wrapper objects that adapt channels to streams, or vice versa. The channel objects returned may not be selectable nor interruptible.

```
public final class Channels
{
    public static ReadableByteChannel newChannel (java.io.InputStream in)
    public static WritableByteChannel newChannel (java.io.OutputStream out)
    public static java.io.InputStream newInputStream (ReadableByteChannel ch)
    public static java.io.OutputStream newOutputStream (WritableByteChannel ch)
    public static java.io.Reader newReader (ReadableByteChannel ch, String csName)
    public static java.io.Reader newReader (ReadableByteChannel ch,
        java.nio.charset.CharsetDecoder dec, int minBufferCap)
    public static java.io.Writer newWriter (WritableByteChannel ch, String csName)
    public static java.io.Writer newWriter (WritableByteChannel ch,
        java.nio.charset.CharsetEncoder enc, int minBufferCap)
}
```

See also: CharsetDecoder, CharsetEncoder, java.io.InputStream, java.io.OutputStream, java.io.Reader, java.io.Writer, ReadableByteChannel, WritableByteChannel

ClosedByInterruptException

ClosedByInterruptException (subclass of IOException) is thrown when a thread is blocked on a channel operation, such as read() or write(), and is interrupted by another thread. The channel on which the thread was sleeping will be closed as a side effect. This exception is similar to AsynchronousCloseException but results when the sleeping thread is directly interrupted.

```
public class ClosedByInterruptException
    extends AsynchronousCloseException
{
    public ClosedByInterruptException()
}
```

See also: AsynchronousCloseException, java.lang.Thread

ClosedChannelException

ClosedChannelException (subclass of IOException) is thrown when an operation is attempted on a channel that has been closed. Some channels, such as SocketChannel, may be closed for some operations but not for others. For example, each side of a SocketChannel may be shut down independently while the other continues to work normally.

```
public class ClosedChannelException
    extends java.io.IOException
{
    public ClosedChannelException()
}
```

See also: Channel

ClosedSelectorException

ClosedSelectorException (unchecked) is thrown when attempting to use a Selector that has been closed.

```
public class ClosedSelectorException
    extends IllegalStateException
{
    public ClosedSelectorException()
}
```

See also: Selector

ConnectionPendingException

ConnectionPendingException (unchecked) is thrown when connect() is invoked on a SocketChannel object in nonblocking mode for which a concurrent connection is already in progress.

```
public class ConnectionPendingException
    extends IllegalStateException
{
    public ConnectionPendingException()
}
```

See also: SocketChannel

DatagramChannel

The DatagramChannel class provides methods to send and receive datagram packets from and to ByteBuffer objects, respectively.

```
public abstract class DatagramChannel
    extends java.nio.channels.spi.AbstractSelectableChannel
    implements ByteChannel, ScatteringByteChannel, GatheringByteChannel
{
```

```
public abstract DatagramChannel connect (java.net.SocketAddress remote)
    throws java.io.IOException;
public abstract DatagramChannel disconnect()
    throws java.io.IOException;
public abstract boolean isConnected();
public static DatagramChannel open()
    throws java.io.IOException
public abstract int read (java.nio.ByteBuffer dst)
    throws java.io.IOException;
public final long read (java.nio.ByteBuffer [] dsts)
    throws java.io.IOException
public abstract long read (java.nio.ByteBuffer [] dsts, int offset, int length)
    throws java.io.IOException;
public abstract java.net.SocketAddress receive (java.nio.ByteBuffer dst)
    throws java.io.IOException;
public abstract int send (java.nio.ByteBuffer src, java.net.SocketAddress target)
    throws java.io.IOException;
public abstract java.net.DatagramSocket socket();
public final int validOps()
public abstract int write (java.nio.ByteBuffer src)
    throws java.io.IOException;
public final long write (java.nio.ByteBuffer [] srcs)
    throws java.io.IOException
public abstract long write (java.nio.ByteBuffer [] srcs, int offset, int length)
    throws java.io.IOException;
}
```

See also: java.net.DatagramSocket

FileChannel

The FileChannel class provides a rich set of file-oriented operations. FileChannel objects can be obtained only by invoking the getChannel() method on a RandomAccessFile, FileInputStream, or FileOutputStream object.

```
public abstract class FileChannel
    extends java.nio.channels.spi.AbstractInterruptibleChannel
    implements ByteChannel, GatheringByteChannel, ScatteringByteChannel
{
    public abstract void force (boolean metaData)
        throws java.io.IOException;
    public final FileLock lock()
        throws java.io.IOException
    public abstract FileLock lock (long position, long size, boolean shared)
        throws java.io.IOException;
    public abstract java.nio.MappedByteBuffer map (FileChannel.MapMode mode,
        long position, long size) throws java.io.IOException;
    public abstract long position()
        throws java.io.IOException;
    public abstract FileChannel position (long newPosition)
        throws java.io.IOException;
    public abstract int read (java.nio.ByteBuffer dst)
        throws java.io.IOException;
```

```
public final long read (java.nio.ByteBuffer [] dsts)
    throws java.io.IOException
public abstract int read (java.nio.ByteBuffer dst, long position)
    throws java.io.IOException;
public abstract long read (java.nio.ByteBuffer [] dsts, int offset, int length)
    throws java.io.IOException;
public abstract long size()
    throws java.io.IOException;
public abstract long transferFrom (ReadableByteChannel src, long position,
    long count) throws java.io.IOException;
public abstract long transferTo (long position, long count,
    WritableByteChannel target) throws java.io.IOException;
public abstract FileChannel truncate (long size)
    throws java.io.IOException;
public final FileLock tryLock()
    throws java.io.IOException
public abstract FileLock tryLock (long position, long size, boolean shared)
    throws java.io.IOException;
public abstract int write (java.nio.ByteBuffer src)
    throws java.io.IOException;
public final long write (java.nio.ByteBuffer || srcs)
    throws java.io.IOException
public abstract int write (java.nio.ByteBuffer src, long position)
    throws java.io.IOException;
public abstract long write (java.nio.ByteBuffer [] srcs, int offset, int length)
    throws java.io.IOException;

public static class FileChannel.MapMode
{
    public static final FileChannel.MapMode PRIVATE
    public static final FileChannel.MapMode READ_ONLY
    public static final FileChannel.MapMode READ_WRITE

    public String toString()
}
}
```

See also: java.io.FileInputStream, java.io.FileOutputStream, java.io.RandomAccessFile, MappedByteBuffer

FileLock

The FileLock class encapsulates a lock region associated with a FileChannel object.

```
public abstract class FileLock
{
    public final FileChannel channel()
    public final boolean isShared()
    public abstract boolean isValid();
    public final boolean overlaps (long position, long size)
    public final long position()
    public abstract void release()
        throws java.io.IOException;
```

```
        public final long size()
        public final String toString()
    }
```

See also: FileChannel

FileLockInterruptionException

FileLockInterruptionException is thrown when a thread blocked waiting for a file lock to be granted is interrupted by another thread. The FileChannel has not been closed, but upon catching this exception, the interrupt status of the interrupted thread was set. If the thread does not clear its interrupt status (by invoking Thread. interrupted()), it will cause the next channel it touches to close.

```
    public class FileLockInterruptionException
        extends java.io.IOException
    {
        public FileLockInterruptionException()
    }
```

See also: FileChannel, FileLock, java.lang.Thread

GatheringByteChannel

The GatheringByteChannel interface defines the methods that perform gathering writes to a channel.

```
    public interface GatheringByteChannel
        extends WritableByteChannel
    {
        public long write (java.nio.ByteBuffer [] srcs)
            throws java.io.IOException;
        public long write (java.nio.ByteBuffer [] srcs, int offset, int length)
            throws java.io.IOException;
    }
```

See also: ByteChannel, ReadableByteChannel, ScatteringByteChannel, WritableByteChannel

IllegalBlockingModeException

IllegalBlockingModeException (unchecked) is thrown when a channel operation that applies only to a specific blocking mode is attempted, and the channel is not currently in the required mode.

```
    public class IllegalBlockingModeException
        extends IllegalStateException
    {
        public IllegalBlockingModeException()
    }
```

See also: SelectableChannel

IllegalSelectorException

IllegalSelectorException (unchecked) is thrown when an attempt is made to register a SelectableChannel with a Selector from a different SelectorProvider class. Selectors work only with channels created by the same provider.

```
public class IllegalSelectorException
    extends IllegalArgumentException
{
    public IllegalSelectorException()
}
```

See also: SelectorProvider

InterruptibleChannel

InterruptibleChannel is a marker interface that, if implemented, indicates that a channel class is interruptible. All selectable channels are interruptible.

```
public interface InterruptibleChannel
    extends Channel
{
    public void close()
        throws java.io.IOException;
}
```

See also: SelectableChannel

NoConnectionPendingException

NoConnectionPendingException (unchecked) is thrown when finishConnect() is invoked on a SocketChannel object in nonblocking mode that has not previously invoked connect() to begin the concurrent connection process.

```
public class NoConnectionPendingException
    extends IllegalStateException
{
    public NoConnectionPendingException()
}
```

See also: SocketChannel

NonReadableChannelException

NonReadableChannelException (unchecked) is thrown when a read() method is invoked on a channel that was not opened with read permission.

```
public class NonReadableChannelException
    extends IllegalStateException
{
```

```
        public NonReadableChannelException()
    }
```
See also: ReadableByteChannel

NonWritableChannelException

NonWritableChannelException (unchecked) is thrown when a write() method is invoked on a channel that was not opened with write permission.

```
    public class NonWritableChannelException
        extends IllegalStateException
    {
        public NonWritableChannelException()
    }
```
See also: WritableByteChannel

NotYetBoundException

NotYetBoundException (unchecked) is thrown when attempting to perform an operation, such as accept(), on a ServerSocketChannel that has not yet been bound to a port.

```
    public class NotYetBoundException
        extends IllegalStateException
    {
        public NotYetBoundException()
    }
```
See also: java.net.ServerSocket

NotYetConnectedException

NotYetConnectedException (unchecked) is thrown when attempting to use a SocketChannel object for I/O before connect() has been called or before a concurrent connection has successfully completed.

```
    public class NotYetConnectedException
        extends IllegalStateException
    {
        public NotYetConnectedException()
    }
```
See also: SocketChannel

OverlappingFileLockException

OverlappingFileLockException (unchecked) is thrown when attempting to acquire a lock on a file region already locked by the same JVM, or when another thread is waiting to lock an overlapping region belonging to the same file.

```
public class OverlappingFileLockException
    extends IllegalStateException
{
    public OverlappingFileLockException()
}
```

See also: FileChannel, FileLock

Pipe

Pipe is an aggregator class that contains a pair of selectable channels. These channels are cross-connected to form a loopback. The SinkChannel object is the write end
of the pipe; whatever is written to it is available for reading on the SourceChannel
object.

```
public abstract class Pipe
{
    public static Pipe open()
        throws java.io.IOException
    public abstract Pipe.SinkChannel sink();
    public abstract Pipe.SourceChannel source();

    public abstract static class Pipe.SinkChannel
        extends java.nio.channels.spi.AbstractSelectableChannel
        implements WritableByteChannel, GatheringByteChannel
    {
        public final int validOps()
    }

    public abstract static class Pipe.SourceChannel
        extends java.nio.channels.spi.AbstractSelectableChannel
        implements ReadableByteChannel, ScatteringByteChannel
    {
        public final int validOps()
    }
}
```

See also: SelectableChannel, Selector

ReadableByteChannel

The ReadableByteChannel interface defines the read() method, which makes it possible for a channel to read data from a channel into a ByteBuffer object.

```
public interface ReadableByteChannel
    extends Channel
{
    public int read (java.nio.ByteBuffer dst)
        throws java.io.IOException;
}
```

See also: ByteBuffer, ByteChannel, WritableByteChannel

ScatteringByteChannel

The ScatteringByteChannel interface defines the methods that perform scattering reads from a channel.

```
public interface ScatteringByteChannel
    extends ReadableByteChannel
{
    public long read (java.nio.ByteBuffer [] dsts)
        throws java.io.IOException;
    public long read (java.nio.ByteBuffer [] dsts, int offset, int length)
        throws java.io.IOException;
}
```

See also: ByteChannel, GatheringByteChannel, ReadableByteChannel, WritableByteChannel

SelectableChannel

SelectableChannel is the common superclass of all channels capable of participating in selection operations controlled by a Selector object. SelectableChannel objects can be placed in nonblocking mode and can only be registered with a Selector while in nonblocking mode. All classes that extend from SelectableChannel also implement InterruptibleChannel.

```
public abstract class SelectableChannel
    extends java.nio.channels.spi.AbstractInterruptibleChannel
    implements Channel
{
    public abstract Object blockingLock();
    public abstract SelectableChannel configureBlocking (boolean block)
        throws java.io.IOException;
    public abstract boolean isBlocking();
    public abstract boolean isRegistered();
    public abstract SelectionKey keyFor (Selector sel);
    public abstract java.nio.channels.spi.SelectorProvider provider();
    public final SelectionKey register (Selector sel, int ops)
        throws ClosedChannelException
    public abstract SelectionKey register (Selector sel, int ops, Object att)
        throws ClosedChannelException;
    public abstract int validOps();
}
```

See also: Selector

SelectionKey

SelectionKey encapsulates the registration of a SelectableChannel object with a Selector object.

```
public abstract class SelectionKey
{
```

```
        public static final int OP_ACCEPT
        public static final int OP_CONNECT
        public static final int OP_READ
        public static final int OP_WRITE

        public final Object attach (Object ob)
        public final Object attachment()
        public abstract void cancel();
        public abstract SelectableChannel channel();
        public abstract int interestOps();
        public abstract SelectionKey interestOps (int ops);
        public final boolean isAcceptable()
        public final boolean isConnectable()
        public final boolean isReadable()
        public abstract boolean isValid();
        public final boolean isWritable()
        public abstract int readyOps();
        public abstract Selector selector();
    }
```

See also: SelectableChannel, Selector

Selector

Selector is the orchestrating class that performs readiness selection of registered SelectableChannel objects and manages the associated keys and state information.

```
    public abstract class Selector
    {
        public abstract void close()
            throws java.io.IOException;
        public abstract boolean isOpen();
        public abstract java.util.Set keys();
        public static Selector open()
            throws java.io.IOException
        public abstract java.nio.channels.spi.SelectorProvider provider();
        public abstract int select()
            throws java.io.IOException;
        public abstract int select (long timeout)
            throws java.io.IOException;
        public abstract int selectNow()
            throws java.io.IOException;
        public abstract java.util.Set selectedKeys();
        public abstract Selector wakeup();
    }
```

See also: SelectableChannel, SelectionKey

ServerSocketChannel

The ServerSocketChannel class listens for incoming socket connections and creates new SocketChannel instances.

```
    public abstract class ServerSocketChannel
```

```
    extends java.nio.channels.spi.AbstractSelectableChannel
{
    public abstract SocketChannel accept()
        throws java.io.IOException;
    public static ServerSocketChannel open()
        throws java.io.IOException
    public abstract java.net.ServerSocket socket();
    public final int validOps()
}
```

See also: java.net.InetSocketAddress, java.net.ServerSocket, java.net.
SocketAddress, SocketChannel

SocketChannel

SocketChannel objects transfer data between byte buffers and network connections.

```
    public abstract class SocketChannel
        extends java.nio.channels.spi.AbstractSelectableChannel
        implements ByteChannel, ScatteringByteChannel, GatheringByteChannel
{
    public abstract boolean connect (java.net.SocketAddress remote)
        throws java.io.IOException;
    public abstract boolean finishConnect()
        throws java.io.IOException;
    public abstract boolean isConnected();
    public abstract boolean isConnectionPending();
    public static SocketChannel open()
        throws java.io.IOException
    public static SocketChannel open (java.net.SocketAddress remote)
        throws java.io.IOException
    public abstract int read (java.nio.ByteBuffer dst)
        throws java.io.IOException;
    public final long read (java.nio.ByteBuffer [] dsts)
        throws java.io.IOException
    public abstract long read (java.nio.ByteBuffer [] dsts, int offset, int length)
        throws java.io.IOException;
    public abstract java.net.Socket socket();
    public final int validOps()
    public abstract int write (java.nio.ByteBuffer src)
        throws java.io.IOException;
    public final long write (java.nio.ByteBuffer [] srcs)
        throws java.io.IOException
    public abstract long write (java.nio.ByteBuffer [] srcs, int offset, int length)
        throws java.io.IOException;
}
```

See also: java.net.InetSocketAddress, java.net.Socket, java.net.SocketAddress,
ServerSocketChannel

UnresolvedAddressException

UnresolvedAddressException (unchecked) is thrown when attempting to use a SocketAddress object cannot be resolved to a real network address.

```
public class UnresolvedAddressException
    extends IllegalArgumentException
{
    public UnresolvedAddressException()
}
```

See also: java.net.InetSocketAddress, java.net.SocketAddress, SocketChannel

UnsupportedAddressTypeException

UnsupportedAddressTypeException (unchecked) is thrown when attempting to connect a socket with a SocketAddress object that represents an address type not supported by the socket implementation.

```
public class UnsupportedAddressTypeException
    extends IllegalArgumentException
{
    public UnsupportedAddressTypeException()
}
```

See also: java.net.InetSocketAddress, java.net.SocketAddress

WritableByteChannel

The WritableByteChannel interface defines the write() method, which makes it possible to write data to a channel from a ByteBuffer.

```
public interface WritableByteChannel
    extends Channel
{
    public int write (java.nio.ByteBuffer src)
        throws java.io.IOException;
}
```

See also: ByteBuffer, ByteChannel, ReadableByteChannel

Package java.nio.channels.spi

The java.nio.channels.spi package contains classes used to create pluggable, selectable channel implementations. Unlike the other packages listed here, the classes in this package also list protected methods. These classes provide common methods to be reused by pluggable implementations, but not all are intended for public consumption.

AbstractInterruptibleChannel

The `AbstractInterruptibleChannel` class provides methods that implement interrupt semantics for subclasses.

```
public abstract class AbstractInterruptibleChannel
    implements java.nio.channels.Channel, java.nio.channels.InterruptibleChannel
{
    protected final void begin()
    public final void close()
        throws java.io.IOException
    protected final void end (boolean completed)
        throws java.nio.channels.AsynchronousCloseException
    protected abstract void implCloseChannel()
        throws java.io.IOException;
    public final boolean isOpen()
}
```

AbstractSelectableChannel

The `AbstractSelectableChannel` is the superclass of all channel implementations eligible to participate in readiness selection.

```
public abstract class AbstractSelectableChannel
    extends java.nio.channels.SelectableChannel
{
    public final Object blockingLock()
    public final java.nio.channels.SelectableChannel configureBlocking
        (boolean block) throws java.io.IOException
    protected final void implCloseChannel()
        throws java.io.IOException
    protected abstract void implCloseSelectableChannel()
        throws java.io.IOException;
    protected abstract void implConfigureBlocking (boolean block)
        throws java.io.IOException;
    public final boolean isBlocking()
    public final boolean isRegistered()
    public final java.nio.channels.SelectionKey keyFor
        (java.nio.channels.Selector sel)
    public final SelectorProvider provider()
    public final java.nio.channels.SelectionKey register
        (java.nio.channels.Selector sel, int ops, Object att)
        throws java.nio.channels.ClosedChannelException
}
```

AbstractSelectionKey

The `AbstractSelectionKey` class provides common routines used by `SelectionKey` implementations.

```
public abstract class AbstractSelectionKey
    extends java.nio.channels.SelectionKey
```

```
{
    public final void cancel()
    public final boolean isValid()
}
```

AbstractSelector

The AbstractSelector class is the superclass of all Selector implementations.

```
public abstract class AbstractSelector
    extends java.nio.channels.Selector
{
    protected final void begin()
    protected final java.util.Set cancelledKeys()
    public final void close()
        throws java.io.IOException
    protected final void deregister (AbstractSelectionKey key)
    protected final void end()
    protected abstract void implCloseSelector()
        throws java.io.IOException;
    public final boolean isOpen()
    public final SelectorProvider provider()
    protected abstract java.nio.channels.SelectionKey register(
        AbstractSelectableChannel ch, int ops, Object att);
}
```

SelectorProvider

The SelectorProvider class is the superclass of all concrete channel provider classes. This class is instantiated only by the Service Provider Interface facility, never directly. The fully qualified names of concrete subclasses should be listed in a file named *META-INF/services/java.nio.channels.spi.SelectorProvider* in the classloader's classpath.

```
public abstract class SelectorProvider
{
    public abstract java.nio.channels.DatagramChannel openDatagramChannel()
        throws java.io.IOException;
    public abstract java.nio.channels.Pipe openPipe()
        throws java.io.IOException;
    public abstract AbstractSelector openSelector()
        throws java.io.IOException;
    public abstract java.nio.channels.ServerSocketChannel openServerSocketChannel()
        throws java.io.IOException;
    public abstract java.nio.channels.SocketChannel openSocketChannel()
        throws java.io.IOException;
    public static SelectorProvider provider()
}
```

Package java.nio.charset

The java.nio.charset package contains classes related to character set manipulation and transcoding.

CharacterCodingException

CharacterCodingException is thrown to indicate that a character set coding error was encountered. This is the parent class of the two specific coding-error exceptions defined in this package. The low-level encoders and decoders do not throw this exception; they return CoderResult objects to indicate which type of error was encountered. In some circumstances it's more appropriate to throw an exception to higher-level code. The CharsetEncoder.encode() and CharsetDecoder.decode() convenience methods may throw this exception. They're convenience wrappers around the lower-level coder methods and use the CoderResult.throwException() method.

```
public class CharacterCodingException
    extends java.io.IOException
{
    public CharacterCodingException()
}
```

See also: CoderResult, MalformedInputException, UnmappableCharacterException

Charset

The Charset class encapsulates a coded character set and associated coding schemes.

```
public abstract class Charset
    implements Comparable
{
    public final java.util.Set aliases()
    public static java.util.SortedMap availableCharsets()
    public boolean canEncode()
    public final int compareTo (Object ob)
    public abstract boolean contains (Charset cs);
    public final java.nio.CharBuffer decode (java.nio.ByteBuffer bb)
    public String displayName()
    public String displayName (java.util.Locale locale)
    public final java.nio.ByteBuffer encode (String str)
    public final java.nio.ByteBuffer encode (java.nio.CharBuffer cb)
    public final boolean equals (Object ob)
    public static Charset forName (String charsetName)
    public final int hashCode()
    public final boolean isRegistered()
    public static boolean isSupported (String charsetName)
    public final String name()
    public abstract CharsetDecoder newDecoder();
    public abstract CharsetEncoder newEncoder();
```

```
        public final String toString()
    }
```

See also: CharsetDecoder, CharsetEncoder

CharsetDecoder

A CharsetDecoder instance transforms an encoded sequence of bytes into a sequence of characters. Instances of this class are stateful.

```
    public abstract class CharsetDecoder
    {
        public final float averageCharsPerByte()
        public final Charset charset()
        public final java.nio.CharBuffer decode (java.nio.ByteBuffer in)
            throws CharacterCodingException
        public final CoderResult decode (java.nio.ByteBuffer in, java.nio.CharBuffer out,
            boolean endOfInput)
        public Charset detectedCharset()
        public final CoderResult flush (java.nio.CharBuffer out)
        public boolean isAutoDetecting()
        public boolean isCharsetDetected()
        public CodingErrorAction malformedInputAction()
        public final float maxCharsPerByte()
        public final CharsetDecoder onMalformedInput (CodingErrorAction newAction)
        public final CharsetDecoder onUnmappableCharacter (CodingErrorAction newAction)
        public final CharsetDecoder replaceWith (String newReplacement)
        public final String replacement()
        public final CharsetDecoder reset()
        public CodingErrorAction unmappableCharacterAction()
    }
```

See also: Charset, CharsetEncoder

CharsetEncoder

A CharsetEncoder instance transforms a character sequence to an encoded sequence of bytes. Instances of this class are stateful.

```
    public abstract class CharsetEncoder
    {
        public final float averageBytesPerChar()
        public boolean canEncode (char c)
        public boolean canEncode (CharSequence cs)
        public final Charset charset()
        public final java.nio.ByteBuffer encode (java.nio.CharBuffer in)
            throws CharacterCodingException
        public final CoderResult encode (java.nio.CharBuffer in, java.nio.ByteBuffer out,
            boolean endOfInput)
        public final CoderResult flush (java.nio.ByteBuffer out)
        public boolean isLegalReplacement (byte [] repl)
        public CodingErrorAction malformedInputAction()
        public final float maxBytesPerChar()
```

```
    public final CharsetEncoder onMalformedInput (CodingErrorAction newAction)
    public final CharsetEncoder onUnmappableCharacter (CodingErrorAction newAction)
    public final CharsetEncoder replaceWith (byte [] newReplacement)
    public final byte [] replacement()
    public final CharsetEncoder reset()
    public CodingErrorAction unmappableCharacterAction()
}
```
See also: Charset, CharsetDecoder

CoderMalfunctionError

CoderMalfunctionError is thrown when the CharsetEncoder.encode() or CharsetDecoder.decode() methods catch an unexpected exception from the low-level encodeLoop() or decodeLoop() methods.

```
public class CoderMalfunctionError
    extends Error
{
    public CoderMalfunctionError (Exception cause)
}
```
See also: CharsetDecoder, CharsetEncoder

CoderResult

A CoderResult object is returned by CharsetDecoder.decode() and CharsetEncoder.encode() to indicate the result of a coding operation.

```
public class CoderResult
{
    public static final CoderResult OVERFLOW
    public static final CoderResult UNDERFLOW

    public boolean isError()
    public boolean isMalformed()
    public boolean isOverflow()
    public boolean isUnderflow()
    public boolean isUnmappable()
    public int length()
    public static CoderResult malformedForLength (int length)
    public void throwException()
        throws CharacterCodingException
    public String toString()
    public static CoderResult unmappableForLength (int length)
}
```
See also: CharacterCodingException, CharsetDecoder, CharsetEncoder

CodingErrorAction

The CodingErrorAction class is a type-safe enumeration. The named instances are passed to CharsetDecoder and CharsetEncoder objects to indicate which action should be taken when coding errors are encountered.

```
public class CodingErrorAction
{
    public static final CodingErrorAction IGNORE
    public static final CodingErrorAction REPLACE
    public static final CodingErrorAction REPORT

    public String toString()
}
```

See also: CharsetDecoder, CharsetEncoder, CoderResult

IllegalCharsetNameException

IllegalCharsetNameException (unchecked) is thrown when a Charset name that does not comply with the charset naming rules is provided. Charset names must consist of ASCII letters (upper- or lowercase), numeric digits, hyphens, colons, underscores, and periods, and the first character must be a letter or a digit.

```
public class IllegalCharsetNameException
    extends IllegalArgumentException
{
    public IllegalCharsetNameException (String charsetName)

    public String getCharsetName()
}
```

See also: Charset

MalformedInputException

MalformedInputException (subclass of IOException) is thrown to indicate that malformed input was detected during a coding operation. The CoderResult object provides a convenience method to generate this exception when needed.

```
public class MalformedInputException
    extends CharacterCodingException
{
    public MalformedInputException (int inputLength)

    public int getInputLength()
    public String getMessage()
}
```

See also: CoderResult, UnmappableCharacterException

UnmappableCharacterException

UnmappableCharacterException (subclass of IOException) is thrown to indicate that the encoder or decoder cannot map one or more characters from an otherwise valid input sequence. The CoderResult object provides a convenience method to generate this exception.

```
public class UnmappableCharacterException
    extends CharacterCodingException
{
    public UnmappableCharacterException (int inputLength)

    public int getInputLength()
    public String getMessage()
}
```

See also: CoderResult, MalformedInputException

UnsupportedCharsetException

UnsupportedCharsetException (unchecked) is thrown when a requested Charset is not supported by the current JVM environment.

```
public class UnsupportedCharsetException
    extends IllegalArgumentException
{
    public UnsupportedCharsetException (String charsetName)

    public String getCharsetName()
}
```

See also: Charset

Package java.nio.charset.spi

The java.nio.charset.spi package contains a single class used by the charset Service Provider Interface mechanism.

CharsetProvider

CharsetProvider facilitates the installation of Charset implementations into the running JVM. The fully qualified names of concrete subclasses should be listed in a file named *META-INF/services/java.nio.charset.spi.CharsetProvider* in the classloader's classpath to activate them via the Service Provider Interface mechanism.

```
public abstract class CharsetProvider
{
    public abstract java.nio.charset.Charset charsetForName (String charsetName);
```

```
        public abstract java.util.Iterator charsets();
    }
```

See also: Charset

Package java.util.regex

The java.util.regex package contains classes used for regular expression processing.

Matcher

A Matcher object is a stateful matching engine that examines an input character sequence to detect regular expression matches and provide information about successful matches.

```
    public final class Matcher
    {
        public Matcher appendReplacement (StringBuffer sb, String replacement)
        public StringBuffer appendTail (StringBuffer sb)
        public int end()
        public int end (int group)
        public boolean find()
        public boolean find (int start)
        public String group()
        public String group (int group)
        public int groupCount()
        public boolean lookingAt()
        public boolean matches()
        public Pattern pattern()
        public String replaceAll (String replacement)
        public String replaceFirst (String replacement)
        public Matcher reset()
        public Matcher reset (CharSequence input)
        public int start()
        public int start (int group)
    }
```

See also: java.lang.CharSequence, java.lang.String, Pattern

Pattern

The Pattern class encapsulates a compiled regular expression.

```
    public final class Pattern
        implements java.io.Serializable
    {
        public static final int CANON_EQ
        public static final int CASE_INSENSITIVE
        public static final int COMMENTS
        public static final int DOTALL
        public static final int MULTILINE
```

```
        public static final int UNICODE_CASE
        public static final int UNIX_LINES

        public static Pattern compile (String regex)
        public static Pattern compile (String regex, int flags)
        public int flags()
        public Matcher matcher (CharSequence input)
        public static boolean matches (String regex, CharSequence input)
        public String pattern()
        public String [] split (CharSequence input)
        public String [] split (CharSequence input, int limit)
    }
```

See also: java.lang.CharSequence, java.lang.String, Matcher

PatternSyntaxException

PatternSyntaxException (unchecked) is thrown by Pattern.compile() (or any of the convenience methods on Pattern or String that take a regular expression parameter) when the provided regular expression string contains syntax errors.

```
    public class PatternSyntaxException
        extends IllegalArgumentException
    {
        public PatternSyntaxException (String desc, String regex, int index)

        public String getDescription()
        public int getIndex()
        public String getMessage()
        public String getPattern()
    }
```

See also: Pattern

Index

We'd like to hear your suggestions for improving our indexes. Send email to *index@oreilly.com*.

About the Author

Ron Hitchens is a California-based computer consultant and educator whose career dates back to the disco era. His first exposure to computers was operating mainframes in the Air Force. His first programming language was COBOL, which he learned from a friend's borrowed textbook. Since that time, Ron has used just about every computer system and programming language you can imagine, from 6502 assembler to XSLT.

Ron spent much of the 1980s at the University of Texas at Austin as a student and staffer, where he burrowed deep into the Unix kernel and assisted with many interesting research projects.

Ron spent the next several years doing kernel work for clients such as IBM and Unisys. He has also developed and taught professional development courses for the same clientele.

Following a brief flirtation with C++, Ron fell in love with Java and has spent the last several years employing server-side Java technologies to build web applications for clients ranging from start-ups to Fortune 500 companies.

Ron is Founder and President of Ronsoft Technologies (*http://www.ronsoft.com*) and lives in California with his wife and co-pilot, Karen, and a dog named Boomer. When Ron isn't working (hah!), he and Karen enjoy snorkeling, bicycling, and walking the dog.

Colophon

Our look is the result of reader comments, our own experimentation, and feedback from distribution channels. Distinctive covers complement our distinctive approach to technical topics, breathing personality and life into potentially dry subjects.

The animal on the cover of *Java NIO* is a pig-footed bandicoot (*Chaeropus ecaudatus*). Though a specimen has not been uncovered since the early 20th century, pig-footed bandicoots were once found throughout central and south Australia and in Victoria. These rabbit-like creatures dwelled in many habitats. In the central deserts, they took up residence in sand dunes. In Victoria, they lived in grassy plains. In other areas, they preferred open woodland with shrubs and grass.

Pig-footed bandicoots grew to be about 230–260 millimeters in length, with a tail of 100–150 millimeters. They had rough, orange-brown fur on the dorsal side of their bodies and a lighter color on their undersides. Their long tails ended in a black tuft. Their bodies were narrow and compact, and they had pointed heads with ears like a rabbit's. Their feet and legs, however, were much different from other bandicoot species'. Its forelegs and hindlegs were long and skinny, ending in strangely shaped feet with nails resembling a pig's hoof. On its hindfeet, the second and third toes were fused, and only the fourth was used in locomotion.

Pig-footed bandicoots are believed to have been solitary animals. Depending on their environment, they may have built nests made of grass or dug short tunnels with a nest at the end. These bandicoots lived on the ground and used their keen sense of smell to find food. The most well-documented behavior of *Chaeropus ecaudatus* was its locomotion. Their movements were often erratic. A slow gait took the form of a bunny hop, while an intermediate gait was a lumbering quadrepedal run with the hind limbs moving alternately. However, Aborigines have reported that the pig-footed bandicoot, if pursued, could reach blazing speeds by breaking into a smooth, galloping sprint.

Little is known about the reproductive cycle of *C. ecaudatus*, but from studying other bandicoots, it can be inferred that pig-footed bandicoots did not carry more than four young per littler. Females had a strong, sturdy pouch that opened on their back-sides. Generally, bandicoots have a short gestation period, around 12 days from conception to birth. Each young weighs about 0.5 grams. When their time in the pouch has ended, baby bandicoots are left in the nest, and around 8–10 days later, they leave with their mother to forage or hunt.

Matt Hutchinson was the production editor and copyeditor for *Java NIO*. Sarah Sherman proofread the book, and Sarah Sherman and Jeffrey Holcomb provided quality control. Angela Howard wrote the index.

Hanna Dyer designed the cover of this book, based on a series design by Edie Freedman. The cover image is a 19th-century engraving from *Animal Creation, Vol. II*. Emma Colby produced the cover layout with QuarkXPress 4.1 using Adobe's ITC Garamond font.

Melanie Wang designed the interior layout, based on a series design by David Futato. This book was converted to FrameMaker 5.5.6 with a format conversion tool created by Erik Ray, Jason McIntosh, Neil Walls, and Mike Sierra that uses Perl and XML technologies. The text font is Linotype Birka; the heading font is Adobe Myriad Condensed; and the code font is LucasFont's TheSans Mono Condensed. The illustrations that appear in the book were produced by Robert Romano and Jessamyn Read using Macromedia FreeHand 9 and Adobe Photoshop 6. The tip and warning icons were drawn by Christopher Bing. This colophon was written by Matt Hutchinson.

Other Titles Available from O'Reilly

Java

Java Performance Tuning, 2nd Edition

By Jack Shirazi
2nd Edition January 2003 (est.)
600 pages (est.), ISBN 0-596-00015-4

Significantly revised and expanded, this second edition not only covers Java 1.4, but adds new coverage of JDBC, NIO, Servlets, EJB and JavaServer Pages. The book remains a valuable resource for teaching developers how to create a tuning strategy, how to use profiling tools to understand a program's behavior, and how to avoid performance penalties from inefficient code, making them more efficient and effective. The result is code that's robust, maintainable and fast!

Java Security, 2nd Edition

By Scott Oaks
2nd Edition May 2001
618 pages, ISBN 0-596-00157-6

The second edition focuses on the platform features of Java that provide security—the class loader, bytecode verifier, and security manager—and recent additions to Java that enhance this security model: digital signatures, security providers, and the access controller. The book covers in depth the security model of Java 2, version 1.3, including the two new security APIs: JAAS and JSSE.

Database Programming with JDBC and Java, 2nd Edition

By George Reese
2nd Edition August 2000
352 pages, ISBN 1-56592-616-1

This book describes the standard Java interfaces that make portable object-oriented access to relational databases possible, and offers a robust model for writing applications that are easy to maintain. The second edition has been completely updated for JDBC 2.0, and includes reference listings for JDBC and the most important RMI classes. The book begins with a quick overview of SQL for developers who may be asked to handle a database for the first time, and goes on to explain how to issue database queries and updates through SQL and JDBC.

Java Network Programming, 2nd Edition

By Elliotte Rusty Harold
2nd Edition August 2000
760 pages, ISBN 1-56592-870-9

Java Network Programming, 2nd Edition, is a complete introduction to developing network programs (both applets and applications) using Java, covering everything from networking fundamentals to remote method invocation (RMI). It includes chapters on TCP and UDP sockets, multicasting protocol and content handlers, and servlets. This second edition also includes coverage of Java 1.1, 1.2 and 1.3. New chapters cover multithreaded network programming, I/O, HTML parsing and display, the Java Mail API, the Java Secure Sockets Extension, and more.

Java Swing, 2nd Edition

By Marc Loy, Robert Eckstein, David Wood, James Elliott & Brian Cole
2nd Edition November 2002 (est.)
1296 pages (est.), ISBN 0-596-00408-7

This second edition of *Java Swing* thoroughly covers all the features available in Java 2 SDK 1.3 and 1.4. More than simply a reference, this new edition takes a practical approach. It is a book by developers for developers, with hundreds of useful examples, from beginning level to advanced, covering every component available in Swing. Whether you're a seasoned Java developer or just trying to find out what Java can do, you'll find *Java Swing*, 2nd edition an indispensable guide.

Java Pr<!---->gramming with Oracle JDBC

By Donald K. Bales
1st Edition December 2001
496 pages, ISBN 0-596-00088-X

Here is the professional's guide to leveraging Java's JDBC in an Oracle environment. Readers learn the all-important mysteries of establishing database corrections; issuing SQL queries and getting results back; and advanced topics such as streaming large objects, calling PL/SQL procedures, and working with Oracle9i's object-oriented features. Also covered: transactions, concurrency management and performance. This is an essential tool for all Java Oracle developers who need to work with both technologies.

O'REILLY®

To order: *800-998-9938* • *order@oreilly.com* • *www.oreilly.com*
Online editions of most O'Reilly titles are available by subscription at *safari.oreilly.com*
Also available at most retail and online bookstores.

How to stay in touch with O'Reilly

1. Visit our award-winning web site

http://www.oreilly.com/

★ "Top 100 Sites on the Web"—PC Magazine
★ CIO Magazine's Web Business 50 Awards

Our web site contains a library of comprehensive product information (including book excerpts and tables of contents), downloadable software, background articles, interviews with technology leaders, links to relevant sites, book cover art, and more. File us in your bookmarks or favorites!

2. Join our email mailing lists

Sign up to get email announcements of new books and conferences, special offers, and O'Reilly Network technology newsletters at:

http://elists.oreilly.com

It's easy to customize your free elists subscription so you'll get exactly the O'Reilly news you want.

3. Get examples from our books

To find example files for a book, go to:

http://www.oreilly.com/catalog

select the book, and follow the "Examples" link.

4. Work with us

Check out our web site for current employment opportunities:

http://jobs.oreilly.com/

5. Register your book

Register your book at:

http://register.oreilly.com

6. Contact us

O'Reilly & Associates, Inc.
1005 Gravenstein Hwy North
Sebastopol, CA 95472 USA
TEL: 707-827-7000 or 800-998-9938
 (6am to 5pm PST)
FAX: 707-829-0104

order@oreilly.com
For answers to problems regarding your order or our products. To place a book order online visit:

http://www.oreilly.com/order_new/

catalog@oreilly.com
To request a copy of our latest catalog.

booktech@oreilly.com
For book content technical questions or corrections.

corporate@oreilly.com
For educational, library, government, and corporate sales.

proposals@oreilly.com
To submit new book proposals to our editors and product managers.

international@oreilly.com
For information about our international distributors or translation queries. For a list of our distributors outside of North America check out:

http://international.oreilly.com/distributors.html

adoption@oreilly.com
For information about academic use of O'Reilly books, visit:

http://academic.oreilly.com

O'REILLY®